IDENTIFYING**TOP**PERFORMERS

Published in 2009 by
CRF United Kingdom
www.crf.com

Kinetic Centre
Theobald Street
Elstree / Herts WD6 4PJ
United Kingdom
T: +44 (0)20 8387 1400
F: +44 (0)20 8387 1410
E: info@crf.com

Regional director Johann Labuschagne
Publisher Tess Lugos
Editor Paul Donkersley
Business development manager Janu Cheng
Account managers Berhane Freyer, Sarah Freyer and Dan Havardi
Administrative assistant Suzanne Bell
Design and production Mark Clubb
Printing and binding Tatra Media, Slovakia

Photography
Badenoch & Clark; BPP College of Professional Studies; Broadway Homelessness & Support;
The Co-operative; Fremantle Media; Friends of the Earth; HCL Technologies; Heart of England NHS
Foundation Trust; Hydrogen Group; IBM UK Ltd; Iceland Foods Ltd; Informa PLC; Innocent Drinks; Irwell
Valley Housing Association; JD Wetherspoon PLC; John Lewis Partnership; John Wood Group PLC; London
and Quadrant Housing Trust; Lloyds TSB; LV=; McCann Erickson Advertising; Moorfields Eye Hospital; Pete
Jones Production; Peter Brett Associates LLP; Shaw Trust; RPS Group PLC; RX Studio; Reliance Security;
Rider Levett Bucknall UK; Tate and Lyle Sugars; TNT UK Ltd; Unite Group PLC; and View

ISBN   978-0-9562015-0-8

Contents

Introduction

CRF is proud to publish *Britain's Top Employers 2009*, the 9th edition of this prestigious project in the UK. It is being released in unprecedented times for economies around the world. Many of the profiles in this book were written before the worst employment effects of the downturn began to happen. That doesn't change one thing – the employers profiled in this book have demonstrated, by international standards, to be front runners in the field of excellent HR management.

Particularly in difficult times, showcasing this excellence is vital. Employees still want to know what they can expect from their employer. Holding Top Employer status is an endorsement of the employer brand, and a powerful opportunity for these organisations to explain this to their employees. After all, leadership means having a vision and implementing this vision, especially in challenging circumstances. This is exactly what the organisations featured here do, and are worthy to distinguish themselves as Top Employers.

"During an economic crisis, being a Top Employer is even more important. By giving their employees a clear picture of what they can expect, employers can gain support and dedication in return. An engaged workforce is crucial to weathering this storm."
(Steven Veenendaal, CEO, CRF)

In recent years, being a good employer was mainly focused on attracting and retaining the best talent. While unemployment is currently on the rise, this is still of great importance. Well-publicised reasons for the shortage of the right people are the persistently growing need for knowledge workers, the outflow of 'baby boomers,' and a limited influx of young talent. The current economic crisis will not alter these fundamental demographic patterns.

A strong employer brand usually generates a tighter bond between employer and employee. The better this relationship, the more commitment the employee will show. In turn, a top employer will be open and receptive to the employee's opinion. A two-way relationship based upon commitment and trust is more likely to lead to stronger performance throughout the organisation.

During an economic downturn, many companies may communicate less, or less effectively, to their employees and to the market. It's never fun to convey bad news and painful decisions. However, keeping a low profile is not a viable option and avoiding dialogue can lead to more criticism. Good leadership is characterised by explaining decisions and sharing an insight to the future. By doing so, criticism can be translated into understanding or even support. It's important that employees who are not made redundant, who after all will usually constitute the vast majority of the workforce, remain connected and engaged. Communicating proactively and clearly is what sets Top Employers apart. It's a time for the leaders to stand up.

During an economic crisis, being a Top Employer is even more important. By giving their employees a clear picture of what they can expect, employers can gain support and dedication in return. An engaged workforce is crucial to weathering this storm.

Testing times like these are providing HR professionals with probably their greatest challenge. Yet they also present a great opportunity to stand up and really make a difference. Never before have their skills been so needed, and the Top Employers in this book are those that demonstrate them in abundance.

Steven Veenendaal
CEO, CRF

Editor's foreword

When CRF invited me to be the editor again of *Britain's Top Employers 2009* (I edited the first two projects a decade ago), I said that the last thing I wanted to do was write a foreword. So indeed, the last thing I am doing is writing a foreword.

This gives me a number of vantage points. I have read all of the profiles, I have benefited from the insights and observations of the experts on CRF's panel. And I can be as up-to-date as possible on the state of the employment market.

Of course, on the latter the daily news is dreadful. But in difficult times there are some things that the best employers do better than others. More on that later.

Seeking calmer waters in turbulent times, I thought I might reflect on some of the 'hot' HR topics and how they have evolved over the last decade. These include diversity, performance-related pay, flexible benefits, managing your own career, work-life balance, and corporate social responsibility (CSR). Then, they represented the brave new world of top employership; today they have become mainstream and are prevalent in many smaller organisations as well as larger ones. Of course they have evolved, as HR professionals have torn into the detail.

Corporate social responsibility was arguably PR as much as CSR. Companies wanted to demonstrate that they were 'doing the right thing'. Nowadays, ethical business behaviour is seen as vital to business success. Often pressure has come from employees themselves. Perhaps as individuals we feel we cannot make a significant impact on environmental and community issues; but in a large organisation, together we can. Employees not only want, but expect their employer to be responsible and be one of the good guys. For that reason, CSR has become an important factor in recruitment.

Another benefit of a strong CSR agenda is that it can help in employee development. Junior employees have opportunities to assume responsibility on CSR committees and task groups, grasping leadership roles that otherwise might not come until later in their career. CSR activities also allow employees to meet colleagues in a different environment: working alongside a senior manager in overalls, splattering school walls with a fresh lick of paint, is a great leveller.

Diversity is surely a subject that has been overdone. A while back, there were targets, monitoring and even quotas. But people found this just wasn't really working – or even relevant anymore. So-called minorities do not always want to be labelled as something different, and be monitored. With racial integration, and many ethnic communities reaching second and third generations, they see themselves as British, plain and simple. Others are maybe coy about revealing their sexual preferences to their employer. And job applicants are allowed to keep their age secret until they have joined the payroll, and often think they are best advised to do precisely that.

Moreover, employers now have sufficient confidence to state the obvious – simply that they want the best person for the job. They have long since recognised that with a diverse customer base, it's a smart move to have a diverse employee base as well. Perhaps what's more important, and more evident 10 years on, is that companies are doing a lot to make themselves more accessible to as wide a section of society as possible – going into schools, choosing where to advertise, open days – in order to open up employment opportunities for all.

Work-life balance is one of today's more prominent topics. Huge work-life balance surveys by bodies such as the old Department of Trade and Industry, and the resulting government legislation, have served to pile pressure on employers. Many businesses, especially smaller ones, found that while the flexible mind was willing, the organisational chart was unable. They were concerned that changing work shifts and patterns would be detrimental to the business, and for some roles, flexible working clearly won't work.

But it's turned out to be not too bad. Why is that? Technology has certainly helped, and if technology is the driver, then trust is the fuel. For example, mums leaving the office early to handle the school run might log online later once the kids are in bed and finish the task in hand. Trust really is the key, and that means from the organisation and from fellow workers. If the job gets done, and gets done well, then employers have realised it doesn't matter where and when it's done. And let's not forget that the best employers don't forget single people; they ensure that flexible working is available to all – not just parents – and avoid any resentment as a result.

Technology has also had a major impact on how we communicate at work. Ten years ago many of us did not have an email address; now we suffer withdrawal symptoms if two minutes pass without an email landing in our Inbox. Company intranets have enabled an explosion in internal communications and staff surveys, and e-learning modules on the web proliferate. Technology has spawned a whole new way of using language in email and tone of voice online. Employers now have to grapple with issues such as email privacy, surfing the Internet in company time and inappropriate material sent as attachments.

The Great Bonus Debate has put performance-related pay in focus. Having a variable element to reward always sounded like a good idea. Employers feel they are paying for value while employees feel valued for striving that little bit harder. But from a company's point of view, implementing performance-related pay fairly can be a nightmare. It's complicated, time consuming and creates collateral damage by suggesting one person's contribution is inferior to another's.

And which performance maps onto variable pay? The individual? The team, or business unit? Or the company overall? And does this mean purely financial performance, or other aspects of work, including competencies, meeting key performance indicators, or living a company's values. Many argue that if a company makes a loss, never mind whether or not it has taken taxpayer's money, then any bonus is out of order. No profit – no bonus. The counter argument is that companies need to give bonuses to retain the top talent. I need hardly mention banks and bonuses for you to know what I mean.

Even measuring roles like sales can get cloudy. A salesperson can be rewarded with commission on new sales; but how much of that success was down to the P.A. who stayed working late the night before to make sure that the client presentation was ready and bound in time?

Flexible benefits schemes have proved to be a big hit and their initial fashionability has lost nothing of their lustre. People love flexible benefits because at different stages of the life cycle, they have different priorities. Having a choice also pampers the spirit of individualism.

But now times are grim. Graduate recruitment is down 17% and this, like many forecasts, may prove to be a massive underestimate. Already new concepts have entered the HR vernacular… partially paid sabbaticals; job sharing; trading off job cuts against pay reductions; and a whole new approach to the bonus culture.

So what next for the British economy? A paper economy built on easy credit, massive personal and public sector debt, and material consumer spending, is no economy at all and clearly unsustainable. Surely there has to be some structural change. Despite expensive government attempts to reflate the consumer bubble and get things 'back to normal', over-inflated asset values have to fall. That could also mean lower salaries and wages as well. A company could theoretically employ twice as many people on half wages. But who wants to work for half their current salary? Maybe people with no jobs at all.

Britain is going to have to rediscover its entrepreneurial culture, and start making things again, not just selling imports to one another and servicing ourselves to death. We'll need to make things that other countries want, to pay for the goods we import from them. We'll need to find real work for millions of people to do.

Managing your own career was a big thing a decade ago and it's never been truer than right now. In difficult times it's vital that people remain active and do something. Because the system has crashed does not mean people should do nothing, even if it just means getting fit, improving the house, or writing that novel. Better still, use downtime to prepare for better times. Look at the emerging trends in the world, anticipate what opportunities they will create, and buy yourself a ticket. Find what training is available and acquire new skills, update existing ones, or embrace new technologies. Research gaps in the market and maybe develop a new idea, approach or product. Arguably you won't get a better time to do it.

Top employers will want all of these things. It's a buyer's market in employment right now, but there are still great jobs, great opportunities, and great employers out there. Many of them can be found in here, as you turn the pages of this book book. With the right policies, the right attitude to training, and a renewed vigour of entrepreneurship, things will change. And when they do, you can expect Britain's top employers to go hunting for Britain's top talent.

Paul Donkersley
Editor

The pressure of pay reviews

Like many other HR activities, setting and managing the base pay of employees is a distinctly cyclical business. Of course, there are many opportunities throughout the year to address salaries for particular posts, say for example when someone leaves and you need to plan for what you will pay to get a replacement. But far and away the most obvious and common demonstration of the way in which working with the cash elements of the reward package is a relatively timetabled activity is the annual pay review.

Now some of you might well have expected that I would have inserted the word 'dreaded' in that previous sentence. For many HR professionals and line managers alike the challenge of delivering a sufficient increase each year to retain good people and keep them motivated whilst managing tight budgets can be enough to make even the most seasoned practitioner blanch.

As the head of a business that deals in market salary data and advice, I am pleased to report that the trade in information to help support this activity is alive and well. And despite the evident difficulties that 2008 has presented to many employers, this year has seen no reduction in the relatively familiar last-minute calls from clients asking for benchmarking data to help them complete the annual pay round.

But there has been one big change this year compared to many of the previous 10 or 15 annual pay review cycles – and to understand what this change is, we just need to look at what drives movements in pay across the market as a whole.

What affects pay movements?

I am fairly confident that most people who work in and around pay and benefits information would agree that the single biggest influence on pay movements is inflation. And no matter what measure you choose to include in the definition, if prices are going up then employees will want their pay to grow in line with these increases – that's why the concept of a 'cost of living increase' has become so enshrined in the annual pay review process.

But inflation in its purest form isn't the only thing that affects pay movements. Genuine and widespread skill shortages can affect whole industries, or can at the very least push entire professions to the top of the pay league over relatively short timeframes. And at a more local level, individual company performance can dictate what an employer feels it can put into the salary pot. So a few years of great results can allow year-on-year salary increases in a particular business to forge ahead of the general market.

Likewise, individual performance can also affect what an employee gains out of a pay review. And in a world where linking pay to performance has become something of a fashion, there are plenty of employers who don't give an across-the-board settlement any more, preferring to take the money available and distributing it along performance-driven lines.

More general business issues too, such as recruitment and retention challenges, can have an impact on salary levels, as an employer seeks to use cash to fix short-term issues, hopefully for the long-term good of the business.

The above are illustrations of factors that put upward pressure on pay levels. There are of course situations where downward pressure is applied to pay movements. This doesn't mean that employers will actually reduce pay in absolute terms during the pay review process, but the effect of a combination of these factors might be that an employee sees his or her take home pay fall in real terms. To help us understand this point, let's think about a couple of examples.

A company employing rare skills in a boom market and in an economy experiencing high inflation will almost certainly need to think about reviewing salaries at an above-average level simply in order to find and keep the right staff.

Conversely, continuing periods of low inflation, poor company performance, difficulties in raising or maintaining prices and tapping into a pool of readily available and perhaps routine skills can all lead to a company being either unable or unwilling to see annual pay movements going up too much.

So what then, is the change that has taken place this year?
In simple terms, it's the mix of factors that are in play in the market. If we scan back over the last 10 or so years, we can see that pay inflation has been steady and very predictable.

The stability of the economy as a whole, coupled with solid growth and relatively favourable market conditions, have meant that most employers have been able to put a reasonable but not excessive amount into the annual pay review 'pot' knowing that employees will be pleased to keep pace with basic cost of living increases. Furthermore, there has been enough scope in the market to see performance-related pay formulae deliver higher than average payments for those making the greatest contributions, while not penalising the solid and important, albeit unspectacular performance that typifies the input of many employees.

For those tasked with managing the annual pay review this period has been something of a breeze – steady upward movement without too much excess. However, the last two to three years have rocked this comfortable arrangement. Undoubtedly that there have been some pretty hefty salaries and bonuses around, most notably in the financial services and banking markets. But the problem is that it's been quite easy to see how these eye-watering sums have been achieved. If you recruit top talent and they perform then the basic principle is that you reward them to match that performance. And although it might be hard to anticipate at the time, it seems pretty inevitable impressive peaks of reward will be followed by equally impressive troughs at some point. Unfortunately, that seems to be precisely what has happened in 2008. And from the great highs in reward of the last 18 months or so, the UK seems now to have plummeted into a new era of austerity.

Yet the fundamental underlying trends in base pay movement haven't really changed yet; any impact will almost certainly be felt first in the areas of bonuses and other cash-based incentives. And so, the latest pay rounds pose something of a challenge. On the one hand inflation in some areas (most notably fuel and food) had been picking up pace, prompting many employees to expect a little more than the 3% increase that typified settlements made during the sustained period of stability.

Conversely though, the general gloom that hangs over the market, the sudden increase in unemployment, falling real inflation, and the stark predictions that 2009 will only bring a worsening picture, all contribute to the feeling for many employers that the next pay reviews will be more challenging than ever before.

In reality, there is a very strong chance that many organisations will still aim for the yardstick 3% pay settlement. But this may have more to do with the tectonic collision of factors that apply pressure on pay and less to do with stability and predictability.

Where might this take us?

This leaves us with a number of unanswered and possibly unanswerable questions. Will employers place more emphasis on variable pay to share the risk and reward? How will employers share out a potentially diminishing 'pot' among the same number of employees? Will there be a fundamental change in the way pay is structured going forward?

In reality, it's pretty difficult to answer any of these questions with any certainty given the overarching economic conditions that we find ourselves in.

There is no doubt that some employers will look at shifting the mix of base to variable pay and probably invoke more demanding or at least more visible mechanisms for linking pay to performance. And let's not fool ourselves that this will just apply to higher earners – there's a good chance that everyone who works in a performance-based environment will have to demonstrate their own value just a little bit more if they want to share in any of the rewards.

But even then it may be that these people are the lucky ones. We're already seeing examples of companies making a choice between keeping heads but on reduced hours and simply cutting back on staff numbers. This notion of sharing out the pain of the current conditions, which is by the way certainly not a new idea, seems to be gathering momentum. The advent of flexible working of course has made the involvement of employees themselves in that decision-making process a slightly more palatable approach. But in short it all boils down to the same thing.

If you've only got a finite amount of money, and that resource is dwindling before your eyes, you have to take decisive and sometime drastic action just to stay afloat.

So I don't think we can make any hard and fast predications about how this current crisis will really affect pay over the next two to three years. But one thing is for sure – there will be an effect and it's unlikely that it will be a positive one for many employees at whatever level and in which ever sector they operate in.

Employers might just need to get a bit more creative about how they construct and communicate their reward packages and couple these more closely to the real things that ultimately affect their ability to make the right moves on annual pay settlements.

Andrew Walker

Andrew Walker is business director at Croner Reward, the specialist pay and benefits arm of Croner, a Wolters Kluwer business. Publishing 60 'off-the-shelf' salary survey titles each year and with a range of salary benchmarking and job evaluation tools, Croner Reward is one of the best known and most respected names in this specialist segment of HR service provision. More information can be found at www.croner-reward.co.uk.

Andrew is a judge for the 2009 edition of *Britain's Top Employers*.

Becoming the employer or employee of choice and coming out on top!

"No problem can be solved from the same consciousness that created it. We must learn to see the world anew." (Albert Einstein)

The year 2009 is shaping up to be a very challenging one, whether you are an employer, an employee, a chief executive, a graduate, or a school leaver looking for a job. For employers, these are particularly interesting times. There is a very strong business case for being an employer of choice; after all, the hardest thing for your competitors to copy is your greatest asset – your people. Being an employer of choice helps with recruitment, retention of talent, creativity and innovation, customer service and becoming an organisation that clients and customers enjoy dealing with.

Wise employers pursue a number of key initiatives. For example, acknowledging that the organisation always needs a healthy flow of new talent – even during a downturn, freezes on recruitment are not productive measures. Employees thrive in an environment where they are allowed to shine and be appreciated and their talents and strengths need to be managed and understood. At the same time, high standards should be set and appraisal systems rigorously organised. Acknowledge and celebrate success, create a happy working environment, and make work fun when possible; these will help to maximise the value and productivity of your people. Live the company values. Strive to understand the different motivations (and demotivations) of different generations: the baby boomers born 1946-1965; the X generation from 1965-1977; and the Y generation born between 1976-1995 (or 1982-2001 depending on the source); and of course the latest work generation, born after 1993, which is about to enter the workforce. Finally, have the right management in place, with high levels of emotional intelligence, and recruit for attitude.

How people feel about the employer brand is increasingly critical to business success or failure, particularly as the next 12 months for most organisations, especially those in the private sector, will be challenging to say the least. Leading companies realise the importance of attracting and engaging the people they need to deliver profitable growth. They are also beginning to recognise that creating a positive brand experience for employees requires the same degree of focus, care and coherence that has long characterised effective management of the customer brand experience.

When it comes to recruitment, different sectors will probably have different fortunes. After the fallout in Banking and Financial Services, a recent graduate milk round survey indicated that this sector was now the least attractive to graduates... no surprises there. It is going to take some considerable time for this sector to regain its lustre. Sectors that show better opportunity are those involved in Energy, Oil and Gas. It is thought that the Nuclear Energy industry will go through a revival, as will the areas of Renewables, Life Sciences and some of the other new groundbreaking sciences and technologies. The public sector is also expected to remain a strong recruiter. However, this is probably not the year to go into the Estate Agency business!

In terms of roles and functions, due to the large and inevitable level of restructuring and integration, we expect to see a greater demand for HR, supply chain and procurement specialists. Despite this backdrop, organisations in any sector can enter a recession as the leader, but end up as a loser coming out. Smarter organisations use downturns to hire the best talent at a time when competitors are battening down the hatches and losing theirs. This is the time to hire people who can help generate new, fresh ideas and solutions more quickly than the competition. Being surrounded by 'yes' people looking for a safe ride out of the downturn can be tantamount to business suicide. To drive creativity organisations need to allow the freedom to experiment with a variety of experience and skills, knowledge and understanding.

The legacy of the Internet age is that everything is so much faster, but the organisations that will succeed in the future are those with a different generation of leaders and entrepreneurs who are more courageous, challenging and ambitious.

Whether you are currently a CEO or a fresh graduate, my advice is universal: as an individual, reflect on the aspirations, beliefs, values and passions that are right for you. Excel at your craft, stay ahead of your game, and turn up the volume. This is certainly the year to improve your personal branding, connect with your market, and get yourself known.

With the Confederation of British Industry (CBI) predicting a 2% contraction this year, and jobless figures expected to peak at approximately three million (the same as during the 1990's recession), none of us can afford to be complacent. In summary my advice is to be visible, demonstrate the value of the work you are doing, and manage your personal brand inside your organisation and in your sector.

Be a 'downturn buster', by aligning your work with the new imperatives of the business. In downturns there is greater emphasis on shorter term wins, cost savings and risk minimisation. Be a leader – take a leadership role in seeing your company through the difficult times. In times of downturn people often become negative, protective and inward facing. Be the opposite. Keep the long-term strategic vision alive. Be positive, helpful, generous and open, and lead by example. Be well networked and keep up-to-date with what your competitors are doing by attending conferences and seminars. Be your company's ear to the ground. Be prepared – if you are concerned your job is at risk, contact recruitment intermediaries and update your CV. Check your savings; securing a new job in 2009 may take longer than you expect – maybe 25% longer than on average, or around 56 days.

At the other end of the scale, if you are a graduate or school leaver, target carefully those organisations that you would like to work for in 2009. If you can contemplate working without pay or at a reduced salary, you may make yourself invaluable to that organisation. 'A sprat to catch a mackerel' – I have seen this strategy by graduates pay healthy dividends.

Despite the downturn, this could very well be the perfect time to approach one of the excellent organisations listed in this year's book, taking your skills, talent and energy where it will be appreciated. We're all in the same boat. And the best will seek out the best. As Coco Chanel once said, and this is probably relevant to both employer and employee, "In order to be irreplaceable, one must always be different."

Clive Sexton

Clive Sexton is a director of Impact Executives, the leading Global Interim Management Providers, a division of Harvey Nash plc, with over 36 offices across Europe, North America and Asia. He has extensive commercial experience gained through general management and board roles within both Plc's and also through running his own businesses. Clive has over 18 years of international experience providing cross-functional resourcing solutions to both global businesses and start-ups.

Clive is a judge for the 2009 edition of *Britain's Top Employers.*

A time for responsible mavericks

The credit crunch took most people by surprise. From the Treasury to bankers, and industry to consumers, we have gone from being 'cautiously optimistic' to downright scared. If there's a lesson in this, it's the need for quick reactions in business. We have been surprised; we will certainly be surprised again. Rather than how *well* we predict and plan the future, perhaps the issue should be how *quickly* we can react. How open are we to new possibilities as they arrive?

Too many organisations cling on to old realities; too many are sure that their success is due to their cleverness and determination rather than just sharing in a rising market. Luck plays a larger role in success at work than most of us like to believe.

New ideas don't usually come out of nowhere. The blinding flash of insight, where an entirely fresh idea leaps full blown into existence is, frankly, a myth. New ways of doing things come from unconventional *connections* – from seeing how a different industry approaches your problem, from drawing on ideas in completely different fields. It's why business leaders are interested in how conductors lead their musicians; it's why the NHS is interested in Toyota's lean production line. Change is about blending the new with the old and joining up unrelated ideas more than fresh creation. Flexible businesses, therefore, use the full range of perspectives and backgrounds in their people – they have many connections and many sources of inspiration. These businesses also avoid the 'group think' that stops people questioning decisions. They have an in-built maverick streak.

It is one thing to recruit a diverse workforce, without discrimination on age, gender, ethnicity, disability or sexual orientation. Indeed both the law and decency require it. But just obeying the law on equality does not do enough for performance. We should be more interested in what's going on in people's minds than what categories they represent. We need a diversity of mindsets and beliefs. It is true that employing a mix of ages, genders, races and cultures is much more likely to provide this; but it may not be enough. Many organisations are actually quite good at destroying mental diversity, however well they tick the boxes on the demographic profiles of their workforce. Do leaders praise and value the dissenter? Do they seek the contrary opinion? Do they take the time to get to know where people come from? Do they help people on how to make their case, and how to deal with conflict well? Do they promote based on ability rather than in their own image? Do they manage people as individuals rather than as categories? Do they give advice that helps people to grow or keep quiet out of political correctness? Do they make it easy for people with different lifestyles to work for them?

People often praise strong company cultures – the clear set of values and widely understood principles that get everybody behind a single vision and teach people how to behave. Sounds good, but dramatic changes in the economy show the limits of culture. Shared values do help, but they can also drown out the dissenting view; that's practically the definition of culture.

The investment bank, Lehman Brothers, was a widely respected 158-year-old firm. Its collapse triggered the latest stage of the financial crisis. The bank's chief executive was brilliant, aggressive and utterly intolerant of dissent or difference. Did this mean that everything he ordered was immediately done? Far from it - people merely hid what they were doing from him. Even worse, no one brought him bad news. Lehman is no more.

There are other benefits to supporting diversity and dissent. Attracting and keeping good staff is one of them. People

tend to join places where they can be themselves and stay if their work makes them proud. Furthermore, if we have a limited amount of time, attention and money with which to reward staff, then targeting those resources at the things that inspire each individual will make those resources go further. One interesting finding of several studies is that good employers tend to pay lower salaries than bad employers. There is a premium to be paid for being an unpleasant place to work. There are lessons to be learned for employers and employees alike. Employers might want to question how they promote mental diversity. Small actions can go a long way – choosing who and what to celebrate, for example; creating 'rituals' where people are actively encouraged to express doubt in meetings; finding out what's different about people and finding ways to use it.

For employees, on the other hand, the question is, how do I become a responsible maverick? Tolerance, courage and the ability to back your gut feel are essential. A responsible maverick also knows when to stop objecting – to put their case strongly but to abide by the final decision and stick to it enthusiastically. There is a difference between a dissenter and a saboteur.

Spotting whether an employer has the right culture is difficult, as it is easy to talk a good game during recruitment. The truth tends to become clear once work has started. Talking to existing staff is one route round this. Who tends to get ahead in this place? How do they match people to projects? When people disagree, what happens? How well respected are members of management below the chief executive? How is experience discovered and recorded? Do people give each other honest feedback?

From the employer's perspective, spotting a responsible maverick in a potential recruit is far easier. They will be willing to disagree with untenable claims and positions; they'll be aware of their feelings and reactions; and they'll take responsibility for group decisions rather than blame others.

The issue of diversity goes far beyond the fashion of 'corporate social responsibility' and into the realm of corporate survival. It moves beyond compliance to culture. These are the only ways to attract more demanding staff and build the creativity and flexibility needed in a harsh economic climate.

Phillip Wright

Phillip Wright is a consultant with Hay Group, a global management consulting firm. See www.haygroup.co.uk for more information.

Phillip is a judge for the 2009 edition of *Britain's Top Employers.*

Methodology

Britain's Top Employers 2009 is an annual research-based HR publishing project designed to assist high-performing organisations with the overall assessment of their HR function.

The aim of *Britain's Top Employers* is to identify, accredit and laud British companies with a demonstrable commitment to and track record in talent management best practice on an annual basis.

> *"To be in a position to attract the best talent, companies are required to align their people management policies and procedures with the right corporate culture, work environment, employer brand and employee offering."*
> **(Alan Hosking, publisher of HR Future)**

CRF's holistic and inclusive research approach to employer framework (HR policies and practices) is unmatched, and for the 2009 project, the company cooperated with Deloitte and CRF International to better improve the HR Benchmark™ survey, which underpins the results of the project.

Developing the employer brand

Employees are not depending on companies anymore. More and more it is the other way around. If employees lose their commitment – or are not engaged anymore – this can have severe impact. In the short run motivation may go down which will also affect others. Secondly talent may start looking around during this difficult time. Since a company is depending on fewer staff doing more, the operational impact will be larger than during times of economic boom.

However during a downturn employees are less willing to shop around. Having said this, when the economy is recovering it will be these more talented people in your company who will be the first to go and it's in this phase when you need them most.

Talking about employer branding during a recession may seem strange. But employer branding is an opportunity for a company to differentiate itself from competition. Strong employer brands can give companies a significant competitive edge, which is more important during a downturn when margins are tight.

Research even suggests that companies seen as top employers even outperform in terms of financial performance, as well as have lower employment costs.

While branding initiatives may have been started when a company was looking to expand, it makes sense to continue with employer branding and keep communicating accordingly.

Make the employer brand work for you – get accredited

Just as the overall company brand is developed to further engage customers and investors, so the employer brand is a construct for the engagement of employees.

International research undertaken by Gallup, the pioneers of this concept, revealed that employee

engagement can be a catalyst for change and transformation. This is in large part due to its link to business outcomes such as:

- Retention
- Productivity
- Effective service delivery or profitability
- Customer engagement, and
- Safety orientation

According to international research commissioned by Robinson, Perryman and Hayday (2004), engaged employees generally displayed the following behaviour patterns:

- Belief in their organisation
- Desire to work towards making things better
- Understanding of business context and the bigger picture
- Respectful of and helpful to their colleagues
- Willingness to go the extra mile
- Keeping up to date with developments on the ground

The exercise of being researched by CRF's HR best practice research survey, the HR Benchmark™, is a good way for companies to assess their employer value proposition relative to the general market, and their industry.
This in turn allows participating companies to adjust their HR strategy in line with what is needed to fully engage employees.

Using this research CRF accredits organisations with the internationally recognised third-party endorsement of their employer value proposition. Only companies who achieve a minimum score in the HR Benchmark™ can be accredited and ultimately published by CRF.

This Top Employer quality seal visibly communicates to talent, both externally and internally, that the company has achieves a benchmark standard in HR best practice.

HR Benchmark™: Areas of research

The following areas are researched through the HR Benchmark™:

Organisational Strategy: What are the organisation's talent management priorities?

The HR Function: The functioning of the HR department and its alignment with the overall business strategy.

Communication: What are the lines of communication between employees and the company, and what is the impact of this?

Diversity Management: How is the company responding to the diversity imperative?

Corporate Social Responsibility: How is the company responding to legal and ethical imperatives and how are employees engaged in order to achieve this?

Knowledge Management: How is this aspect of the business managed, and how does this translate into organisational success as knowledge is gained and shared?

Talent Management and Engagement: Assesses 'vital' statistics on employee entry and exit, and how this is managed.

Employee Development: How are employees nurtured, mentored and developed in order for both them and the organisation to reach their goals?

Performance Management: Performance agreements and competency framework assessment.

Reward and Recognition: How are employees recognised and rewarded for their achievements and successes?

The questionnaire offers a range of options per question, and many of the questions invite companies to include more information in an open field option contained in the question.

Each area has an overall score that can be achieved, and some areas are weighted more heavily than others. The scores that all participating firms achieved in the following criteria are presented as stars, ranging from 3 stars (good) to 5 stars (excellent):

- Pay and Benefits
- Training and Development
- Career Development
- Working Conditions
- Company Culture

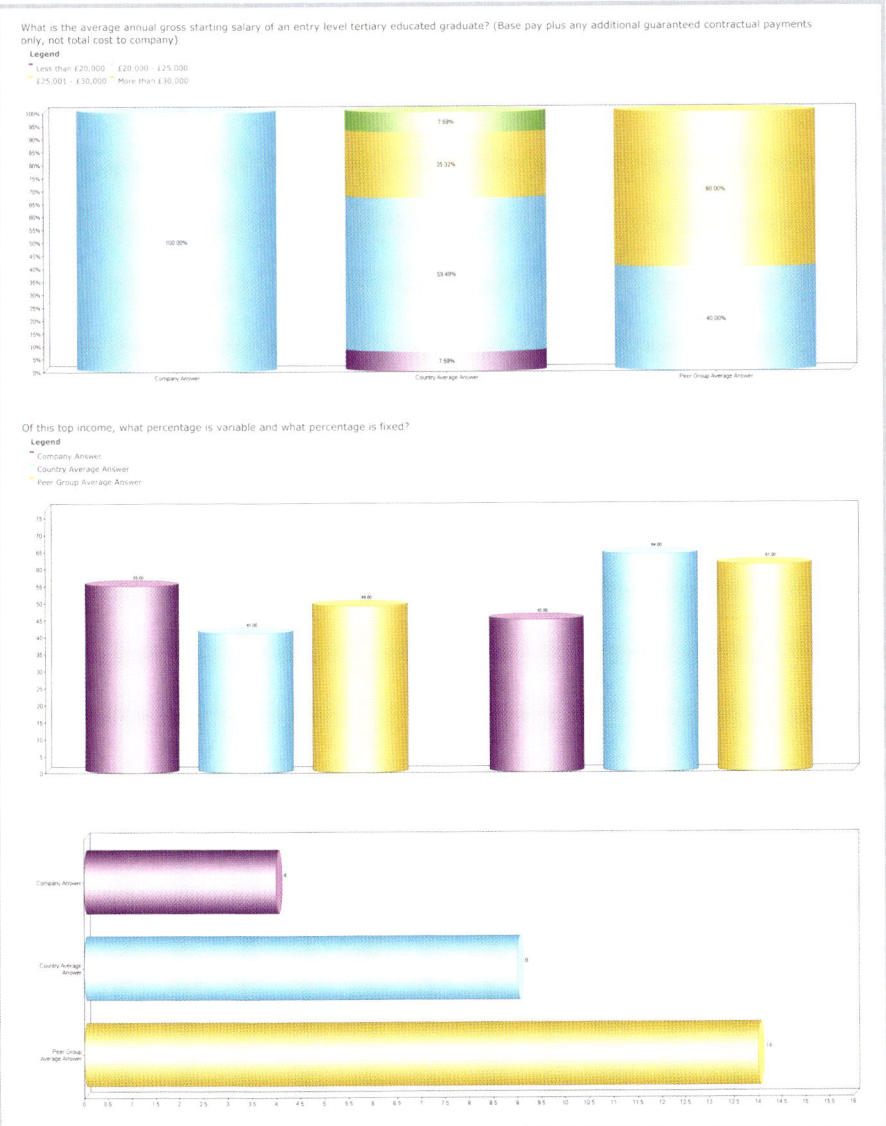

What is the average annual gross starting salary of an entry level tertiary educated graduate? (Base pay plus any additional guaranteed contractual payments only, not total cost to company)

Legend
- Less than £20,000
- £20,000 - £25,000
- £25,001 - £30,000
- More than £30,000

Of this top income, what percentage is variable and what percentage is fixed?

Legend
- Company Answer
- Country Average Answer
- Peer-Group Average Answer

Sample pages from an HR Benchmark™ report

Participating companies that do not meet the requirements will not receive the CRF Quality Seal, nor will their results or profile be published. However, they do get a full report on their performance and position as an employer in the form of the HR Benchmark™, so that they can gain insight into their strengths, weaknesses and possible areas for improvement.

Only accredited Top Employers are published in the annual book *Top Employers UK* for the relevant year.

The research process for each project also includes desk research, analysis and interviews with the senior management of the participating organisations, which is then compiled with the questionnaire results.

Companies

AimiA foods

astbury marsden

Badenoch & Clark

BPP BUSINESS SCHOOL · BPP LAW SCHOOL ·

BROADWAY

The co-operative

DentonWildeSapte...

DLA PIPER

FREMANTLEMEDIA

Friends of the Earth

gsk GlaxoSmithKline

HCL

NHS · HEART of ENGLAND NHS Foundation Trust

hydrogen

IBM

Iceland

IG GROUP

informa

innocent

Irwell Valley

J·D·WETHERSPOON

John Lewis Partnership

WG WOOD GROUP

L&Q HOUSING TRUST

LV= LIVERPOOL VICTORIA

Aimia Foods Ltd

Penny Lane
Haydock
Merseyside WA11 0QZ

Telephone: 01942 408600
Fax: 01942 272831
Email: info@aimiafoods.com
www.aimiafoods.com

Pay and Benefits	★ ★ ★ ☆ ☆
Training and Development	★ ★ ★ ☆ ☆
Career Development	★ ★ ★ ★ ⯪
Working Conditions	★ ★ ★ ⯪ ☆
Company Culture	★ ★ ★ ⯪ ☆

Biggest Plus
Ability to react quickly to changes in the marketplace and come up with suitable products.

Greatest challenge
Retaining the confidence of the big brands in a fickle and changing market.

Summary

Aimia Foods may not be a household name yet its business is steeped in household names and international brands. If you pop your money into a vending machine for a drink, the chances are that your purchase started life at Aimia. Or when you scour the supermarket shelves for beverages and your eye catches products from the likes of Galaxy, Maltesers, Milky Way, WeightWatchers, Slazenger and Outspan, their first home was probably at Aimia Foods in Haydock. As a leading supplier of beverages to the retail, foodservice and vending markets, Aimia is everywhere. In addition, it also co-packs major household brands on behalf of international blue chip clients such as Nestle, Kraft, Premier, Cadbury and GSK.

About the organisation

Aimia Foods is a family business run as a family business. That might sound inappropriate for a business that employs 250 people on three sites, distributes products throughout the UK, and has a turnover approaching £55m and a pre-tax profit of £2m. But a family firm it very much is.

The company was started by brothers Ian and Gary Unsworth in 1981, became Nichols Foods in 1986 after a takeover, and in 2004 ownership returned to the Unsworth family after an MBO. While rubbing shoulders with international brand giants the family is anything but aloof and is caring and thoughtful with its staff.

The MBO brought key changes to the organisation. Gary and Ian have recently taken on non-executive roles as consultants. Gary's wife Jackie, with the business since day one in charge of human resources, now works part-time, looking after the culture side of the business. Lorraine Mercer, who has a Unilever and Meridian background, is now in charge of HR and Gary's son Rob, a chartered accountant, is now managing director. There are now five non-family members of the board, four of which represented internal promotions. Rob Unsworth says: "Lots of family businesses try to keep it under family control and I think the way we have changed is quite enlightening."

Major investment has brought a state-of-the-art stock management system at a new 5,000 pallet capacity warehouse close to the company HQ and Aimia has just commissioned a 65,000 sq. ft. bespoke factory for an international, US-based cereal firm. For this client, Aimia ensures the cereal packing process from » start to finish is of world-class standards of quality, whilst providing outstanding customer service, all done on a long-term partnership. This is part of the growing outsourcing business and this coup shows that Aimia knows where it is going – and how it is going to get there.

Company Culture

Dave Taggart collects a visitor at Wigan railway station and when asked about working at Aimia he says his wife had an illness which lasted 15 months and it meant he frequently had to get time off to care for her. "They bent over backwards to help me. I never lost a penny of my salary." This unsolicited testimonial is not unusual from Aimia employees.

Dave is a member of a management and staff committee that meets once a month and calls itself 'How Are We Doing?' This is the focal point for any complaints or suggestions and action is taken. A bike shed is requested. Staff discuss and agree a date and theme for the next fun day. Night shift workers did not get a share of a celebration cake – so a further one was made. All seemingly mundane stuff but an essential part of team bonding all round.

Managing director Rob Unsworth explains: "Companies talk about communication but they believe it is from the top down. We try to do it the other way round – we like to have open, honest meetings and address any concerns."

His mother Jackie adds: "We are all team players – there are no prima donnas."

The company lists its core values as partnership, people, energy, integrity and passion and stresses that these can be achieved only through a valued workforce.

The staff handbook states: "As individuals we are all free-thinking, creative and innovative, but at the same time commercially aware. The culture of our business really encourages team spirit and fun but, above all, we seek to act with integrity."

Gary Unsworth says there is another important ingredient: "They are the intangibles. We look for them in people. They are harder to measure but we believe in looking for them."

Innovation and Creativity

Aimia's amazing distinction is the trust placed in it by international brands to develop, manufacture, pack and deliver their products to their exacting specifications. It's not a misplaced trust but it is not all about following instructions and delivering what is being asked for.

A crucial part of the business is recognising consumer trends and approaching their customers with ideas and suggestions. If, for example, they have an idea for a new WeightWatchers product they knock on the WeightWatchers door and talk about it (that's already happened and a new WeightWatchers product is on the way). As Rob Unsworth puts it: "We have to understand what the consumer will need – before he knows it."

"The way we have changed is quite enlightening"
(Rob Unsworth, managing director)

Consequently, Chris Durling, general manager of research and development, has 500 different product lines and he constantly has to stay ahead of the game. If Jamie Oliver forces education authorities to find something different for school meal menus Chris makes sure that Aimia is working on it before they get round to asking.

He's even innovative with the words he uses. 'Premiumisation' is fully exploiting respected brand names; while 'virtuousity' is providing products and procurement which show the Fairtrade pundits that their concerns are shared.

Pay and Benefits

Aimia is about much more than food and drink. It uses pioneering technology to package and distribute products so that its strength is just as much in the factory as in the laboratory. That demands a wide variety of skills, competing in different sectors of the market for top quality people. Aimia gets them – and keeps them – by offering more than the competition. The process means constantly benchmarking what local companies are up to so that they can stay ahead of the game in attracting and keeping the calibre of people to keep pushing the company forward.

Incentives abound – and have to be earned. A new staff incentive scheme gives employees the chance to earn up to £500 extra if they achieve certain objectives. The company contributes £75 per employee for all staff towards celebrating success at summer and Christmas nights out.

There is a defined contribution pension scheme, life cover and a health cash plan providing payments towards healthcare costs and unexpected medical bills. As part of a new Health Sure plan that has been implemented all staff opting for it qualify not only for healthcare benefits but also free and confidential counselling and a debt advisory service.

There is an occupational health nurse available, an on-site chiropody service, bereavement, maternity, paternity, adoption and parental leave, and a turkey and six bottles of wine and Easter egg for all staff!

And there's more. There's free use of the company's holiday homes in the UK, Spain and Florida, a social club, a staff recognition scheme called 'You Are a Star' for those who go that extra mile when delivering »

"If you are good enough, flaunt it"
(Ghazanfer Ali, QSHE manager)

internal customer service, a childcare voucher scheme for parents with children under the age of 16 and cash awards for those who complete 10, 15 and 20 years' plus service.

Career Development

Aimia believes that its independent family-owned status means that there are perhaps more opportunities than in a larger multinational organisation to move through the company in pursuit of your career goals.

A case in point is the decision in January 2008, to reorganise the hierarchy. This elevated Rob Unsworth to managing director, and brought in five non-family members to help run the business. Four of them joined the board from within the company – Dameon Bamber to purchasing director, Malcolm Downing to operations director, David Drabble to finance director and Steve Johnson to business development director. The next move is to roll out incentives to keep them at Aimia for the long-term.

A revised personal development review system has been introduced, backed by a determination to ensure that it is used fairly and consistently. This encourages participation from employees by asking them to give their own views on achievement of objectives and assessment of core skills.

To ensure that this is tailored to the needs of staff and managers, stakeholder interviews are held with a wide range of personnel. From the completed personal development reviews, individual training needs are identified and the required training programme is delivered. A new role of technical trainer has been established to push training along and as a result, training hours per employee have increased significantly.

In partnership with the local college a significant number of production operatives have completed NVQ Level 2 in Food and Drink Manufacturing and this is ongoing.

At a different level the company stresses that it is committed to management development and 'upskilling' by providing the opportunity to attend two-day training and development sessions on essential management skills. The company believes that together with in-house learning lunches this forms a solid foundation to build upon.

Corporate Social Responsibility

Ghazanfer Ali joined the company in February 2008 as QSHE manager, responsible for quality, safety, hygiene and

the environment. These subjects had always been given due care and attention but the appointment of the man from Mars – one of Aimia's top three brand partners – heralded an even more serious approach.

Recycling, segregating materials and managing waste have been a way of life at Aimia for some time but Ghaz has a mission to step it up. He says: "I have taken it one step forward. We want to minimise our impact on the environment. It might not seem to some the greatest priority but it is morally the right way to go about it. We are looking to reduce wastage by 20% in the next 12 months with similar savings on energy."

He is determined to take it all to the nth degree and to let suppliers – and indeed, the world – know about it. He says: "If you are good enough, flaunt it, and in our business we have to do that. Sometimes we don't sell ourselves enough."

The company complies with and exceeds all regulatory requirements in respect of wastage, pollution and health and safety standards for employees. Wherever practicable the company uses recycled material in packaging, marking packaging for easy separation of recyclable elements and its corporate literature and sales materials are produced on paper certified as originating from sustainable sources.

It has a clear commitment to the principal of equal opportunity in employment and it says that all employees have a duty not to discriminate unlawfully against fellow employees, customers, suppliers or members of the public. Cross the line and it is a disciplinary offence, maybe even gross misconduct.

On corporate governance, as Aimia is not a publicly quoted company it does not have to conform to Stock Exchange rules and regulations regarding shareholders and market-sensitive information. But the company view is that corporate governance is not just about legal compliance but also about surpassing legal and customer expectations.

Ethics are a cornerstone of how Aimia conducts itself in the marketplace. As the business is centred around its people the HR department offers equal opportunities for all and is constantly benchmarking local companies to ensure the business attracts and retains the best people. The business has now been accredited with Investor In People for over 10 years.

Facts and figures

Total number of staff: 250
Office location: Haydock, Lancashire
Industry sector: Food packaging
Annual turnover: £55m

astbury marsden

Astbury Marsden

Augustine House
6a Austin Friars
London EC2N 2HA

Telephone: 020 7065 1222
www.astburymarsden.com

Pay and Benefits	★ ★ ★ ⯪ ☆
Training and Development	★ ★ ★ ★ ⯪
Career Development	★ ★ ★ ★ ⯪
Working Conditions	★ ★ ★ ☆ ☆
Company Culture	★ ★ ★ ★ ☆

Biggest plus
The company can and will do everything to help 'make it happen'.

Greatest challenge
Finding those people who want to make it happen.

Summary

Founded in 1995, Astbury Marsden is a City based recruitment firm that places mid-to-senior level professionals within banking, financial services and specialist markets throughout Europe and Asia. Clients include Barclays, JP Morgan, HSBC and Deloitte.

Astbury Marsden is on track to have four offices outside of its London headquarters by 2012, with the first opening in Hong Kong in the first quarter of 2009. The second international office in the Middle East should follow shortly after in the first half of the year.

The company's sales have grown rapidly from £1.9m in 2002 to £12.1m in 2005 to over £30m today. In 2007 managing director Jonathan Nicholson and chief operating officer Mark Cameron led a management buyout backed by NVM Private Equity with a view to continuing to invest in the business.

About the organisation

"Since the management buyout we have been reviewing our company strategy" says Cameron. "Our key focus is to become the leading international recruitment firm delivering mid-to-senior level talent to banking, financial services and specialist markets clients throughout the UK, Europe, the Middle East and Asia. We have consolidated our Professional Services and Commerce business into a specialist markets unit. This gives us the opportunity to allow more entrepreneurial people to grow new, niche businesses within our existing business."

To become the leading international recruiter by 2012, Cameron points to four key objectives the firm has set:

1) **To identify and develop leading people.** This means having the best people and teams in the market. Astbury Marsden wants to be an inspirational employer with more ownership from within the business. Since the MBO, five more stakeholders have been appointed.

»

2) **To create a market leading brand.** "Recruitment businesses are essentially the same. The distinguishing factor between them is the quality of people and the way they engage with clients and candidates. We aspire to be something different to the competition by the way we position ourselves and engage with people."

3) **Build relationships with leading market players.** "Our client base is a reflection of us as an organisation."

4) **Deliver an industry leading performance.** "By 2012 we aim to have a turnover of £50m. To achieve this we need 140 employees across four to five international offices," says Cameron.

Already, the firm has delivered recruitment solutions across Europe, the Middle East and Asia and is currently in the process of setting up local offices.

The business has been recognised in the Sunday Times Fast Track 100 as one of the fastest growing in the UK for the last two years. It was also identified as the 'One to Watch' in 2008 by *Best Companies*, listed 53rd in the *Real Business Hot 100*, and was a finalist in 'The Recruiter's Best Financial Services Recruiter' category.

Company Culture

Astbury Marsden instils a culture of personal pride and ownership, where people feel they own a business within a business. "If a vertical market can be built from a desk, people should feel proud of the business they have created," says Cameron. "There are many opportunities at Astbury Marsden for people who want to make that happen."

The business operates a flat structure. A large open plan office means anyone can walk up to the managing director or COO's desk as they share the same space as everyone else. There are no partitioned offices, although there are naturally a few meeting rooms. There is an honest culture here – if you ask a question you will always get an answer. "People understand that we are quite open," says Cameron.

On offering a work-life balance, the firm impresses on its people that it is a performance business, a sales environment where the more you sell the better you will do. If you can make it happen here, you can achieve a rewarding work-life balance. Some employees who have been doing particularly well have changed their working hours to fit in with their personal activities.

"If you perform well, you can choose how much input your require from the business day-to-day," says Cameron. "Performance is the currency in our organisation."

A group, comprising the MD, COO, HR training and development manager and internal recruitment executive, meets twice a month to work out how to attract the right people. Once on board, how does the company retain them, develop them and ensure they surprise themselves? "We are keen to engage our employees on an ongoing basis to understand how we can meet their needs," says Cameron.

"The distinguishing factor between them [recruitment businesses] is the quality of the people and the way they engage with clients and candidates" (Mark Cameron, chief operating officer)

"If you expect to win,
you're more likely
to be successful in
business; people
need to understand
the biggest influence
on the end game
is them"
(Jonathan Nicholson,
managing director)

Innovation and Creativity

An impromptu quarterly MD Forum is held for anyone who wants to ask questions. This is well attended and provides "a forum to allow people to engage directly," says Cameron. "We encourage people to come armed with solutions rather than problems and for teams to come up with their own ideas. The ultimate aim is for people to be empowered to run their owned business."

Astbury Marsden is a people business and creativity comes through its employees. "It is knowledge and connections that we sell," says Cameron. "We encourage creativity in our employees; we want them to come to us with their solutions and ideas on how we can meet client requirements more effectively and how we can engage with them."

This is not a breakthrough industry; Astbury Marsden is a consulting firm where innovation comes from the people. It improves the quality of organisations, offering strategic solutions to their problems, and seeking their leaders of tomorrow. "Solving client's problems is the first step," says Cameron.

To do this, Astbury Marsden seeks natural ability from its staff and a hunger to succeed. "We help our people by providing them with the skills to perform at their best," says Cameron.

Pay and Benefits

"We want to be competitive with our peer organisations on pay and rewards. We don't set out to be the best payer, we set out to give people the opportunity to achieve the sort of income that they want to in our organisation," says Cameron. "If people exceed expectations and perform well, we're happy for them to share in the fruits of their labour."

Remuneration is made up from a base salary plus commission and an opportunity to receive a performance bonus. The rewards are commission-related and down to the individual – the more you bill, the greater share of your billing you will get. Managers receive a base salary with a bonus scheme tied to deliverable objectives.

Senior consultants and staff who have been with the company for two years are invited to join the group »

"Work is as interesting as you want to make it"
(Mark Cameron, chief operating officer)

personal pension scheme, where the company matches staff contributions up to 4% of salary. Everyone can join the stakeholder pension scheme and death-in-service (four times salary) benefit after three months. The firm is keen to promote healthy living and its health cover (available to all staff and provided for managers and those who have been with the firm for two years) provides members with financial incentives to go to the gym, eat well and participate in a healthy lifestyle. Holiday allowance is 25 days, plus Bank Holidays.

There is also a share option scheme. To qualify you must demonstrate you have created something of significant value in the business, and you must continue to show repeat increases in such business. This year five people have been invited into the scheme through excellent performance-related work.

Career Development

"The drive behind our desire to grow the organisation is so we can provide more career opportunities," says Cameron.

The two career tracks in the organisation are concerned with management and sales. There are programmes underpinning the two routes – there is a recruitment excellence programme (a rolling event run every two weeks) focussing on a consultant's work and there are business development courses to hone skills (e.g. closing a deal). Beyond this there are emerging talent and management programmes to develop management skills.

The sales route offers advanced sales training and a range of specialist courses. Personal development plans are available for everyone covering personal goals, professional goals and what progress is being achieved. Plans are reviewed every six months.

"Work is as interesting as you want to make it," says Cameron. "We run competitions where everyone will swap teams and we can see who delivers the best results. It's a good way both of meeting other staff and gaining invaluable experience."

International opportunities now exist through the Hong Kong and Middle East offices.

Corporate Social Responsibility

"We are very supportive of CSR, but not as a box-ticking exercise," says Cameron. "Because we are a people business, we are interested in what employees think and what motivates them." There are three key foundations underpinning the company's social responsibility:

1) The environment: There are well-advanced plans to become a carbon neutral company; this covers everything from recycling initiatives through to notices to switch PCs off at night. A Ride to Work bicycle scheme also operates where the firm assists employees to pay for equipment and accessories.

2) Employee well-being: there is an employee advice line which offers confidential legal advice, bereavement support and employment advice and a medical scheme which offers a cash-back facility for people who seek to stay healthy.

3) Community initiatives: This is where the firm will partner with organisations e.g. the firm will run CV writing and interview training classes for school leavers.

"The CSR committee is run by people in the business" says Cameron. "The committee meets once a month. I support the committee's endeavours and represent them and their initiatives at boardroom level. Consequently there is the support to deliver the change the employees want."

"We understand that our people are the key to our success. To recognise this, we offer a number of rewards and benefits and encourage all our people to take full advantage of what we have to offer," says Nicholson.

Facts and figures

Total number of staff: 68, with planned growth to 130
Office location: London, opening in Hong Kong and Middle East (2009)
Industry sector: Recruitment, in banking, financial services and specialist areas
Annual turnover: over £30m

A member of MPS Group International

Badenoch & Clark

Millennium Bridge House
2 Lambeth Hill
London
EC4V 4BG

Telephone: 020 7583 0073
Fax: 020 7429 5001
www.badenochandclark.com

Pay and Benefits	★ ★ ★ ⯪ ☆
Training and Development	★ ★ ★ ★ ★
Career Development	★ ★ ★ ★ ★
Working Conditions	★ ★ ★ ☆ ☆
Company Culture	★ ★ ★ ★ ☆

Biggest plus
A commitment to improve consistently the service provided to clients and to candidates.

Greatest challenge
Going beyond the standard recruitment process to act more as a trusted adviser to its clients.

Summary

Badenoch & Clark is a recruitment company that is best known for dealing in finance, accountancy and legal staff, but it has evolved into a wide-ranging business that also covers the public sector, information technology and human resources markets. Badenoch & Clark started in 1980, when founder Alexander Badenoch began supplying permanent and temporary accountancy and finance staff. It soon took off on the back of the rising demand for these workers. Now part of MPS Group, a listed US company that sees the business as a key to European expansion, it has 15 offices around the UK in addition to London and a developing European network.

About the organisation

Now headed by managing director Neil Wilson, the company expanded rapidly on the back of both the 1980s economic boom and the growing demand for temporary professional services workers, to become a leading provider of temporary, contract and permanent staff in various specialisms within the public and private sectors.

In 1997, Badenoch sold the business to a US company now known as MPS Group, which is based in Jacksonville, Florida and is a leading provider of staffing and consulting services in the United States, Canada and Europe.

The company now employs 500 people in the UK. More than half are based in London, with the rest spread among 15 regional offices, stretching from Bristol to Edinburgh. The business, which had a turnover in 2007 of £239m, also has subsidiary companies operating in Germany, Luxemburg and the Netherlands. The main subsidiaries include Faraday Clark, a recruitment agency based in Frankfurt, and Corinthe Executive Search, a temporary and permanent professional finance recruitment agency based in the Netherlands. There is also a human resources solutions company, PPS. The company's latest acquisition, made in August 2007, was Judd Farris, a recruitment company operating in the property and construction sectors around the world.

The company has set out its strategic priorities as becoming widely recognised as a leading international recruitment business; having a reputation founded on outstanding service and an extensive database of high-quality candidates; being known for offering its staff compelling careers; and for having a top management team with a culture that drives commercial success and is embodied by everybody.

Wilson says: "The challenge we set ourselves is to be the best we can be. We are never complacent; even when we are doing a great job we are looking for ways to improve."

"Our values influence
everything that we do
as a company"
(Neil Wilson,
managing director)

Company Culture

Badenoch & Clark believes it has achieved a distinctive identity in a crowded and highly competitive market through sticking to a set of core values. It says the values of teamwork, innovation, fun, achievement and excellence are "the backbone of the company." In the booklet explaining these values that is distributed to each member of staff, Wilson writes: "Our values influence everything that we do as a company. They define our priorities, both commercially and in the way in which we deal with others around us at work."

Sarah Toal, resourcing team leader, adds: "Everybody is expected to live the culture." She explains that in order to promote the values, members of staff can send colleagues 'values cards' if they feel they have done something in their work that particularly upholds the company values.

Badenoch & Clark sets great store by recruiting from within. Wilson rose to become managing director after starting as a consultant, for example. But the company also recognises the need to hire from outside in order to gain access to wider knowledge, so human resources director Keith Nash was recruited from Coca Cola four years ago and he has been pivotal in setting out clear career paths.

Management takes an open approach and employees are surveyed regularly and the findings are acted upon, as in the case of benefits, which were reviewed after the largely young workforce indicated that pensions were not as valuable to them as some other benefits.

Above all, though, the company encourages a happy working environment. Due to the nature of the work, it is difficult to work flexibly, but long hours are not the rule and there is a crossover between employees' working and social lives, with sports teams, 'Champagne Fridays' at the end of sales periods, and other gatherings.

Innovation and Creativity

Innovation is one of Badenoch & Clark's core values and the company is always seeking ways to improve its services to both clients and candidates. For example, it says initiatives in areas such as candidate sourcing and services ensure that it remains cutting edge and so of special value to clients as well as making it an attractive place to work.

In addition to its dedication to understanding the precise needs of its clients and using its collaborative approach to answer them, Badenoch & Clark has other initiatives designed to set itself apart from its competitors.

For example, it publishes a quarterly client-focused magazine *Connections* that provides market commentary on topics such as the state of the economy and aspects of employment legislation and features statistics relevant to recruitment. It also carries out regular salary surveys that include comments on such issues as individuals' views on work-life balance and career paths available to them.

It is increasingly using technology to promote itself and its clients. For example, it sends to its clients a quarterly commentary via an html link, designed to keep customers and other contacts up to date with developments in the various markets in which the company operates. Another example is the opportunity for clients to be promoted as employers of choice on the company's new website. This is being combined with the use of Google ad-words to drive fresh traffic from Google to the featured employers.

Pay and Benefits

Badenoch & Clark aims to pay in the upper quartile for its sector, as judged by regular surveys carried out by compensation specialists.

The proportion of commission within total pay varies according to the type of team. For instance, in a low-margin, fast-paced team placing temporary workers there would be a strong team ethic and so commission might be split 75% on team performance and 25% on the individual. Consultants in other areas might work over longer timescales and so receive commission on a more individual basis. But all teams will have a team element to their commission in order to encourage best practice.

There are no set salaries other than for graduates and industrial placements. This is because employees join from a variety of backgrounds. When setting their initial salary, each individual's experience is taken into account.

Staff usually receive pay reviews annually. These reviews take into account both changes in the cost of living and the individual's performance over the year. Managers are paid according to a 'balanced scorecard' of financial and non-financial factors in order to encourage an all-round contribution to the business.

Badenoch & Clark offers a range of benefits. Key among them are a non-contributory pension scheme that starts after the end of the probation period with the company's contribution rising after five years' service; »

"Everybody is expected to live the culture" (Sarah Toal, resourcing team leader)

"Even when we are
doing a great job, we
are looking for ways
to improve"
(Neil Wilson,
managing director)

interest-free loans for travel season tickets and clothing; childcare vouchers; and after three years' service, a choice of private medical insurance or gym membership allowance. All employees receive 20 days of annual holiday, rising first to 24 days after the first year and then to 26 days. Managers are entitled to more.

Career Development

Badenoch & Clark takes on about 200 new people a year. The graduate intake fluctuates depending on business needs, varying between 10 and 50 a year. All those hired go through courses provided by the company's dedicated training department.

The idea is that the trainers' extensive experience of the recruitment industry enables them to identify, develop and deliver courses that will truly benefit consultants in their work and on a more personal level. The policy of promoting from within also helps to retain knowledge within the organisation.

All consultants go through a rigorous training course followed by a written examination. The course covers areas such as employment law, interviewing, CV writing, client development and advertisement writing. Afterwards there are various forms of training, along with regular performance appraisals and career discussions. In addition to monthly reviews, there are more thorough six-monthly reviews, which include feedback from clients and contractors.

The graduate scheme runs over 12 months and offers graduates structured training in a range of different roles to help them develop premium recruitment consultancy skills and so become a leading fee-earner within the business.

Badenoch & Clark sees developing and motivating its employees as the key to retaining them and so uses various methods to ensure that each employee feels valued and is able to develop both in terms of their career and as a person. At the centre is career path mapping, whereby the company is developing a structured, documented career path for every role and business area within the company. Recognising that people have different goals and expectations, with some, for example, wanting to manage teams and others more keen on developing niche expertise, the company provides flexible opportunities to accommodate its employees' differing needs.

Every consultant also has a personal development plan designed to help them enhance their key client relationships and these are reviewed at least monthly to check against their targets.

In addition, the company acknowledges the importance of effective leadership and has developed a range of courses covering the different aspects of effective management, including people, operations and the business.

Corporate Social Responsibility

Badenoch & Clark is seeking to embed CSR in the company so that it encourages innovation and creativity that delivers benefits to customers. It is committed to developing and maintaining ethical practices and to ensuring that it acts responsibly in the communities in which it operates. It also aims to be carbon neutral.

However, it recognises that for CSR to be integrated within its business strategy, decision-making and account-planning processes, it needs to change individual behaviours. Realising that this requires effort and communication, it has set up a CSR committee and given CSR responsibilities to people with other jobs and encouraged them to act as role models to ensure that CSR principles are integrated into daily practices. It is also stressing the importance placed on the issue by the leadership team.

In keeping with its role of supplying many public-sector organisations, the company is committed to sound and sustainable procurement practices, with resources and working methods managed in order to minimise environmental impact and maximise social value. The goal is to reduce emissions as rapidly as possible, with similar commitments made to reducing energy use, managing waste and making travel more efficient.

The company is also promoting community involvement by allowing every individual the opportunity to become involved in charitable events and projects. The company is aiming for 25% of staff to give up a day for community projects by 2010.

Badenoch & Clark wants to be recognised as a leading recruitment agency taking CSR seriously and, as a result, aims to help customers with diversity initiatives, building and developing new skills and finding new ways to operate more efficiently.

The company is committed to a policy of equal opportunities for all and runs the business as a strict meritocracy. To make sure it continues to adhere to this policy it reviews all aspects of the business regularly to check for unlawful or undesirable discrimination.

Facts and figures

Total number of staff: 500 (280 in London)
Office location: London (head office); 15 other UK offices
Industry sector: Recruitment
Turnover: £239m

BUSINESS SCHOOL ® **LAW SCHOOL** ®

BPP College of Professional Studies Ltd

68-70 Red Lion Street
London
WC1R 4NY

Telephone: 020 7430 2304
Email: lawrecruitment@bpp.com or businessrecruitment@bpp.com
www.bppuc.com

Pay and Benefits	★ ★ ★ ☆ ☆
Training and Development	★ ★ ★ ★ ☆
Career Development	★ ★ ★ ★ ⯪
Working Conditions	★ ★ ★ ☆ ☆
Company Culture	★ ★ ★ ☆ ☆

Biggest plus
A friendly, professional and highly focused environment with few of the pressures of working for a City law firm.

Greatest challenge
To establish its position as the number one provider of legal and other professional training in the UK.

Summary

BPP College of Professional Studies is one of the UK's largest providers of postgraduate legal training for solicitors and barristers. In 2008/9 it will train more than 5,000 students at its four schools: two in London, and one each in Manchester and Leeds. The college, split into law and business schools, has about 400 staff and is part of BPP Professional Education plc, a group that employs 1,300 people and provides professional business training Europe-wide for qualifications in areas such as accountancy, tax, financial services and marketing. In September 2007, the Privy Council granted the college powers to award its own undergraduate and postgraduate degrees. In 2009, BPP College's fledgling business school will launch a series of new courses in business, finance, management and other areas.

About the organisation

BPP Professional Education was founded in 1976 by Alan Brierley, Richard Price and Charles Prior, accountants who saw the opportunity to provide professional training in their own and other areas; it became a plc in 1986. In 1992 the group established BPP College, now among its fastest growing businesses, contributing £36.8m to the group's overall £150m turnover in 2007.

The college claims about 25% of market share for its Legal Practice Course (for solicitors) and 30% for its Graduate Diploma in Law (conversion course for non-law graduates). It also trains nearly 20% of those studying for the bar, and its business school works with clients including the BBC and Tesco.

BPP College's legal training is distinguished by the depth and longevity of its relationships with top legal employers: it is the sole training provider for 11 of the City's largest law firms (Freshfields Bruckhaus Deringer, Herbert Smith, Lovells, Norton Rose, Slaughter and May, Addleshaw Goddard, CMS Cameron McKenna, Macfarlanes, Simmons & Simmons, SJ Berwin and Jones Day).

"Our unique selling point is our level of engagement with employers," says Peter Crisp, the college's chief executive. "We work very closely with these firms to design and tailor our programme, and we get a huge amount of input at a really detailed level. That gives us a huge competitive advantage over other providers of legal education, and we would see that continuing and deepening."

In 2009, the law school introduces an undergraduate law degree, though not one aimed at school leavers. "We treat our students as business clients, and our courses are aimed at the mature working adult – we provide as flexible and portable an experience as possible, but not a wraparound experience," explains Crisp.

"Our unique selling point is our level of engagement with employers. We work very closely with the City's top law firms to design and tailor our programme."
(Peter Crisp, chief executive)

With the UK market for business and law postgraduate degree studies worth at least £800m, and City shrinkage causing more professionals to consider retraining, BPP College expects demand for its courses only to increase in coming years.

Company Culture

BPP College describes its culture as "professional and friendly". It is proud of the way this has evolved and is maintained by staff and students, the latter being among the most focused in any of the UK's learning environments. About half of those taking legal training are sponsored by firms, with the remainder paying their own fees.

Despite its business-like approach, the college avoids putting staff under the kind of pressure they might experience elsewhere in the corporate world. Courses are run during the working day, but also in the evenings and at weekends, offering teaching staff a high degree of flexibility. They can vary their shifts, work on an hourly basis, or (if circumstances demand it) negotiate late starts and early finishes. Most work from home one day a week, and about a fifth work for the college part-time. After three years of service, all employees can take a year's sabbatical.

While college staff are "a diverse group of people," they share a similar approach, according to HR manager Rachel Hope. To thrive at BPP College, teaching staff (who make up the majority of employees) must show "a real willingness to engage with students" and "want to help them to become successful and celebrate success when it comes." Some support staff are sponsored through college courses, and all are encouraged to develop professionally by accessing the education available.

There is a high level of staff involvement in decision-making, with a joint consultative committee meeting four times a year to take on board everyone's views. A scheme allows employees to make suggestions or raise concerns, and an academic council is responsible for maintaining standards. In addition, the college is updating its information services system, which from 2009 will empower staff to deal with data relating to their own employment and hours.

Innovation and Creativity

As the structure of higher education in the UK changes, BPP College's corporate approach, employer relationships and growing reputation give it clear advantages in the new landscape. Seeing students as 'clients, rather than nuisances,' the college offers a high-tech learning environment, including remote access to textbooks and other materials. "We are investing a lot of time and money in our e-learning strategy – the aim is to have an online version of every classroom experience," explains Crisp. Students can opt to view lectures on their computers, rather than attend in person, and many do.

Other aspects to electronic and interactive learning include a simulation module on the legal practice course, which teaches students to handle a residential property transaction online, with telephone feedback from a 'partner,' played by an actor. The college is also building an impressive archive of discussions on a range of legal topics, which students can access online. Elsewhere, its relationships with employers have led to the development of tailor-made training modules, most recently with Macfarlanes.

Internally, the college's new information services system, to go live in early 2009, will "encourage people to look for information for themselves, about finance, learning and development – it will all be there for them," according to Hope.

Pay and Benefits

As a private sector organisation in a market dominated by public sector bodies such as universities, BPP College looks to pay its staff well above the average salary. Teaching staff in particular can increase their pay by taking responsibility for evening and weekend courses, although teaching hours are capped at 16 per week.

Salaries are individually negotiated, and pay reviews are based on company and individual performance. A bonus scheme marks the achievements of those who meet annual targets. Conversely, Crisp says, "We don't reward time-serving". People are also paid £750 if they make a successful referral of a new staff member. The college recently introduced a new sharesave scheme, Save As You Earn (SAYE), and offers executive share options to senior staff.

In 2008, the college established an annual award in memory of a young staff member to recognise the efforts of support staff. "With recognition, though, a 'thank you' can be nicer and gratitude counts for a lot," Hope points out. "We often do that quite publicly, so that half the college or team is copied in on an email."

The basic holiday allowance for teaching staff is 30 days, and for support staff 25 days (rising to 30 days after six years' service), with two no-questions-asked sick leave, or 'duvet days.' Currently, the flexible benefits package allows staff to exchange holiday leave for additional salary, pension contributions and childcare vouchers. »

"A 'thank you' to an employee can be nicer than a monetary gift – and we often do that quite publicly." (Rachel Hope, HR manager)

"We are investing a lot of time and money in our e-learning strategy – the aim is to have an online version of every classroom experience." (Peter Crisp, chief executive)

Staff can also access an onsite gym, a personal trainer, and a free massage every three months, as well as a counselling service. There is a discount club for all employees, offering money off a range of products and services.

"We are using external consultants to review our benefits package at group level, to see if we can do things better, and keep it fresh," says Hope. "We want to give employees the chance to have more control."

Career Development

Staff at BPP College work in teaching, management or support roles. With the growth of the college and the opening of new campuses, teaching staff can expect to be promoted quickly if they are motivated to succeed and meet promotion criteria.

The college's promotions board meets quarterly to review positions. Crisp, who himself joined the college as a tutor in 1997, explains: "People progress through open competition for positions. The first step would be to take responsibility for a particular area, then to head up a module, then to head up a programme."

Recruitment depends on student numbers and areas of growth. In 2008, for example, senior roles were created to oversee the development of talent management, with a programme to be offered by the business school in 2009.

All staff have a budget to design their own training package, monitored through appraisals, but while there is some freedom to pursue individual interests, teaching staff are mandated to attend specific courses. A member of staff on the legal practice course would start with a five-day introductory training programme, while an annual conference adds another two days of compulsory training.

Law school tutors must pass an annual Teaching and Learning Certificate (TLC), while middle managers are entered for a part-time management development programme with the Chartered Institute of Management. At a senior level, the company is paying for several of its managers to study MBA courses.

"A lot of professional development goes on here," says Crisp. "We are very fortunate within BPP College that our staff can attend any course free of charge, and we have a good take-up of one-day courses, since there are a huge number on offer."

Since BPP Professional Education plc is active throughout Europe, there are opportunities to teach abroad, though these are relatively limited.

Corporate Social Responsibility

BPP College is proud of its diverse make-up, and sees this as key to its success. More than half of staff, and nearly half the board, are women, while a quarter are from religious or ethnic minorities, reflecting the student body's ratio.

Since class can be a factor that prevents diversity, the college provides an annual £300,000 in bursaries to help those from disadvantaged backgrounds to attend its courses, while two diversity access schemes assist students to get work experience placements. One scheme, run in conjunction with the law firm Addleshaw Goddard, saw two out of six of its participants win training contracts in 2008, and has been nominated for a Business in the Community 'Race for Opportunity' award. The college also helps students to find mentors from within 100 participating firms.

Individual staff members participate in charitable events such as the JP Morgan Chase Challenge, and the college itself gave £80,000 in 2008 to help keep open the Mary Ward Legal Centre. BPP College also has an extensive pro bono presence, offering students the chance to be involved in 30 different projects; about half of the teaching staff also give time to these. The college hosts the annual conference of the human rights organisation Liberty, and offers its facilities to other charities.

BPP College is regulated by the Law Society and the Bar Council, and complies with corporate best practice as part of BPP Professional Education plc. The law school employs a data protection officer and risk assessment team, and uses random checks to monitor course quality. Accolades and awards have included an 'excellent' rating for its London legal practice course from the Law Society.

BPP College formulated an environmental policy in 2007 after wide consultation with staff. Since its campuses are in city centres, most staff travel to work by bike or on public transport; the college offers interest-free loans for season tickets, and provides bike racks and loans to purchase bicycles.

Hope says that the college is committed to make "incremental improvements" in all its operations. Examples include locating recycling bins on each floor, putting office lights on a sensor system, and ensuring that cups in vending machines are recyclable. The college also participates in green schemes such as London Better Together and Manchester City Green Pledge, and ensures that old textbooks and computer equipment are recycled or reused.

Facts and figures

Total number of staff: 1,300
Office location: London, Manchester and Leeds
Industry sector: Law
Budget: £36.8m in 2007

Broadway

15 Half Moon Court
Bartholomew Close
LONDON
EC1A 7HF

Telephone: 020 7089 9500
Fax: 020 7089 9501
www.broadwaylondon.org

Pay and Benefits	★ ★ ★ ½ ☆
Training and Development	★ ★ ★ ★ ☆
Career Development	★ ★ ★ ★ ☆
Working Conditions	★ ★ ★ ☆ ☆
Company Culture	★ ★ ★ ★ ☆

Biggest plus
The opportunity to do rewarding work in a demanding environment where best practice and excellent standards are rigorously enforced.

Greatest challenge
Working with homeless clients requires particular skills and a high level of commitment.

Summary

Broadway is a leading homelessness charity that supports people across London to make the journey off the streets and into their own homes. It employs 180 staff and 60 volunteers, and offers a range of services including specialist housing, work and learning support, advice on health, welfare and debt management, and consultancy to other organisations. The charity regularly wins awards and more than 80% of clients in 2008 said they were satisfied or very satisfied with the help they received. Broadway's income is around £9m annually.

About the organisation

Broadway was formed in 2002 from the merger of Riverpoint, a charity at the forefront of the Rough Sleepers Initiative, and Camden-based Housing Services Agency, an expert in housing, resettlement and homelessness research. With 150,000 single homeless people in London, Broadway's vision is to offer support and guidance through integrated services to help each person find and keep a home.

The charity runs five hostels, four outreach contracts and a day centre, together with supported housing schemes and 'floating' support for those who are resettled. It has work, learning and vocational programmes, a trading arm, debt advice, an HR consultancy, a research and policy unit, and a private sector leasing pilot scheme. The aim is to develop innovative, flexible services both to benefit clients directly and to provide support to other agencies, raising standards of practice across the board.

Accredited by Investors in People, Broadway has won several top awards for the quality of its human resources, including Third Sector's Best Employer (2008). In future years it plans to expand its operations outside London. "Many organisations, including very large ones, are keen to work in partnership with us, because our services are so good and the quality of our staff is very well known, but we intend to remain independent and not enter into any sort of group structure," says Helen Giles MBE, Broadway's HR director.

Clients speak of the charity giving them 'confidence and a future' through its support. Meanwhile, chief executive Howard Sinclair believes the working environment is second to none. "The staff at Broadway are the best people I have ever worked with, and they are the reason I am happier here than anywhere else in my working life."

"Broadway allows you to be who you are and provides you with the tools to become who you can be"
(unnamed employee)

Company Culture

Broadway aims to be personal, committed and innovative, and its people management values include openness, honesty, diversity, creativity, challenge, approachability and professionalism. The senior management team is committed to the principles of authentic leadership, while its chief executive visits all services frequently, often doing sleep-in shifts.

Since working with dispossessed and marginalised people can be demanding, clarity about expectations is key. All new employees are briefed on what the charity offers them, and they can feed back about how the delivery measures up; in turn, management takes a zero tolerance approach to underperformance.

Underlying a range of high-commitment practices is a progressive HR strategy, which focuses on recruiting those with a track record of ability to engage; it wants people who are dynamic, intelligent, committed and client-centred. Dress code is casual and the office vibe is non-hierarchical. Managers are expected to be coaches, not bosses, and all employees are involved in setting standards and improving client services.

In surveys, the charity gets marked highly on work-life balance: 92% of employees said they felt able to balance work and home life without hindering their career. "We allow people as much flexibility as we can," says Giles. "The core hours for non-shift staff are 10.30am to 3.30pm, and we don't expect anyone to do unpaid overtime." Staff can accrue up to 21 hours per month to take as flexi-leave, and can access up to 10 days of dependency or compassionate leave. Some employees have ongoing alternative arrangements, such as condensed working weeks. After four years, there's an entitlement to a year's unpaid sabbatical.

Giles says: "Our clients and staff are at the heart of everything we do: we only employ the best and most committed staff because we believe our homeless clients deserve the best, and we are in the business of providing excellent services that turn people's lives around. The quality of our staff is reflected in low absence rates and a high level of engagement."

Innovation and Creativity

At Broadway, creativity is seen as the ability to look at a problem or issue in a new or different way, and innovation is seen as the ability to put a creative idea into practice. Both abilities are highly valued, and together they constitute one of the areas on which employees are judged annually during appraisal. "Innovation and creativity is so important to us that it's one of the competencies that we support through training," says Giles.

The charity is involved in a number of initiatives, including the London-wide debt advice partnership, Capitalise, and a government-led private sector leasing pilot, Real Lettings. It also undertakes extensive research to influence policy makers and to improve its own services; the design and delivery of projects is informed, wherever possible, by people who themselves have experienced homelessness.

In 2007 Broadway launched a new and unique training scheme to develop leaders and managers who work in the homelessness sector. Leading Places of Change is run in association with the Chartered Institute of Housing and Homeless Link, and sessions are delivered across the UK in cities including London, Exeter and York. Formerly aimed at the staff of bodies in receipt of capital funding for the improvement of accommodation-based services, it has proved so popular that places on the scheme are in future to be open to employees from any homeless charity.

Pay and Benefits

In previous years Broadway has aimed to pay staff salaries as near to the upper quartile as possible. However, the current economic and funding climate means that, in common with other charities, it has had to revise pay towards the median. Nevertheless, it has a set of 'good, old-fashioned incremental pay scales' that are 'transparent and fair,' with no element of performance-related pay or bonus.

Giles says: "Our pay is guided by affordability. We pay all staff as much as we can possibly afford to pay, given our income streams, and this is equitable for all levels of staff and management. Our staff surveys show pay is seen to be fair and to compare well with earnings for comparable work elsewhere."

The benefits package is broad: the charity makes a 5% contribution to a stakeholder pension scheme for all staff, and offers its employees a minimum of 25 days' annual leave, rising in stages to 30 days after five years of service. Other benefits include life insurance, enhanced maternity and paternity leave entitlement, interest-free season ticket loans, childcare vouchers, and loans to purchase bicycles. Employees also have access to an assistance programme that provides information, advice and counselling for staff and their families. »

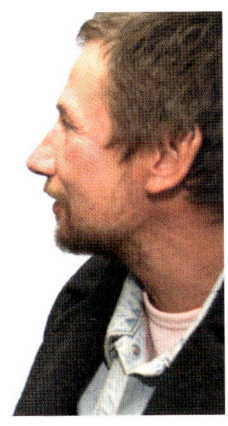

"People only get the position of line manager at Broadway if they demonstrate a clear desire and ability to take an interest in other people" (Helen Giles, HR director)

There are no formal reward or recognition schemes, says Giles. "We consulted our staff on whether they would like a bonus or reward for nominated people, but they are very much against it. What they want is what they get: recognition and thanks for a job well done."

Broadway holds its staff party in December, and has events through the year that often involve clients, such as an annual picnic in the park. Staff organise their own activities locally, such as a five-a-side football team and a yoga club.

Career Development

At Broadway, the majority of staff work on the front line with homeless people, either in hostels, outreach, supported housing or floating support work. Of the rest, a large number are involved in education, training and vocational guidance.

Each year the charity takes on about 20 trainees, young and older people who show real enthusiasm and commitment to work with clients. Although the scheme lasts a year, often they move into permanent positions after eight or nine months. "We choose people who show excellent levels of transferable competencies and an extremely committed attitude. Our employees like the fact that they are working with people who are as committed as they are," says Giles.

There is no automatic promotion. With the help of personal development plans, a modular management development scheme, and a performance management system that gives regular feedback against goals and assessment of learning needs, employees are expected to self-manage their progress and to use every available opportunity to develop and progress. For example, all trainees are mentored, and those chosen to be mentors can use this role as a first step into line management.

The charity advertises permanent jobs internally and externally at the same time, but 70% of management jobs are filled from inside. "It's a great validation that we are providing a good learning environment," says Giles. "Not everyone is cut out to be a line manager, and people only get that position at Broadway if they demonstrate a clear desire and ability to take an interest in other people." Line managers are also assessed through 360-degree feedback.

Some support is given for managers to take external qualifications, for example through the Chartered Institute of Personnel & Development, or the Chartered Institute of Housing accredited leadership programme, Leading Places of Change. In addition, it is relatively common for employees to move between functions, such as managing day

centres and corporate fundraising. One employee summed it up in a quote frequently used by the charity: "Broadway allows you to be who you are and provides you with the tools to become who you can be."

Corporate Social Responsibility

Broadway says it is committed to responsible and sustainable business practice that delivers value to stakeholders, including clients and customers, funders and investors, business partners, suppliers, employees and the community. A strong code of ethics underpins its work practices, and it manages risk proactively while maintaining a commitment to be a 'decent company both to work for and to work with.'

Its quality strategy includes a programme of audits for all housing-related support services, audits on specific issues to ensure services are operating to a high standard, monthly performance targets for each team, 'listening lunches' at which clients help to develop service delivery policies and procedures, and client survey benchmarking.

With its mission to integrate homeless clients with the community, Broadway is on the front line of corporate social responsibility. Its CSR strategy is developed and supervised by a working group that meets regularly to review best practice in areas such as diversity, community work, and the environment. It also offers many different ways for volunteers to get involved in its work.

The charity's employee base is hugely diverse: in 2008, more than a quarter of employees came from Black and Minority Ethnic (BME) backgrounds, and nearly three-quarters were women; about 5% had declared disabilities, and 8% were lesbian, gay or bisexual. The charity monitors its impact on the environment and sends out regular bulletins to staff about how to save energy – anything from recycling stamps for charity to using the stairs instead of a lift. It buys Fairtrade products for its hostels, projects and offices, recycles wherever possible, and promotes the use of public transport for work. It also encourages non hostel-based staff to spend time on the front line.

Managers and staff are asked to abide by a clear code of conduct, while at board level there is a strictly applied code of governance for trustees. "We advertise vacancies for trustees – it's not done by word of mouth," explains Giles. "We look very carefully at people's skills and aptitudes before we appoint them to the board and we hold a joint annual appraisal, where we look at the contribution of individuals." Trustees are also asked to hold regular surgeries, which involve going out to hostels so that clients can 'meet the board.'

Facts and figures

Total number of staff: 240
Office location: Central London
Industry sector: Charity
Income: £9m

The **co-operative**

The Co-operative

The Co-operative Trading Group
New Century House
Corporation Street
Manchester
M60 4ES

Telephone: 0161 834 1212
www.co-operative.coop

Pay and Benefits	★ ★ ★ ★ ☆
Training and Development	★ ★ ★ ☆ ☆
Career Development	★ ★ ★ ☆ ☆
Working Conditions	★ ★ ★ ☆ ☆
Company Culture	★ ★ ★ ★ ☆

Biggest plus
Enhancing the lives of its staff and the communities in which it trades.

Greatest challenge
Building a career development infrastructure.

Summary

The Co-operative Trading Group is a major player in the UK retail market with more than 4,300 outlets. Following the acquisition of Somerfield (early 2009) the Group will be the UK's fifth largest food retailer, operating more than 3,000 grocery stores, and the UK's third largest retail pharmacy chain. The Co-operative is also Europe's largest funeral services provider , the largest independent travel business, and the UK's largest farmer. It currently employs 75,000 people. The Group headquarters are in Manchester. As a true co-operative, the Group is owned and democratically run by its three million members.

About the organisation

As well as delivering on financial and operational goals, co-operatives also set themselves social goals. Operating in a sustainable way and trading ethically are key principles of the Co-operative Group. As an example, it's the UK's biggest supermarket supporter of Fairtrade, through introducing, stocking and advertising its goods.

The Co-operative Group evolved gradually over 140 years through mergers of many independent co-operative societies. The biggest of these occurred in 2007 when the Group merged with United Co-operatives, the UK's second largest co-operative.

Growth is still on the agenda and in 2008 the Group agreed to purchase the rival Somerfield business for £1.565bn in a move that catapulted the chain to owning more than 3,000 grocery stores and an anticipated 9% share of the UK food market. Peter Marks, chief executive of the Co-operative Trading Group, describes this deal as "transformational."

The business is fully aware that the UK co-operative movement had been in decline since the 1950s and 60s, due to market consolidation and competition. Through consolidation and acquisition, combined with what it claims is the largest re-branding exercise in UK corporate history, the Co-operative Group is changing this. "The acquisition of Somerfield will provide the rocket fuel for our three-year growth plan. We are revitalising our retail estate under a single unified brand – modernising our stores, improving our product offer and service levels for customers and members, and reinforcing our co-operative difference," says Marks.

These actions are already paying off. For 2007, revenue for the Co-operative Trading Group was up by £1bn to £8.3bn, while operating profit rose 8.6% to £431.6m. For the first six months of 2008, sales were up 34% to £4.02bn on the first six months of 2007, with operating profits up 35.6% to £191.1m.

Company Culture

Co-operative values define the business and are core to what attracts people to working for the Group. »

Its vision is 'to be the best co-operative business in the world' by striving for world class levels of business performance and enhancing the lives of its people, members, customers, and the communities in which it trades.

The model is obviously important to Marks. His first job was with a co-operative society and he's stuck with the movement since 1967. The values also strike a chord with graduate job seekers. For its 2008 graduate intake the Co-operative Trading Group saw 2,500 people applying for the 12 places on its trainee scheme.

But it also appeals to people with PLC experience like Richard Bide, director of Human Resources. "It's in our DNA caring about issues, rather than a marketing exercise. People who join from PLCs find what we stand for very attractive," he says. "We like to recruit people who buy into our ethos - our social agenda is important."

As an illustration, the Co-operative food ethical policy was guided and endorsed by polling its members at the end of 2007 and 100,000 of them responded. Employees don't have to be co-operative members, but it's rewarded and strongly encouraged, with employee membership now approaching 90%. "We believe being part of this organisation, being a member, goes with the territory," says Bide. "You ought to want to buy into what we stand for in order to be an advocate for it."

Employee engagement is the centrepiece of the Group's HR strategy, and one of the ways it's measured is through the annual 'Talkback' staff survey. Questions include staff's assessment of how their managers value staff contributions, display a number of specific leadership skills, and also how they provide feedback to staff on how their work is helping the Group's business.

Innovation and Creativity

The Co-operative sees its competitive advantage as coming from its different way of doing business, in other words by marrying financial and social goals. It's been championing an ethical approach for decades, and continues to lead the market in this aspect.

Nearly 20 years ago it became the first supermarket to ban animal testing on own-brand toiletries. It pioneered the introduction of Braille on packaging, and in 2002 launched Britain's first fully degradable plastic carrier bag.

Co-operative values define the business and are core to what attracts people to working for the Group.

Just because the Co-operative Group has a social agenda... doesn't mean that salaries aren't competitive with rival PLCs.

It is currently saving around 20 tonnes of glass a year through the launch in 2006 of the world's lightest whisky bottle, and this was extended in 2008 to 26 different Co-operative wines that will save a further 450 tonnes per year. "We do make profit, but it's what we do with it," says Bide. "Part of our reason for being is to improve communities. PLCs care about other things."

The Co-operative also recognises that success will stem in part from having skilled, educated and supported managers. As well as a professional staff magazine called *Us* to aid communication across the business, it has created *Mag:ma*, a management magazine, for its top 5,000 managers. "It's a bit weightier," says Bide. Subjects covered include understanding and developing the organisation's culture, staff engagement, transferable skills and brand values.

Pay and Benefits

Just because the Co-operative Group has a social agenda, and its recruits tend not to see money as 'the be all and end all,' it doesn't mean that salaries aren't competitive with rival PLCs. "We pay competitive packages," says Bide. "They're suitable and attractive to the market – they have to be."

The graduate starting salary for 2009 will be £23,000. Above that there is a salary range, but pay becomes individually based, with managers receiving annual bonuses to recognise financial and non-financial performance including employee engagement levels. There are annual performance and salary appraisals. Base levels of executive pay correlate to around market median, and there are long-term incentive plans, employing cumulative targets across a three-year period.

"Five years ago we were an organisation that was struggling," says Bide. "Our approach to reward was traditional, but now we've introduced a lot of incentivisation."

These include competitive annual leave arrangements, defined benefit pension, free life assurance, a reduction of 35% on BUPA insurance and an employee discount card entitling staff to up to 10% off Co-operative goods and services. The Group's Employee Member Benefits package offers benefits that range from car breakdown insurance to family days out and are in addition to the new range of employee member discounts and employee member dividend.

»

Trainees are given the opportunity to have a senior manager as a mentor, and to work with staff at all levels in the business.

Where it can't compete is with share options, but Co-operative employee members benefited from dividend payments doubling up from £45.6m to £94.7m in 2008 – around a £500 pay-out. On pensions, employees will be able to continue in the scheme past 65 years of age.

Career Development

The Co-operative Trading Group employs a wide variety of people – funeral directors, pharmacists, travel advisors, accountants, lawyers, IT professionals, retail managers and customer service assistants, to name but some.

Graduates joining as general management trainees will work on real business projects across the entire organisation over an 18-month period. As well as study-time and sponsorship towards relevant post-graduate or professional qualifications, they receive intensive, individual development, focusing on building core management skills, working strategically, leadership and introducing and driving change. Trainees are given the opportunity to have a senior manager as a mentor, and to work with staff at all levels in the business. They should move into their first management role upon completion of the programme, with a £2,000 pay rise, depending on their performance.

The Co-operative states: 'We do not map your long-term career development or fit you into predetermined career paths. This allows for excellent flexibility, breadth, scope and advancement if you have the tenacity and ability to drive your own career development within the Group.'

Bide concedes that career development is an area the Co-operative is still working on, but recognises it is vital to its plans. For 2009, a major succession planning exercise is planned.

Bide assesses the graduate trainee retention rate of the Co-operative Group to be a creditable 75%, and qualifies this by saying, "The reasons for leaving tend to be good ones – a partner gets a job elsewhere in the country, or they decide on a complete career change."

Corporate Social Responsibility

The Co-operative Group walks the talk when it comes to its ethical business behaviour, social responsibility, environmental policies and attitude to diversity.

It is the only major retailer to have all its own-brand toiletries and household products accredited to the British Union for the Abolition of Vivisection (BUAV) non-animal testing standards. It launched the UK's first Fairtrade bananas and mangos; it was the first supermarket with own-brand Fairtrade coffee; and the first retailer to launch fairly traded red and white wine. It extended the concept by producing the UK's first supermarket Fairtrade chocolate cake, using Fairtrade sugar and cocoa.

The Co-operative Group has more than 4,000 branches powered by renewable energy, and each business reports on its energy consumption and carbon emissions – the latter have been cut by 89% since 2003. An £18m efficiency programme has been launched to reduce electricity and gas consumption even further by 2012.

The business has an in-house office waste recycling facility and in 2006 it recycled over 27,000 tonnes of waste cardboard and polythene packaging. Co-operative farming land in Cambridgeshire houses eight wind turbines generating enough electricity to power over 9,000 UK homes, and the Group has invested £1m to fund the installation of free photovoltaic or solar panels in UK schools.

The business has set up the Co-operative Group Volunteer Programme that aims to engage staff with local communities where they work. In 2007, 9,898 employees gave 120,000 hours in work time to fundraising and community activities. In 2008 it announced it had raised £2.9m for its charities of the year – The Children's Society and Diabetes UK.

The Co-operative embraces diversity and instigates policies and education to make sure it manages this effectively. The Group has been awarded the title of 'Age Positive Employer Champion,' a Government-recognised status, and among the steps it has taken to get this is the removal of the retirement age of 65.

It has also retained its top 100 place in the Stonewall Workplace Equality Index, the highest placed retailer in the index and the only food retailer in the top 100. On top of this it has won the Race for Opportunity Chairman's award for business impact for its work in the provision of ethnic minority funerals. The work has so far resulted in a 15% increase in business from multi-faith communities.

It's all impressive stuff but the Co-operative Group has high standards. "Diversity expresses a lot about the values of an organisation. We believe that the Co-operative Group has a fantastic future ahead of it. But in order to realise the businesses' full potential we need to attract, develop and retain the best talent. That means being the UK's most successful ethical business. In recent years we've made great strides in achieving that objective. The people we recruit over the next few years will have a crucial role in taking us to the next level. There never has been a better and more exciting time to be part of the Co-operative Group'" says Bide.

Facts and figures

Total number of staff: 85,000
Office location: Manchester
Industry sector: Retail
Annual turnover: £8.3bn

DentonWildeSapte...

Denton Wilde Sapte LLP

One Fleet Place
London EC4M 7MS

Telephone: 020 7242 1212
Fax: 020 7246 7777
Email: info@dentonwildesapte.com
www.dentonwildesapte.com

Pay and Benefits	★ ★ ★ ★ ✯
Training and Development	★ ★ ★ ★ ✯
Career Development	★ ★ ★ ★ ✯
Working Conditions	★ ★ ★ ★ ★
Company Culture	★ ★ ★ ★ ☆

Biggest plus
Presence in emerging markets and strong sector focus.

Greatest challenge
Offering a work-life balance whilst competing with the top law firms in the world.

Summary

Created by the merger of two of the City of London's oldest law firms in 2000, Denton Wilde Sapte traces its roots back over 200 years, and is now one of the world's major international firms. With 1,570 employees operating from offices across Europe, the Middle East, Africa and Asia, the firm's global footprint is reflective of its focus on four key business sectors: banking and finance; energy and infrastructure; technology, media and telecoms (TMT) and real estate. Denton Wilde Sapte has over 180 partners and employs over 640 legal staff globally, of which 350 are based in the UK, where the firm has offices in London and Milton Keynes.

About the organisation

Denton Wilde Sapte was one of the first UK law firms to embark on significant international expansion, and as a result, now has the largest presence of any international law firm in the Middle East and is the largest law firm in the CIS. The firm is also one of the few to have a network of associated offices across Africa. Since June 2007 the firm has opened new offices and associated offices in Riyadh, Doha, Amman (Jordan), Kuwait and created associations with firms in St Petersburg and Algiers. The firm reinforced its commitment to its global footprint with the relocation of chairman and energy partner James Dallas to the Dubai office in February 2008.

The firm was also one of the first to focus its business around servicing core industry sectors, and its lawyers are trained to be well-versed in those sectors in order to really understand their clients' work. The firm's clients range from the major international banks – where it acts for eight of the top nine – to the likes of Arabic news network Al Jazeera, which chief executive Howard Morris describes as "a very important client for a foreign law firm operating in the Arab world".

In the financial year that ended April 2008, Denton Wilde Sapte's turnover was £164.4m, up 6% on the previous year, and its profits were up 10% to £40.4m.

Morris says that the firm's eclectic business mix leads to an inclusive and diverse culture: "There's a big difference between a lawyer who handles new media and someone who does sovereign bond issues," he » says. "Our culture is open, supportive, inclusive and team-focused. Success comes from teamwork, so when people have problems or are under pressure, there are always people around looking to help, and getting stuck in without having to be asked."

Company Culture

Denton Wilde Sapte prides itself on its flat management structure, and adopts an informal yet professional attitude. Each legal department and each support department has a leader who reports to the chief executive, and these are backed up by a team of managers. In a staff survey in 2007, 64% of respondents said that their manager encouraged open, honest, two-way communication, and 75% described Morris as an accessible leader.

Internal communications are a key issue for the firm, and Morris hosts a monthly breakfast meeting that is open to all staff, providing an update on the business. There is also an in-house electronic news magazine published monthly, and a weekly email update detailing media coverage that the firm has received.

Another fundamental concern is work-life balance, with 16% of the firm's employees working flexibly, including 8% of partners. Morris says: "It's part of our culture that people here aren't stretched to breaking point. We maintain a balance, allowing our people flexibility, whilst also ensuring that we have adequate resources and are able to work hard to compete with the best law firms in the world. We are able to work with the same intensity as everybody else."

A perfect illustration of the firm's culture is Mark Andrews, the firm's head of insolvency and one of the UK's top lawyers advising companies facing financial difficulties. Despite regularly tackling engagements to help clients in dire straits at short notice, he finds time to perform as a concert musician, having played the French horn at a high level since childhood. Andrews says he has never missed a performance or had to let a client down, thanks in part to the firm's supportive environment.

In a staff survey, 70% of Denton Wilde Sapte's employees said that the hours they were expected to work were reasonable, and whilst regularly extended days, Monday to Friday, are normal for the legal profession, the firm's base salaries reflect that.

Innovation and Creativity

As one of the first firms to put client sectors at the heart of its strategy when it reorganised the business in 2003, Denton Wilde Sapte has been courageous in its commitment to differentiation in an often monochrome legal market. Mike Gannaway, the firm's marketing director, says: "We say that we are the natural choice for clients in those sectors. We are a very good commercial firm for clients outside those sectors, but we don't claim to be a natural choice for them."

Much of the firm's day-to-day activity involves creativity, particularly in areas such as energy and TMT, where the firm's experts have been at the cutting edge of developments in areas such as carbon storage projects, wind farms and nuclear energy in the UK, and are now taking that knowhow to new markets like Abu Dhabi.

"Success comes from teamwork, so when people have problems or are under pressure, there are always people around looking to help."
(Howard Morris, chief executive)

"People here aren't stretched to
breaking point"
(Howard Morris, chief executive,
on the firm's work-life balance)

In terms of career structures, Denton Wilde Sapte has broken down some of the traditional norms in the legal industry to introduce an alternative role to partner, called a managing associate, and has removed the traditional progression based purely on post-qualification experience to instead allow lawyers to move forward at their own pace.

Finally, the firm has introduced an Email Free Day to encourage more face-to-face meetings and telephone conversations, and donates the saved storage fees to charity.

Pay and Benefits

When it comes to lawyer remuneration, Denton Wilde Sapte aims to compete with the best in its market. Human resources director Margaret Brooks says: "We think our salaries are competitive. For someone working the sort of hours that are expected in Magic Circle law firms, we would pay close to their level, because we offer a combination of basic salary and bonuses. People who don't want to work such long hours still get good salaries."

Salaries are reviewed annually, and from May 2008, newly qualified lawyers could expect to earn £64,000 a year, rising to between £87,000 and £95,000 after five years' experience. Fee-earners have an annual minimum target of 1,540 hours to complete, and there is a bonus paid depending on the number of hours achieved, including time spent on pro bono work. Part of the bonus can be exchanged for extra holiday entitlement. Furthermore, each department has a fixed cash pot from which to reward specific contributions in sector, client service and departmental projects.

Denton Wilde Sapte operates a profit sharing scheme, where senior associates get an additional 1% of salary for every 2% by which the firm exceeds budget, up to a maximum of 10% of salary. Support staff can get bonuses of up to 5% if the firm hits target, and 10% if it is above target. There are other schemes for more senior staff.

>>

"We were the first City law firm to introduce flexible benefits"
(Margaret Brooks,
human resources director)

When it comes to benefits, Brooks says: "We like to think we are leaders in the legal field. We were the first City law firm to introduce flexible benefits, and we look at those every year." Employees can pick and choose the benefits that meet their needs, on top of core benefits of 24 to 26 days holiday (plus eight statutory days); life assurance cover of two times salary, and income protection insurance. Additional benefits include the ability to increase or decrease annual holiday, holiday travel insurance, critical illness insurance, private medical insurance, childcare vouchers, dental insurance, sports club membership allowance, a concierge service, bikes for work, and a Carbon Neutral facility that allows individuals to contribute to charity to offset their annual carbon footprint.

Career Development

Denton Wilde Sapte recruits approximately 35 graduate trainees each year, who join the firm two years later after completing law school. Trainee interviews include psychometric tests to assess critical thinking and the presentation of a case study to assess analytical skills. Candidates meet as many of the team as possible, including partners and support staff.

The firm has developed a bespoke microsite on its website to deal with trainee recruitment enquiries. It pays its trainees' law school fees and pays a maintenance allowance, and then when they arrive, trainees spend two years learning at the firm before qualification. In 2008, 89% of newly-qualifieds stayed when they finished their training contracts. Trainees are offered secondments to clients and overseas offices as part of their training.

All new-joiners to the firm receive a buddy, who introduces them around the department and the office, and there are also mentoring schemes.

For qualified lawyers, Denton Wilde Sapte offers more than 2,000 hours of legal and personal development training each year, and in the 12 months to October 2007 the firm ran more than 1,500 internal training sessions in its offices worldwide. Legal training includes regular updates on key areas of law and introductions to new areas, while staff can also attend courses in presentation skills, negotiation skills, business development, interviewing, time management, and plain language, amongst others.

The firm's recently reviewed career structure allows solicitors to develop their careers at different paces, and offers an alternative to partnership that requires the management, leadership and client skills of a partner without the full business and practice development demands.

Those wishing to develop their careers can do secondments to clients including Royal Bank of Scotland and Shell, to increase their understanding of those businesses, as well as to international offices.

Corporate Social Responsibility

There are five components to Denton Wilde Sapte's CSR policy: environmental sustainability; pro bono; community work; charitable giving; and Equal Opportunities and diversity.

The environmental policy looks at waste, energy and water consumption, travel and sustainable purchasing, and working groups have been established in London and Milton Keynes that have led to initiatives such as the introduction of recycling facilities for paper, plastic, metal and organic materials, reducing the amount the London office sends to landfill by 60%. The firm also provides cups and glasses to all staff and uses refillable water bottles for meetings.

In 2007, Denton Wilde Sapte staff completed over 3,800 hours of pro bono work for projects such as the PopLaw legal advice clinic in Tower Hamlets, Unicef UK, the Campaign for Female Education and the HIV/AIDS Alliance.

Other community work includes around 15 volunteers providing at least one hour a week to support an Inner City Reading Scheme, and fortnightly volunteers helping the Whitechapel Mission, offering breakfasts and washing facilities to the homeless of East London.

The firm has a strong relationship with City Gateway, which mentors young people in Tower Hamlets. Groups of students have come into the firm for work experience days and career advice. In August 2008 the firm made a donation of £50,000 of dormant client funds to Birkbeck, University of London, in order to set up a bursary for postgraduate students.

The firm's social committee holds fundraising events throughout the year and gives proceeds to a chosen annual charity, which in 2008 was Breakthrough Breast Cancer. In 2007, the firm raised £10,000 for the St Francis and Willen hospices.

Diversity is a hot topic for Denton Wilde Sapte, and its partnership is 23% female and includes 7% from declared ethnic minorities, while the firm as a whole employs 61% women and 9% declared ethnic minorities. The firm has made a concerted effort to combat ageism as a key issue, and has staff ranging in age from 20 to 65, with the average age being 38. The firm has had a handful of requests from people to continue working beyond 65 and has agreed the vast majority.

Facts and figures

Total staff: 1,570 employees, of which over 180 are partners and 640 are lawyers
Office locations: London, plus 15 offices and associated offices across the UK, Europe, Middle East, CIS and Africa
Industry sector: Legal
Annual turnover: £164.4m

DLA Piper UK LLP

3 Noble Street
London EC2V 7EE
Telephone: 08700 111 111

www.dlapiper.com

Pay and Benefits	★ ★ ★ ★ ☆
Training and Development	★ ★ ★ ★ ⯨
Career Development	★ ★ ★ ★ ⯨
Working Conditions	★ ★ ★ ⯨ ☆
Company Culture	★ ★ ★ ★ ⯨

Biggest plus
Our attractiveness, and what sets DLA Piper apart, is our people and through them our culture. It is the people who make our firm what it is and help bring the brand to life for our clients.

Greatest challenge
As a firm which has, and continues to expand so rapidly, the biggest challenge is ensuring that we integrate diverse local cultures whilst aligning our operating procedures. We believe this is key to making our employees feel part of the broader business.

Summary

DLA Piper is one of the world's largest legal services organisations that has undergone a dramatic transformation over the last 20 years, such that it now competes with the very top law firms in the world. Thanks to a series of mergers in Europe, Asia, and North America, DLA Piper is almost peerless for its international coverage and continues to expand. DLA Piper now has more than 60 offices worldwide and a total of 3,700 lawyers located in over 20 countries. As a full-service practice, DLA Piper is best-known for its expertise in real estate; technology, media and communications; legislative and regulatory matters; litigation; corporate, finance and employment, pensions and benefits.

About the organisation

DLA Piper began life in the UK as a regional firm in Yorkshire. A succession of mergers, culminating in a transformative deal in 2005 with two American law firms – Piper Rudnick and Gray Cary Ware & Friedenrich – propelled DLA Piper to the forefront of the legal sector.

Despite this global outlook, DLA Piper remains mindful of its origins. It is the fifth largest legal services organisation in the UK by turnover, employing 2,800 people across Birmingham, Edinburgh, Glasgow, Leeds, Liverpool, London, Manchester and Sheffield, and generating some £540m in revenues.

What sets DLA Piper apart is its 'can-do' attitude, borne from its rapid elevation to the top-tier of its sector. What has driven the expansion has been a belief in servicing clients, whatever their needs and wherever they are in the world, and that fundamental driver informs the whole practice. Ailsa Martin, the head of human resources projects in the UK, says: "The lawyers here tend to think laterally about the best business solution for the client. To succeed here, you need to be prepared to know the clients back to front, know what's important to them, and then think about how you can help."

Lawyers at DLA Piper like to be considered as part of the business solution, rather than the typical problem-solvers or risk assessors found elsewhere. They continue to innovate to stay ahead in what is a highly competitive market. DLA Piper is frequently at the cutting edge not only of legal developments, but also on pushing the industry to do more around alternative career structures, CSR and environmental initiatives, and the use of technology to benefit clients.

Company Culture

Given its background, it is perhaps no surprise that DLA Piper's UK business is consistently described as 'down to earth and approachable.' Martin says: "We are not elitist, and we are not populated by fourth-generation lawyers. We are nationally spread across the UK, and we are global, which gives us a rounder view of the world. This is a very diverse community."

DLA Piper does not have a UK head office, and as such there is no sense that one place is more important than another. While the London practice has grown tremendously in recent years, the IT function continues to be run from Leeds and Human Resources out of Birmingham thereby fostering a team-based culture.

DLA Piper's values statement focuses on people, clients and communities, while the vision statement sets out the strategy 'To be the leading global business law firm, delivering quality, value-added services to our clients, globally and locally.'

Joint chief executive Nigel Knowles is afforded much of the credit for DLA Piper's transformation and »

"We serve our clients, locally, nationally and globally by providing outstanding legal advice and business insight. We understand that attracting and retaining talented and gifted people is critical to our success..."
(Joint CEO, Nigel Knowles)

is a big personality in the legal industry. Known as an approachable northerner, Martin says of Knowles: "He's very down to earth, realistic and hard-working, and he's a really good communicator. We have a very approachable management team and an open, honest style."

There are communications groups in each office, including members from each team, who meet regularly to discuss issues ranging from business and client matters through to day-to-day operational details.

For the human resources department, a priority is performance management, with DLA Piper renowned for its meritocratic style. Martin says: "Performance management is a really big issue. It's all about managing the top performers and working with the under-performers, being clear about what you want people to do, and offering open and honest feedback."

Innovation and Creativity

The legal market has seen few innovations as radical as DLA Piper's transformation to international player. The bringing together of DLA Piper's European and Asian businesses with two American legal firms was one of the first transatlantic mergers in the industry, and was by far the largest and most complex, described as the first true 'merger of equals' in law.

Now, DLA Piper is pioneering the legal industry's move towards more corporate management styles, with its aggressively meritocratic compensation culture just one example of its move away from industry norms of rewarding individuals based purely on seniority.

On a smaller scale, DLA Piper has pioneered technology allowing staff easy online access to their human resources records and entitlements, and Knowles has been the driving force setting up the Legal Sector Alliance,

a grouping of law firms committed to working together to encourage the profession to deal with environmental sustainability.

Pay and Benefits

DLA Piper seeks to be an employer of choice, and remains competitive with the leading players in each of its markets in terms of pay and benefits. Nancy Furness, DLA Piper's UK HR manager, says: "We look at what our competitors are paying. The legal sector is some way ahead of general salaries anyway, so we feel comfortable that we are able to reward all our people."

For the first few years of their careers, lawyers are paid according to fixed bands, with less room for performance-related rewards. Beyond that, the percentage increases are very much merit-based, with department heads taking decisions over the salaries of individuals based on their total contributions. In 2008, DLA Piper launched a fee-earner bonus scheme that is based on a matrix taking into account the hours worked, performance in areas such as management, client development, teamwork and technical expertise. Furness says: "We wanted to avoid basing bonuses purely on hours worked, so this way we encourage some of DLA Piper's values, like teamwork." Support staff are eligible for bonuses up to a maximum of £750 a year, and also receive a £200 bonus after ten years' service.

In terms of benefits, DLA Piper offers the usual package associated with major legal employers, including a good pension scheme, private medical insurance and 25 days' holiday. There is a 'service holiday scheme' that entitles employees to the equivalent of a fortnight's extra holiday over a two-year period after each three years' of service, and there are also enhanced maternity and paternity benefits.

Unusual perks include a LifeWorks service that offers confidential counselling and support to staff on anything from bereavements to dealing with elderly dependents, and a concierge that helps the time-poor, cash-rich, by arranging anything from foreign holidays to tickets for sporting events on their behalf.

Career Development

Following its transatlantic merger in 2005, DLA Piper moved to harmonise its global approach to career development as much as possible, and introduced four career levels for lawyers across DLA Piper. In the UK it is typical to spend two years as a trainee before qualifying as a solicitor, typically spending six to seven years at this level before being promoted to associate. Associates then have the opportunity to go for either partnership or legal director responsibility.

DLA Piper takes on about 100 trainees each year in the UK and they spend six months in four departments before qualifying, often including a stint overseas. Sally Carthy, the head of graduate recruitment, says: "We are looking for a certain level of intellectual rigour, demonstrated through academic progress, plus communications skills, motivation for the profession, and a can-do attitude." »

"DLA Piper looks after its people and provides a framework of outstanding training that enables real career development."

> "Our people know that DLA Piper has always recognised their talent and diversity. This, allied with clear vision and strategic goals, has allowed the business to grow to more than 60 offices in 25 countries. We will continue to offer the very best opportunities for all our people wherever they work."
> (Joint CEO, Nigel Knowles)

The practice welcomes applicants who may have come from other professions or from atypical academic backgrounds, and the organisation recently triumphed in the Target Jobs National Graduate Recruitment Awards as a result of its diversity in recruitment.

The performance management process now includes twice-yearly reviews at which partnership prospects and development criteria are discussed, and various residential training courses are organised to prepare candidates for senior associate and partnership level. DLA Piper was one of the first legal firms to introduce the legal director role as an alternative to partnership.

David Halliwell is the head of knowledge management for DLA Piper in Europe and Asia, and organises a raft of in-house training programmes covering both legal and business skills. He says: "We are not just a firm of lawyers, we also have other professionals. In our finance team in Sheffield we have people with finance and accountancy qualifications that they need to maintain, so we have recruited someone to specifically look after that. The same is true in IT," he adds.

Corporate Social Responsibility

Everyone at DLA Piper is encouraged to participate in CSR activities – from school reading schemes and team challenges through to pro bono matters of international importance. Last year, 55% of the UK staff chose to get involved, giving nearly 20,000 hours to community and environmental causes.

In September 2008, DLA Piper published its first global CSR Review, detailing its efforts to improve its impact on the environment and local community in each of its locations. As one of the first of its kind to publish such a statement,

DLA Piper reveals information about at least 40 projects it has been involved with, and sets out its objectives around climate change.

DLA Piper has conducted its first global staff survey around Responsible Business in the last 12 months, and found that 94% of its employees were either moderately or extremely concerned about climate change. "That validates our position on that agenda," says Elaine Radford, head of CSR. "We are now building that into discussions with other departments to make sure our policies as a firm reflect what is important to our people."

DLA Piper's CSR function is divided into into four categories, covering education, employability and enterprise; pro bono; people and communities; and sustainability. Recent examples of its work include a nation-wide project in the UK called 'Building Better Lives,' which DLA Piper developed in partnership with The Prince's Trust. This brought together a number of construction companies to help disadvantaged young people across the UK to learn skills needed by the industry, including carpentry, plastering, bricklaying, painting and decorating, and allowing them to qualify for a Construction Skills Certificate Scheme.

The project goes on to offer apprenticeships and job opportunities, and is supported by the Olympic Delivery Authority, working towards London 2012. So far, 320 disadvantaged young people have attended courses, of which 50% have gone straight into employment and 22% have gone on to further education.

Another similar scheme in Paris is called Mobi 3, which brings together young people with blue-chip companies like Nokia and IBM, who challenge students with a real-life business opportunity. Last year, 120 students designed and marketed a new mobile phone, giving disadvantaged youngsters an insight into the private sector.

In 2007, DLA Piper introduced a Global Sustainability Initiative to reduce its environmental impact, and has set carbon emission reduction targets that include reducing air travel by 1% and obtaining 50% of its energy from renewable sources. Chief executive Nigel Knowles has set up the Legal Sector Alliance, bringing together law firms to share knowhow on reducing the industry's environmental impact.

Facts and figures

Total number of staff: 2,800 staff in the UK
Office location: London, Birmingham, Edinburgh, Glasgow, Leeds, Liverpool, Manchester and Sheffield in the UK, and more than 60 offices worldwide in over 20 countries
Industry sector: Legal
Annual turnover: £540 million across Europe and Asia

FremantleMedia

1 Stephen Street
London
W1T 1AL

Telephone: 020 7691 6000
Fax: 020 7691 6100
www.fremantlemedia.com

Pay and Benefits	★ ★ ★ ☆ ☆
Training and Development	★ ★ ★ ★ ⯪
Career Development	★ ★ ★ ★ ⯪
Working Conditions	★ ★ ★ ★ ☆
Company Culture	★ ★ ★ ★ ⯪

Biggest plus
People love what they do, which is producing some of the best entertainment formats on TV.

Greatest challenge
Achieving consistency and standard processes across a diverse and eclectic workforce.

Summary

FremantleMedia is one of the world's largest international creators, producers and distributors of entertainment brands, with leading prime time drama, entertainment and factual entertainment programming in over 40 countries. FremantleMedia's global headquarters is in London, and its UK businesses are FremantleMedia Enterprises and talkbackTHAMES, one of the UK's largest content production companies responsible for over 500 hours of award-winning programmes a year across all genres, for all major broadcasters. These include *The X Factor, Britain's Got Talent, Grand Designs, The Bill, QI* and *The Apprentice*. FremantleMedia employs 3,000 salaried staff globally and 750 in the UK, many in Soho in London's West End.

About the organisation

FremantleMedia exists 'to create amazing entertainment experiences that capture the richness of life.' FremantleMedia owns and works with local production companies around the world to produce long-running hits and successful entertainment global brands that appeal to a broad range of audiences. FremantleMedia is particularly successful in the UK, US, Germany and Australia.

The Idols format has become a global phenomenon, sold to 43 countries. *The Apprentice* has become one of the fastest-selling formats of all time, having been produced in 12 countries. FremantleMedia's vast game show catalogue includes the hugely popular *The Price is Right*, which is the world's longest-running game show and produced locally in 33 countries. FremantleMedia also produces the evergreen Australian soap opera, *Neighbours*.

If you're watching a talkbackTHAMES programme then you're watching a No.1 hit. In 2008, *Grand Designs* was the UK's highest-rated property show, while *The Apprentice* was one of BBC1's most successful series of the year. The *X Factor* series 5 broke all records to win an audience of 14.1 million viewers, making it the UK's highest-rated entertainment show of 2008 and the best-performing talent show this decade. In second position was *Britain's Got Talent*, with an audience of 13.9 million viewers and an incredible audience share of 56% for the finale of series 2.

FremantleMedia Enterprises is responsible for exploiting and developing the company's properties off-screen in areas such as merchandising, the Internet, interactive television and wireless, as well as licensing rights.

FremantleMedia's business model of developing entertainment and drama formats and then rolling them out internationally has proved to be very successful. The company has increased its profit every year since 2000, with turnover reaching €1.132bn in 2007.

››

FremantleMedia creates value by attracting and retaining the best talent, developing great ideas, building formats and controlling rights...

Company culture

"We don't want one culture. It wouldn't work in different countries and in different parts of the business," suggests Nicky Gray, HR director. "But we do want alignment behind our values and attitudes."

That makes a lot of sense. There's a diverse workforce – eclectic even – with hundreds of freelancers, and people do come and go. Different programmes have very different people, who tend to identify strongly with the individual programme, which usually has its own location in and around London. "That's why we need processes," adds Gray.

If FremantleMedia stands for one thing, it's about connecting creativity. This is a wonderful environment where creative people flourish. Producers, script developers, directors and writers are passionate about devising brilliant formats. But it's also a hard-nosed commercial business. With many others fighting for a piece of the pie, and broadcasting companies setting up their own production outfits, it must be commercial.

FremantleMedia creates value by attracting and retaining the best talent, developing great ideas, building formats and controlling rights, producing 'must see' entertainment hits, and rolling these out to create global brands. That's why collaboration is such an important aspect of the culture.

"Even if you're not a 'creative,' you must be able to work in a creative environment," says Gray. Professionals in finance, legal, HR and IT need to flex their style and apply their skills with a light touch to influence successful business outcomes.

This is a fun, informal environment and people really do love their work. But for anyone who is desperate to work in TV at any cost, lured by apparent glamour and celebrities, the message is clear. It's not like that. It's hard work, and the company has become very adept at screening out 'wannabees.'

Talking of celebrities, perhaps the best way to glean insights to the culture is through their words. Simon Cowell said "talkbackTHAMES has the ability to find really good talent and train them up to be superb," while Sarah Beeny said "I love working with the people at talkbackTHAMES."

Innovation and Creativity

"We strive to make every programme the best in class of its type," says Lorraine Hegessey, chief executive of talkbackTHAMES. "We put as much thought and care into returning formats as new ones, making them bigger and better. It's the best way to engage viewers, who we never take for granted."

FremantleMedia's international creative network provides local companies with instant access to ideas, expertise and trends from around the world. Sharing ideas and whatever is 'hot' in the business produces results. For example, with

Hole in the Wall, FremantleMedia made sure that teams knew how it's made and how to network it; it's now FremantleMedia's fastest-selling show ever.

When producers from the UK and Germany met at a global brainstorming workshop, one outcome was an innovative joint two-part drama production of *The Bill*, filmed in both Britain and Germany and now shown in both languages.

talkbackTHAMES is particularly agile in developing partnerships and joint ventures with emerging, independent labels and talents, ensuring a vibrant and continual flow of fresh ideas. Recent partnerships include a joint venture company, Arbie, with Rob Bydon and Miles Ross, and a stake in Trevor Eve's production company, Projector.

FremantleMedia has established FMX to develop personalised, participatory media entertainment across new platforms enabled by emerging technology, including mobile, broadband, games consoles and Internet Protocol Television (IPTV). Meanwhile talkbackTHAMES also launched its first digital project, *Toyboize*, on YouTube and realised one million views in just a month.

Pay and Benefits

"Because of the nature of the business we have a number of unique roles. We therefore don't follow a fixed approach to reward," says Gray. Pay is often determined by local market factors, although FremantleMedia participates in various benchmarking surveys and looks to structure packages.

The staff profit share scheme can add 5% to everyone's salary, based on the company hitting its profitability targets. For the last five years, this has paid out at the maximum. Senior executives have various bonus schemes, calculated on both company profitability and individual targets set over one to three years. Recognition schemes are being looked at but managers often reward individual employees with an ad hoc bottle of champagne for a job particularly well done.

A defined contributions pension scheme is available to all. There are 25 days' annual holiday, plus a couple of extra 'free' days over Christmas. Private health insurance and company cars are granted at certain levels. »

"We hire for attitude and alignment with our values"
(Nicky Gray, HR director)

"Even if you're not a 'creative,' you must be able to work in a creative environment"
(Nicky Gray, HR director)

Employees also benefit from life insurance, childcare vouchers, season ticket loans, the cycle to work scheme (there are showers and changing facilities provided) and retail discount vouchers offering substantial reductions on things such as Apple products. talkbackTHAMES has coffee bars and baked potatoes at all its sites, and free yoga and massages. Perhaps the best perk is free tickets to see the blockbusting live shows!

The company knows how to party. The Christmas bash at the Natural History Museum was anything but bare bones and attended by 700 people. There are also traditional 'Wrap' parties at the end of each individual programme production. Presenters, stars of the show and celebrities often attend.

Career Development

There's a real mix of roles at FremantleMedia. All the programme production skills you would expect, including developers, scriptwriters, sound, camera, lighting, directors and producers. On the management side of production there are heads of entertainment, drama, comedy, with their support teams. In the commercial division are sales and other specialist roles in brand exploitation. And of course the corporate business has professional functions in strategy, legal, marketing, communications, IT, finance and HR. Recruitment for production roles is often informal, with the 'who you know' network playing a part. In management and the professions, it's more conventional, using head-hunters, behavioural interviewing and psychometric testing. "In all cases, we first get prospects to meet the people they would be working with," says Gray. "We also hire for attitude and alignment with our values."

FremantleMedia plans to recruit six people into its graduate recruitment scheme in 2009. "They will move through different areas of the business, to become generalists," says Gray. The company develops its people by using 360-degree feedback, training, coaching and mentoring. "We deliberately cross-match mentors from completely different parts of the business," says Gray. "That way they can share networks and gain a different perspective."

Training courses are numerous and include presentation skills, interviewing, and finance for non-financial managers. talkbackTHAMES also holds regular master classes open to all and given by producers such the producers of *The Bill*, where they talk about what worked, what didn't, and lessons learned.

'Jumpstart' is the annual gathering of over 100 creatives from around the world, held this year in Paris. External speakers, trends analysis and ideas workshops ensure this is a fertile development opportunity for networking and brainstorming.

What type of person does well at FremantleMedia? Those who relish working collaboratively, sharing knowledge, with a real interest in what others are doing. Add to that strong business skills and being comfortable working with creative individuals, and you have the real winning format the company is happy to roll out.

Corporate Social Responsibility

The three priorities on FremantleMedia's CSR agenda are community, charity and environment. Managers are also trained in ethical business behaviour and the company is very much an equal opportunity employer. Staff survey feedback gave a clear message that they wanted the company to do more and they wanted to be personally involved. So a dedicated UK CSR team was established to give something back, using the skills at its disposal.

In one project, Business in the Community, FremantleMedia staff are mentors and job interview coaches for homeless people to help them secure work (they film interviewing techniques!). With results. One person now holds a position at M&S while another even works for Ann Summers!

London is a city of both affluence and deprivation and FremantleMedia has developed strong community links with Newham in East London. A donation of £50,000 has enabled a number of good things, including a safe play area 'The Ark' and training two former users of the Ark as community and social workers. "It's about helping people as well as providing infrastructure," says Gray. "We also staged a special 'Newham's Got Talent' show for kids. It was a fantastic event, and provided a tour of where *The Bill* is filmed."

Through the CARES project, FremantleMedia staff carry out volunteer community work such as gardening and painting jobs for good causes. They also spend days reading in local primary schools. Staff can volunteer for up to three days' community work annually, on projects of their own choice; all the company asks is that each request is signed off by their line manager.

"We believe passionately in using volunteering and sitting on CSR committees as opportunities for our people to develop broader skills," says Gray. FremantleMedia has received national recognition (ISO 40001) for its commitment to environmental initiatives. Smart IT systems, switching off lights and computers when not needed, recycling paper, cartridges, and mobile phones all feature.

The company is also reducing its carbon footprint by replacing international travel with videoconferencing. Cooking oils from the canteen are recycled to run company vehicles and, while not for the faint-hearted, there's a company wormery to ensure that waste food is not wasted.

Facts and figures

Total number of staff: 3,000 worldwide; 750 in the UK
Office location: London
Industry sector: Entertainment
Turnover: €1.132bn (2007)

Friends of
the Earth

Friends of the Earth

26-28 Underwood Street
London
N1 7JQ

Telephone: 020 7490 1555
Fax: 020 7490 0881
www.foe.co.uk

Pay and Benefits	★ ★ ★ ⯪ ☆
Training and Development	★ ★ ★ ☆ ☆
Career Development	★ ★ ★ ☆ ☆
Working Conditions	★ ★ ★ ☆ ☆
Company Culture	★ ★ ★ ☆ ☆

Biggest plus
A real team organisation where everyone plays a part.

Greatest challenge
Getting government to recognise the challenges of global climate change and seize the opportunity to lead Britain to a greener and more prosperous future.

Summary

Friends of the Earth is the UK's most influential environmental campaigning organisation. It has a unique network of local campaigning groups, working in over 220 communities throughout England, Wales and Northern Ireland. Friends of the Earth has a track record of mobilising people to drive major political change and believes that this is the best way to find solutions to the global environmental challenges we all face. It is part of the world's most extensive environmental network, with almost one million supporters across five continents and more than 70 national organisations worldwide.

About the organisation

Since 1971, Friends of the Earth has been inspiring people to care about environmental issues and make a difference locally, nationally and internationally. Most of its staff work in its London headquarters, but the organisation also comprises 220 autonomous groups across England, Wales and Northern Ireland (EWNI) – Friends of the Earth Scotland operates independently.

The organisation is heavily dependent on volunteers: over 2,000 of them at the last count. It is also largely funded by individual donations, with 90% of its £11.9m income in the financial year ending May 31 2008 coming from that source.

The UK has changed markedly since Friends of the Earth was founded. Today there are many single-issue pressure groups, creating competition for the scarce resources of time and money. Friends of the Earth remains unique, however, in its opportunities to get involved at a local level, and also to make a difference nationally and globally.

Its main focus has been on climate change, with campaigns on issues including recycling, energy efficiency, protecting the countryside, keeping genetically modified food off the menu, and persuading big companies to behave better. In June 2008 it launched a new five-year plan, concentrating on the issues of climate change and the loss of biodiversity. These are big, complex concerns: however, as executive director Andy Atkins says, "Big change happens in steps."

A good example of this was the Climate Change Act which received cross-party support and became law in November 2008 as a direct result of Friends of the Earth's Big Ask campaign. Over 200,000 people » took action in support of the climate change law – contacting virtually every MP in the country to ask for their support. As a result, ministers bowed to pressure to increase the target for cutting emissions from 60% to 80% by 2050 and closing a loophole that would have excluded emissions from international aviation and shipping. The new law makes the UK the first country in the world to commit to legally binding cuts in greenhouse gas emissions.

Company Culture

What is it like to work for Friends of the Earth? Carol Hughes, HR manager: "Inspiring, friendly – and busy! It's great reading in the newspaper that something has changed for the better because of work you've been involved in. People smile and laugh a lot here. And Friends of the Earth will always be busy, because there are always things that need doing in order to safeguard the environment for future generations."

The work is often intellectually challenging, including juggling facts and figures from disparate sources to create compelling arguments. It can also be hard work, as the organisation does lots of ground-breaking research in its areas of concern.

It is certainly empowering, however. Everyone in the organisation can make a difference, and anyone involved in a project can offer a view, knowing it will be listened to. Friends of the Earth people are very diverse, and there are many opportunities to put different skills to use. IT and finance staff mingle with campaigners, who feel passionate about their area, and fundraisers, who work across the different campaigns. The latter also need to build relationships with advocates such as Thom Yorke of Radiohead and Razorlight's Johnny Borrell.

Those likely to succeed at Friends of the Earth are people who know their job, can work with other people well, and are eager to keep learning. Hughes said: "It's not about getting your head down and charging; we need to pull together and make our campaigns work on every level."

The organisation is evolving, and there's a need to address every audience professionally, from supporters and donors to lawmakers. Perhaps surprisingly for a charity, there is quite a sophisticated business environment. The organisation needs to stay up to date with everything happening that affects its work, and its people need to be able to able to communicate using the latest technology.

Innovation and Creativity

One of the most innovative aspects of Friends of the Earth is the way it engages people, particularly decision-

"It's great reading in the newspaper that something has changed for the better because of work you've been involved in" (Carol Hughes, HR manager)

"I came to Friends of the Earth because I wanted to make a difference" (Andy Atkins, executive director)

makers. It did this with its Solutions Day in 2007, aimed at journalists and designed to show them the beneficial effects of a stronger climate change law, from carbon-free motorbikes to low-carbon buses.

Its Big Ask campaign, which culminated in 2008, galvanised the opinion of over 200,000 UK citizens and brought real pressure to bear on the Government on climate change. It also enlisted the help of celebrities, including Jude Law, Gillian Anderson and Stephen Fry, to boost public interest and involvement. Emily Thornberry, Labour MP for Islington South & Finsbury Park, commented: "The response to the Big Ask in my constituency has been very strong indeed, and it's come from all sectors of society."

Inside the organisation, its skill share programme has proved very successful. Previously based on sharing a wide set of skills, both internally and externally focused, this is now being relaunched with more of an emphasis on matching up with the five-year strategic plan.

Pay and Benefits

Although Friends of the Earth is definitely rewarding to work for, the real reward tends to be non-financial. As new executive director Andy Atkins said: "I came to Friends of the Earth because I wanted to make a difference" – a view evidently shared by most if not all of his colleagues.

Having said that, bills still need to be paid and the organisation has upped its salary offering in recent years. It checks its salaries annually against the rest of the not-for-profit sector. Salaries range from around £20,000 for junior roles to roughly £58,000 for the highest-paid member of the management team. The fact that the top salary is just three times' that of the lowest says much about the organisation's flat, non-hierarchic structure.

Holiday entitlement is very good, starting at 25 days and rising to 30 days according to length of service. There are also bonus days at the five, ten and fifteen year mark. New fathers are entitled to four weeks of paternity leave at full salary, maternity leave goes beyond the statutory minimum, and childcare vouchers are available through salary sacrifice.

»

"Big change happens
in steps"
(Andy Atkins,
executive director)

Work-life balance is very important in the organisation. Anyone can ask for flexible working, and many people have restructured their jobs around family life. Some have chosen to relocate to other Friends of the Earth offices in cities such as Leeds and Bristol. The organisation is introducing a fully fledged extranet to allow staff to access their files and networks remotely, and make it easier to work from home.

There is an ethical pension scheme with a choice of funds, and employee contributions are matched up to 7% following an increase of 1% in 2008. There is also free life assurance. Friends of the Earth is introducing a telephone/internet confidential employee assistance programme.

Career Development

Every employee has his or her own development plan, which is put together as part of the annual appraisal process. Hughes said: "We will support the things people need in order to do their jobs. We invest not only money but also time and energy to our staff so they can develop."

There is a mix of internal and external training. The former is focused on imparting knowledge in areas such as project management skills, targeting development to the areas that will make the most difference to the daily work. This can involve mentoring and coaching, and also sharing best practice across different areas.

External training promotes diversity learning, management skills and leadership abilities. There is also lots of professional or vocational training, with a number of people acquiring master's degrees, accountancy or HR qualifications.

The two largest work groups are campaigners and fundraisers, and these people have more structured career paths. Other staff in the organisation have less formal scope for promotion, but do have considerable opportunity to work on a range of projects. In any case, promotion in itself is less of an issue here than in many organisations, given the vocational nature of the work and the flat structure (just six strata from top to bottom).

Although Friends of the Earth EWNI is part of an international network, national operations are highly autonomous. Nevertheless, some people do find themselves working with partner organisations overseas. This may occur as part of the EWNI operation's specific projects. For example, a recent research study into the use of palm oil and its impact on local communities required a number of EWNI staff to work in the Far East for a while.

Corporate Social Responsibility

While many companies in this book are committed to acting as sustainable and socially responsible organisations, such commitment is the core purpose of Friends of the Earth. Not surprisingly therefore, this thinking informs everything it does. The induction process includes the company's green approach, showing employees what they can do to support it at work and also at home. All computer monitors are switched off unless they are being used. All staff receive free cotton bags, so they don't need to use plastic bags when shopping.

Documents are all printed double-sided, and energy-saving bulbs are used throughout the organisation's premises. Almost all waste is recycled, in separate bins for white paper, coloured paper, cans and cartons. There is even a teabag and food waste composting service. The staff run their own clothes swaps, bringing in unwanted clothes and exchanging them for others, rather than both parties throwing them away and buying new ones.

Cycling to work is a popular option and over a quarter of the London staff do so. They are encouraged both by a cycle rack on the premises and by an interest-free loan for bicycle purchase available from the company.

New staff have a one-to-one session on how to reduce their carbon footprint. Many staff are also involved in similar activities in their own communities and local areas. Carol Hughes, for example, was recently involved in organising a low carbon conference for South London, and also spoke at a charity HR networking event on environmental issues.

Most of the campaigns organised by the organisation run under the Friends of the Earth Trust, while Friends of the Earth Limited carries out the political work. Each organisation has its own board, with its own chair. Ten regional voluntary members are elected to the board for a three-year term. These meet quarterly with an annual residential weekend to explore wider strategies. Over 30% of board members are women.

Facts and figures

Total number of staff: 175
Office location: London
Industry sector: Charity, not-for-profit
Total income: £11.9m

GlaxoSmithKline

GSK House
980 Great West Road
Brentford
Middlesex TW8 9GS

Telephone: 020 8047 5000
www.gsk.com

Pay and Benefits	★ ★ ★ ★ ☆
Training and Development	★ ★ ★ ★ ☆
Career Development	★ ★ ★ ★ ☆
Working Conditions	★ ★ ★ ★ ☆
Company Culture	★ ★ ★ ★ ★

Biggest plus
A high performance culture with a strong sense of purpose in healthcare.

Greatest challenge
Keeping its product pipeline reloaded to offset drug patent expiry.

Summary

GlaxoSmithKline (GSK) is a world leader in research-based pharmaceuticals with a stated mission 'to improve the quality of human life by enabling people to do more, feel better and live longer.' GSK has a 7% share of the global pharmaceutical market and produces medicines that treat the major disease areas of asthma, virus control, infections, mental health, diabetes and digestive conditions. GSK is big in vaccines and also has a consumer products business. With headquarters in the UK and significant operations in the US, GSK employs around 100,000 people in 114 countries, with around 18,000 based in the UK.

About the organisation

GSK has three main business areas: pharmaceuticals, vaccines and consumer products.

GSK's pharmaceutical product portfolio covers many therapeutic areas including cardiovascular and metabolic, neurosciences, oncology, respiratory and infectious diseases. It is one of the few pharmaceutical companies researching both medicines and vaccines for the World Health Organisation's three priority diseases – HIV/AIDS, tuberculosis and malaria. Its consumer healthcare division manufactures many household name brands, including Ribena, Horlicks, Lucozade, Aquafresh, Sensodyne and Panadol.

GSK is a company with a firm foundation in science and a flair for research. It can point to a long and strong track record of converting that research into powerful, marketable drugs. Every hour GSK spends more than £300,000 on discovering new medicines.

In May 2008 JP Garnier retired as chief executive and was succeeded, through an internal succession appointment, by Andrew Witty, who has a strong commercial background gained over 23 years since joining GSK as a graduate. Under his leadership, GSK is transforming the way it undertakes research, making it more commercially based and focused on the value of products to patients.

In 2007 GSK had a turnover of £22.7bn and an operating profit of £7.6bn. Geographically its turnover is split roughly one-third each in Europe, the US and the rest of the world.

Looking forward, while GSK is historically known for 'blockbusting' pharmaceutical drugs, it expects both vaccines and consumer products to be key areas for investment and growth. Nonetheless, replacing and more importantly reloading its product pipeline of pharmaceutical drugs as current products go off-patent » will remain the vital challenge that GSK must rise to and meet. There may be stormy seas ahead in the industry, but of all the boats on the water, GSK looks to be one of the sturdiest.

Company Culture

"Andrew Witty, GSK's new CEO, is a leader who is passionate about leadership, ethical conduct and getting the best out of every employee," says Adrian Machon, Director Leadership Development. "As an initial symbolic act, he moved his new Central Executive Team from the twelfth floor of the tower block in GSK's west London Headquarters, to the ground floor 'Street' to ensure that they were fully accessible and connected with everything that's happening."

'The Street' is just that – a series of shops and amenities that run along the central concourse of the main building. They include restaurants, a coffee shop, grocery store, hairdresser and a bike shop complete with a bicycle doctor to provide staff with superb conveniences at an out-of-town location. The Central Executive Team's suite of offices is now slap bang in the middle of it.

GSK has always been a high performance culture designed to deliver growth. 'Operational Excellence' was launched in 2007 aimed at simplifying business practices and enabling faster decision making.

Andrew Witty has distributed a five point global strategy to focus the whole organisation. This is a holistic model that also emphasises individual empowerment – not as a directive, but as a process of engagement, communication and motivation. "It's about working together to get the system to change," says Machon. "At Andrew Witty's town hall meetings, you can sense people feeling 'Wow! I want to be part of this.'"

The GSK Spirit defines the qualities that the company expects all its employees to embrace. These include: performance with integrity; entrepreneurial spirit; a focus on innovation; a sense of urgency; and passion for achievement.

"We want our people to be able to do their best work in a way that meets not only the needs of the business but their own personal needs as well," says Martin Swain, Director Policy, Employee Relations and Diversity & Inclusion. GSK's Flexible Working Policy, which applies to all staff, covers a host of working patterns including home working, part-time working, annualised hours and term-time working. In its lifestyle survey, over 75% of GSK employees said they had enough flexibility to balance their work and personal responsibilities.

Innovation and Creativity

"There's been a shift in culture over the last 3-5 years," suggests Swain. "Innovation has always been linked to our R&D activities. But every human being is creative and the shift to individual empowerment is intended to unlock that creative potential in all areas."

GSK has an innovative leadership framework which in addition to behaviours and expertise, focuses on self-awareness. It's a differentiating factor which gets GSK leaders to look at how they manage and lead their own resource, providing the fuel for the rest of the framework.

There is a shadow advisory board for the Central Executive Team. "It's made up of talent from across the businesses, from different nationalities," explains Machon. "It's all about senior executives tapping into a broader range of views."

R&D now follows a new model and process flow for drug discovery. GSK's Drug Discovery Groups are effectively small bio-pharma businesses, bidding for available development funds. Discovery Performance Units are small groups around which drug formulation is centred. Centres of Excellence for Drug Discovery are hubs of innovation for therapeutic areas, from which potential drugs move in the Discovery Performance Units. There is also an internal forum called 'SciNovations,' a science fest in which GSK researchers explain their work.

Pay and Benefits

GSK's compensation package is called TotalReward. It's a comprehensive and well-balanced package combining TotalCash (salary plus bonus), Savings choices (pension, longer-term savings and incentives), and a host of lifestyle benefits.

Basic salaries are not pitched at the very top of the market, but on average target the median of the external market with flexibility through salary ranges to pay above or below this, based on performance and capability. TotalCash is bolstered by an annual bonus based on individual performance and the performance of your business unit and the company. This bonus is typically 12-25% of salary and currently the average TotalCash package is £50,000. "We'll be looking to invigorate the package next year to see that we're getting the most out of it," says Jacky Weller, UK Policy & Employee Relations manager.

There are three ways to save earnings with GSK. There's a money purchase pension plan, under which the company matches contributions up to 4%. There are also two medium-term savings vehicles: ShareSave, a three-year plan which pays a guaranteed tax-free bonus and the option to buy discounted GSK shares; and ShareReward, a buy one, get-one-free savings plan. Take-up is very healthy, at around 85%.

"Your personal development plan is most definitely your document"
(Martin Swain, director Policy, Employee Relations and Diversity & Inclusion)

"We couldn't successfully deploy people through the organisation in the numbers that we do if we didn't give people the right career development"
(Jacky Weller, UK Policy & Employee Relations manager)

Softer lifestyle benefits are geared towards supporting employee health and enabling a work-home balance. These include a healthcare plan, which covers 90% of the cost of medical treatment; LifeWorks, an employee assistance programme; and family support in the form of emergency childcare. Employees may use salary sacrifice to buy a bicycle for work travel or to undergo a health assessment. There's also 26-28 days' holiday each year and a range of discounted products and services to choose from.

For more senior managers the greatest earning potential lies in the form of long-term incentive plans – a share value plan and a share option plan – that are designed to provide a real stake in the business' success. There is also a choice between a car allowance and car purchase through a car ownership scheme.

Career Development

"We select candidates based around high-performance behaviours," says Machon, "as these will be the same behaviours they will be developed by once they are in the organisation." Naturally there are a lot of science-based backgrounds but GSK is looking innovatively at different skills and technologies and how they might be applied to pharmaceuticals. As you would expect, GSK has strong relationships with universities.

Everyone has a personal development plan (PDP) which is usually reviewed on a quarterly basis. "Your PDP is most definitely your document," says Swain. "We recognise that the employee should be driving that plan – it's not for the business or the manager."

Under each plan individual performance is measured against annual objectives and how tasks have been carried out. They are also an opportunity to focus on development objectives and ultimately career aspirations. The size and global reach of GSK mean that for many employees these can be fulfilled by remaining where they are. Accordingly overall turnover is low at around 5-6%.

If you perform well, chances are you'll be noticed and given the opportunity to progress through the business. A talent management process identifies top performers, and GSK supports this with a range of leadership courses to suit managers at all levels.

The value of mentoring is understood. It's seen as a great way of transferring knowledge and to emphasise this, GSK trains staff members in how to teach mentoring skills to others. Another useful tool is myLearning, a global website where individuals can shape their own learning plan, including registering on a training course, accessing online education, or simply finding recommended reading.

"We couldn't successfully deploy people through the organisation in the numbers that we do if we didn't give people the right career development," says Weller.

Corporate Social Responsibility

On CSR, GSK tries to think global and act local. Obviously much of its opportunity is health related. "There's a direct link between our products and ethics," says Swain. "When CSR reflects your business then it can become sustainable and you can really involve employees; CSR becomes motivational with the right business ethos." Many initiatives take place at a global level, such as a major push to eliminate lymphatic filariasis, or running 'Global Wash Your Hands' Day.

Given its position in the industry, GSK takes a position of responsible leadership. It cares about the impact that it has on the people and places touched by its mission to improve health around the world. This includes helping developing countries where debilitating disease affects millions of people and access to life-changing medicines and vaccines is a problem. "Providing discounted medicines where they are needed most is a difficult balancing act," says Swain. GSK has separate production lines to create bright orange medicines to avoid their illegal on-sale. "One of the drivers behind the commercialisation of R&D is a wish to be transparent to the patient about what they are paying for," he adds.

In the UK GSK makes awards to at least ten charities and supports many more initiatives and community partnerships at local level. Orange Day allows employees to perform voluntary work for a local charity. GSK claims to top the list of FTSE-100 companies in putting money back into the community and this effort is measured in hundreds of millions of pounds.

GSK has a business ethics process that every manager has to certify that they understand and comply with every element. This covers 'everything' – customers, shareholders, integration, environment and communities.

The environment is a major issue, particularly GSK's environmental footprint in manufacturing, in terms of carbon emissions, energy usage, water and waste management. Each global site is tasked with reducing these measures year-on-year. This drive is supported by high-level CEO awards for best practice. In head office, recycling is taken to a personal level – all individual waste bins have been taken away.

GSK has a clear policy on diversity and a number of steering groups to drive it forward. "We track the numbers and all the trends are positive," says Swain. Global initiatives go way beyond age and gender issues. 'If the public spotlight shone on GSK, what would it expect us to focus our efforts on,' the company asked itself. The answer was disability. GSK has subsequently made a public commitment to be a disability-friendly company.

Facts and figures

Total number of staff: 100,000 (19,000 in the UK)
Office location: Head office in London; operations in 114 countries
Industry sector: Pharmaceuticals
Annual turnover: £22.7bn

HCL Technologies

7th floor
68 King William Street
London
EC4N 7DZ

Telephone: 020 7105 8600
www.hcltech.com

Pay and Benefits	★ ★ ★ ★ ★
Training and Development	★ ★ ★ ⯪ ☆
Career Development	★ ★ ★ ⯪ ☆
Working Conditions	★ ★ ★ ☆ ☆
Company Culture	★ ★ ★ ★ ⯪

Biggest plus
HCL's egalitarian principles combined with trust, transparency and flexibility.

Greatest challenge
To deliver fiscal improvements year-on-year while providing excellent customer satisfaction for lower cost and striving for carbon neutral status.

Summary

Part of the HCL Group, HCL Technologies of India is a global IT services company, providing software-led IT solutions, business process outsourcing (BPO) and remote infrastructure management (RIM) services. It has annual revenue of US$2bn (HCL Group: US$5bn). HCL currently employs some 51,000 professionals worldwide, 3,500 in the UK. HCL makes use of an extensive offshore infrastructure and a global network of offices in 19 countries to deliver solutions across sectors including banking, insurance, retail, aerospace, healthcare, media and entertainment, automotive, semiconductors, life sciences and telecommunications. HCL is unique in its ability to source operations almost anywhere across the globe and the breadth of its outsourcing capabilities.

About the organisation

Since moving into IT services, HCL Technologies focused on technology and R&D outsourcing. While it realised offshore models may provide profitability, sustainability could only be secured if the right talent and operations could be developed for clients across the globe. The company has a strategy to create a sustainable revenue stream by offering the right outsourcing location for any client – replacing offshore outsourcing with the right shore, set against a philosophy of 'the employee comes first.' Near-shore operations will typically involve locations in Eastern Europe.

"Transformation is the basic agenda," says S. Ramachandran (Ram), director of HR. "Enabling transformation in employees leads to value creation for all stakeholders."

To drive profitability and build on 2007/8 revenues of US$2bn, HCL is continuing to position itself around integrated services offerings to solve business problems. "It's our blue ocean strategy," says Ram. "We have now established true end-to-end services offerings, solving customers' problems rather than just offering services." A three-tier operation is available, involving countries where customers operate, countries near to the client (i.e. near shore) and offshore locations.

Rajeev Dawhney, HCL president, Europe, says, "For the past four years we have registered significant year-on-year growth of 60%. The role Europe plays in the global business has also significantly grown to constitute 30% of overall HCL business. We expect to improve on this over the next three years."

Meanwhile the US market still represents a significant chunk at 58%. The UK component is not resting, contributing through both organic and inorganic activity. HCL acquired the consultancy group Axon in a surprise »

"For the past four years we have registered significant year-on-year growth of 60%" (Rajeev Dawhney, HCL president, Europe)

move in September 2008, with at least one other US$850m deal in the pipeline, apart from a few mid-sized acquisitions in the US$50m-US$100m area. Interestingly, Axon's entrepreneurial employee culture was similar to that at HCL.

Company Culture

"Three key attributes that drive our behaviour and policies are trust, transparency and flexibility. Emphasising these attributes are the egalitarian principles on which the company is run. All benefits apply equally to all employees at all levels."

"For people with ambition who want to take the initiatives and deliver something, then HCL is the place to be," says Ram. "There is encouragement at all levels in the organisation to be proactive in skills and there are continual efforts from the company to achieve higher excellence."

"A key attraction of HCL is the spirit of entrepreneurship and the flexibility in the whole system. If someone has an idea – to improve a process for example – the ethos is 'go for it.' And people do," says Ram, which melds with the overarching initiative that the employee comes first.

As an offshore outsourcing expert, HCL has had to fuse this entrepreneurial culture with clear accountability. In the UK, HCL has fostered links with the Financial Services Authority in a drive to regulate offshore operations.

As a result of this transparency, qualifications are key within HCL. Some 20% of staff have achieved postgraduate qualifications (for example, MBA, MSc, MTech) and 60% have graduate qualifications. Such highly qualified people need a strong work/life balance and a range of policies exist within the workplace to protect and focus their efforts. "We flex for certain categories of staff to enable working from home wherever practical. However, software engineers do mostly have to be at a client site." There are policies and procedures in place to prevent bullying and harassment, but there have never been problems – nor with absenteeism. This is a sales-driven company at the forefront of technology that's clearly moving forwards. There's a buzz to HCL, reflected in the positive atmosphere on its sites.

Innovation and Creativity

HCL Technologies is at the heart of developing industry standard technology. Today, the mantra running through the company is that 'customers want more for a lesser price,' and the only way to service this is through innovation and creativity. That HCL has been successful is proof of how innovation happens here.

An internal blog initiated by the CEO called U&I addresses all of the company's 51,000+ employees. Here any employee can raise any issue – and the CEO also asks employees, "how do we build innovation?"

HCL gained the world's first BS15000 certification for a customer-dedicated offshore development centre. BS7799 security accreditation has been achieved, plus COPC, the most coveted certification in the customer service provider industry. AS9100 certification, the de facto quality standard for the demanding aerospace industry, and ISO13485:2003 quality standard applicable to the design, development and manufacture of medical devices have also been awarded.

HCL innovation can be found in almost any industry. Some 35% of car electronics and the software behind the latest dashboards come from HCL. RIM is a service offering pioneered by HCL – multi-location, multi-facility infrastructure management can be handled not just centrally but remotely. HCL is a one-stop-shop IT partner to its clients, with flexibility a key attribute.

Pay and Benefits

HCL recognises that it operates in a competitive market and must offer attractive packages to its staff. "Our remuneration packages range from better than average graduate salaries (starting at approximately £26,000) potentially up to six-figure sums for professionals with a range of global responsibilities," says Ram.

"We offer a relatively simple formula of two components – fixed salary and bonus," says Ram. "Our performance bonus structure runs from July to June in line with the company's financial year, the bonus being paid in October. Recently, for our sales staff, we moved to offering quarterly performance bonus payments, strengthened the sales organisation by doubling its size, and have now increased it by 30% to grow the business aggressively and penetrate new markets."

The company has a strong egalitarian principle. For benefits, generous BUPA medical and travel insurance are offered not only to employees but to their dependants as well. Uniquely, the travel cover also applies to leisure activities. The company offers stakeholder and money purchase pension schemes, a permanent health insurance plan, critical disability cover of twice salary, and life insurance of four times salary. "We're focusing on the long-term sustainability of the business," says Ram.

"A key attraction of HCL is the spirit of entrepreneurship and the flexibility in the whole system" (S. Ramachandran, director of HR)

"All benefits apply equally
to all employees at
all levels"
(S. Ramachandran,
director of HR)

"The global company is listed on the Indian Stock Exchange and our stock option plan applies to 20% of our global population," says Ram. Long-term service awards are offered for five, 10, 15, 20 and 25 years' service and can take various forms. Flexible support is offered to all sales and corporate staff with each person receiving a laptop and BlackBerry. "There is very much a family feel to the company," says Ram. "People can work from home depending on project demands, client needs and managers' discretion. Flexible working arrangements are also available subject to fitting in with workloads and project demands."

Career Development

Within HCL, training is delivered through a mix of on-site, classroom training at an offshore centre, computer-based methods and employee-driven self-initiatives. The thrust is that training and development is self-managed, with responsibility shared by employees. The number of courses on offer has doubled and the US$10m iLearn e-learning system introduced. Career Power is a self-managed tool which employees utilise to manage their careers. Rolled out in summer 2008, the system assesses capability and competence, showing gaps and learning needs, defining career goals and leading to opportunities (the internal job market). Meanwhile, the new US$3m Eagles' Nest programme gives 400 sales staff a bird's eye view of HCL.

There's focus on three groups on training – sales and marketing, project/service delivery, and corporate functions. HCL currently imparts an average of 11.72 training days/employee/year. Just over half (53%) of the training focuses on technical skills, 30% on soft skills and the rest is divided between management/quality and engineering skills.

HCL also exploits its international infrastructure to develop its staff. Based out of its Belfast Apollo contact centre, the Business Exchange Programme enables tranches of 10 people to go to India for periods of six months to a year. Conversely, 10 people from India also head to Belfast for 3-9 months. This international perspective of training provision has already paid dividends as staff within Apollo can speak six languages.

"We have a lot of movement of people globally," says Ram. "There's phenomenal movement of software engineers/consultants." Consequently, HCL has invested a great deal in acclimatising employees to foreign cultures.

As training placements depend on client requirements and the skills needed, the training courses also create future business unit leaders. With HCL's 30% growth per annum, key emphasis is placed upon employee learning and development.

Corporate Social Responsibility

A senior executive appointment has been made to cover Corporate Social Responsibility (CSR). The company continues to focus on good corporate governance in line with local and global standards. Its primary objective is to create and adhere to a corporate culture of conscience and consciousness, integrity, transparency and accountability for efficient and ethical conduct of business in meeting its obligations towards shareholders and other stakeholders.

Corporate governance is an integral part of the philosophy of the company in pursuit of excellence, growth and value creation. HCL recognises that strong corporate governance is indispensable to safeguarding the interests of shareholders and other stakeholders.

As technology is at the heart of HCL's operations, most of the investment within HCL is focused on IT. Technology development is crucial to the development of HCL as a company. Building on HCL's history of innovation, the company intends to continue leading outsourcing throughout a number of key markets, particularly with its driven philosophy that 'the employee comes first.'

Given its global operations, HCL has a presence in some countries where education is not as easily available to all strata of society as it is in the West. HCL operates foundations run by the chairman's office to remedy this need. The SSN Foundation, for example, runs schools and colleges to cater to the needy, such as the SSN College of Engineering, located on a campus on the Rajiv Gandhi Salai ('Cyber Corridor') of Chennai in India. The SSN College of Engineering follows an admission policy that strongly favours merit, even as it enables access to education for students from all strata of society.

Ram points to the per capita footprint (PCF) which is expected to decrease while per capita income (PCI) increases. "PCI is going up alongside revenues increasing to US$2bn and employee growth reaching 51,000; we are global and service customers where they are located. All of which means (international) travelling is unavoidable," says Ram. "We use videoconferencing judiciously – for example, two from a team of 10 might physically travel, while the rest of the team communicates by video conference."

HCL appreciates that it's equally important to change the behaviour of employees, such as leaving light switches off, switching computers off and sensible use of printing. "The intention is to have mechanisms in place to measure continuously to ensure PCF reduces," says Ram. "The goal is to achieve carbon neutral status." ∎

Facts and figures

Total number of staff: 51,000 worldwide, 3,500 in the UK
Office location: London, with a network of offices in 19 countries
Industry sector: IT services
Turnover: US$2bn, out of HCL Group's US$5bn

Heart of England

Heart of England NHS Foundation Trust
Birmingham Heartlands Hospital
Bordesley Green East
Birmingham B9 5SS

Telephone: 0121 424 1334
Email: mandy.coalter@heartofengland.nhs.uk
www.heartofengland.nhs.uk

Pay and Benefits	★ ★ ★ ★ ☆
Training and Development	★ ★ ★ ★ ☆
Career Development	★ ★ ★ ★ ☆
Working Conditions	★ ★ ★ ★ ☆
Company Culture	★ ★ ★ ★ ☆

Biggest plus
A financially stable employer with strong people-management skills.

Greatest challenge
To ensure its clinical staff and board members reflect the community it serves.

Summary

Heart of England became a Foundation Trust (HEFT) hospital in 2005, and is one of the largest trusts in England. It runs four sites: its main unit in Birmingham Heartlands Hospital; a site at Solihull Hospital; the Birmingham Chest Clinic; and the newly acquired Good Hope Hospital in Sutton Coldfield. Its workforce totals 10,000, serving over one million patients. A specialist in treating MRSA, heart and kidney disease, cancer, HIV and AIDS, it also has the largest maternity unit in Europe, leading in premature baby care. Internationally it has forged links with healthcare providers in the US and Europe.

About the organisation

"We work as one team with one ambition: to be the best we can for our patients and our community," says Dr Mark Goldman, chief executive of the Trust.

The development of Heart of England into a Foundation Trust hospital historically has been by way of merger and acquisition. Originally the Little Bromwich Hospital, a fever unit and sanatorium on Birmingham's outskirts, it acquired the Marston Green Maternity Hospital and in 1992 became the first Acute Trust in Birmingham. The Birmingham Chest Clinic and Solihull Hospital were acquired in 1993 and 1995 respectively.

The national regulator Monitor oversees the Trust, which has been repeatedly rated highly for its performance and strong finances. It has had an annual turnover of just under £500m for the past two years. With a £200m kitty to invest in its sites over the next 10 years, such financial muscle enabled the Trust to carry out its most significant move to date – the acquisition of Good Hope Hospital in April 2007 – without having to borrow a penny. The deal is also unique as it is the first acquisition by a Foundation Trust hospital of another hospital.

This 'merger by absorption' has given Heart of England a strong market share in Birmingham's North East and South regions, with a total of almost 1,500 beds. Consolidating the takeover has been a main focus for the Trust over the past 12 months.

The Trust is seen by the sector as one of the highest-performing hospitals in the UK, and it has been recognised accordingly with an award for Acute Trust of the Year at the Health Service Journal Awards in 2006. In 2008 its public relations team won the Chartered Institute of Public Relations gold award for the most outstanding team and a Silver Award for its 'Beat the Bugs' infection control campaign. It has also been shortlisted for the Chartered Institute of Personnel and Development award and won the HR Excellence 2008 Award for 'most successful change management' for the acquisition and integration of Good Hope Hospital into the Trust. »

"We've been pushing an agenda of doctors being leaders here for many years, which the NHS is just waking up to"
(Mandy Coalter, director of HR)

Company Culture

The Trust's mission statement is ambitious – to be the most exciting and influential healthcare provider worldwide. From that is born its 'quality as a business' strategy. Quality is defined as patient and staff experience and value for money. Everything the Trust does is aligned to these outcomes and delivering quality standards is the responsibility of every leader.

The aims of the £200m development plan back this up – the priorities are infection control; choice; privacy and dignity for patients; and staff satisfaction through creating a better working environment.

Large displays of art and crafts created by staff ranging from cleaners to senior executives adorn the walls and communal areas of a spotless hospital. Staff take pride in their workplace, and patients and visitors directly benefit from their creative input.

The Trust is keen for all of its hospitals to be part of a community rather than a huge, monolithic organisation. Staff engagement is seen as paramount to the Trust's success and everyone can attend a monthly briefing with the chief executive. Its Intranet, currently being revamped, provides updated news and 'computers on wheels' are taken round the wards so that staff can have access while they work. Around 70% of staff read the bi-monthly newsletter. Staff surveys are conducted regularly, covering all aspects of working at the Trust, monitoring staff attitudes and opinions on new proposals and daily issues.

As all staff deal with stressful situations on a daily basis, the Trust offers everyone counselling, a discounted gym, aromatherapy and massages. With 80% of its workforce being female, it readily offers flexible working, including career breaks, job sharing and term-time contracts. It takes someone who is personable and resilient in a fast-paced and demanding environment to thrive at the Trust, although considerable training and support are provided to enable staff to do their jobs effectively.

Innovation and Creativity

The Trust believes passionately that clinicians should hold leadership roles. The board has two medical directors and a nursing director, while a number of clinical directors are responsible for budgets and staff in their department. The CEO was previously a consultant vascular surgeon and medical director for surgery at the Trust. Mandy Coalter, director of human resources and organisational development, says this is unusual in the NHS. "Most leaders come from

management and finance. We've been pushing an agenda of doctors being leaders here for many years, which the NHS is just waking up to."

HEFT has a leadership academy and a quality dashboard for each directorate is being developed to measure outcome, patient and staff experience, and satisfaction of each of the Trust's clinical directors. In doing so, the Trust hopes to pinpoint any problems and hold clinicians to account.

"We've given staff tools to change the way wards work; we've got managers and nurses quite passionate about ward efficiency," says Coalter. "There's no template from the NHS. We define our own qualities and how someone performs clinically. We're a very confident organisation and feel we can shape our destiny, which isn't always the case, particularly in non-foundation trust organisations."

Pay and Benefits

Salaries are bound by the NHS pay framework introduced in 2004. HEFT offers different pay levels for different groups of staff. For example, band 1 currently covers porter/security level roles with 2008 pay levels at £12,517-£13,617. Staff nurses fall into band 5: £20,225-£26,123. Team manager salaries can range from £14,834 to £64,118, depending on the work and qualifications involved.

Pay is an area that the Trust wants to review. It doesn't offer bonuses but it does have a final salary pension scheme. It also has good annual leave provisions. For a new employee, that means 28 days plus Bank Holidays, increasing to 33 days after 10 years' service. Coalter says: "We are just about to adopt a new strategy on reward to take into account what matters to staff, how we can adapt the national pay framework and look at the pay rewards and benefits."

The Trust runs a staff recognition programme, which provides a prize of £500, and nominations are made both by staff and by patients. The ceremony is a rather glitzy affair that is held off-site. The Trust also invests in health services for staff such as online counselling and a proactive health promotion roadshow. It also provides staff with the flu jab and will fast track them for other treatments such as physiotherapy. The thinking is to invest in the strong team of people that the Trust has and to use its money wisely – for instance, investing in human resources and ensuring that staff benefit from good services.

'We work as one team with one ambition: to be the best we can for our patients and our community'
(Dr Mark Goldman, chief executive)

"The NHS as a concept really is still the envy of the world. We should value the system we have in this country"
(Mandy Coalter, director of HR)

Career Development

The national pay structure heavily influences career paths in a process approved by Trade Union colleagues within the Trust. For example, newly qualified nurses joining on band 5 can easily see how to progress through the band levels and what is required to reach that next level.

Training is a key part of staff development. Upon joining, staff are given a two-day induction to immerse them in the Trust's values and also to cover specific workplace issues such as infection control. The Trust has a dedicated learning and development website that makes staff aware of training opportunities and support, and courses can be booked online. Essentially the Trust is a teaching hospital and in any one year it could have 300-400 junior doctors training.

The HEFT leadership academy provides different levels of training for its different levels of managers and leaders. For example, if you are managing a ward, you receive training based around managing people and resources. Those managing a department receive more strategic leadership development. Staff are also using training to manage sickness and working patterns on the wards, something that the Department of Health has been keen to observe at the Trust. Over the past two years, about 400-500 people have received such training.

The Trust uses Birmingham UCE University for training nurses. It is looking at forming an alumni to encourage former trainees to return there to work. Non-professional development is also provided by way of NVQ levels 1-3.

The Trust has also formed a number of international links, namely with institutions in the US, Sweden, Canada and Italy. Research has been carried out with the American health organisation Kaiser Permanente, which is well-known in the healthcare world and is held up as a yardstick to good healthcare in the US. Coalter says, "The NHS as a concept really still is the envy of the world, particularly in the US. We should value the system we have in this country."

Corporate Social Responsibility

The very nature of what HEFT does is social responsibility. Month in, month out, its news releases detail fundraising efforts by staff at all levels, and charity and community events taking place across all of its sites.

There are two main elements of governance: corporate and clinical. A director of governance and standards ensures that all business regulations and codes are complied with. Clinical governance requires that the Trust is up-to-date on

risk issues, like safety and infection control. A healthcare directorate ensures information security, effective handling of complaints, staff security and safety. Policies and guidelines come from national bodies such as the National Institute of Clinical Excellence and National Service Frameworks.

As part of the Government's academy programme, the Trust is sponsoring an academy school in the Solihull area. A high level of response to these programmes originally came from the private sector, but the Trust is one of the first hospitals to be involved in the scheme. It will effectively mean that the Trust runs the school. The voluntary scheme is due to start in 2010. As well as being seen by the Trust as giving something back to the community, it's also viewed as being a future 'talent pipeline.'

The Trust also works hard to make sure that its staff make-up reflects the communities it serves. Diversity statistics on ethnic minorities, published in September 2008, showed that overall the Trust's staffing levels accurately reflected the make-up of ethnic groups in the communities it serves – in this case 24%. The gender balance is slightly tipped in favour of women, who comprise 80% of the workforce. Its executive team is well-balanced by gender.

Environmentally, much is done around recycling and waste management. The Trust has a carbon management programme in place. It encourages cycling to work through discounts and interest-free loans on cycles and also has cycle storage facilities and an annual bike to work day; the Trust is still working on installing shower facilities at all sites. Car sharing is encouraged and is rewarded by the Trust waiving the £11 parking fee for those that do. A shuttle bus service takes staff between the Solihull and Good Hope sites.

Facts and figures

Total number of staff: 10,000, including 5,000 nurses and healthcare assistants, and 800 doctors
Office location: Birmingham
Industry sector: Healthcare
Turnover: £265m

hydrogen

Hydrogen Group plc

16 Old Bailey
London
EC4M 7EG

Telephone: 020 845 4200
www.hydrogengroup.com

Pay and Benefits	★ ★ ★ ★ ★
Training and Development	★ ★ ★ ★ ⯪
Career Development	★ ★ ★ ★ ★
Working Conditions	★ ★ ★ ★ ★
Company Culture	★ ★ ★ ★ ★

Biggest plus
People here tend to be more successful in career and productivity terms than they are at competitors.

Greatest challenge
To successfully internationalise the business, using global processes but with a local aspect.

Summary

Hydrogen is an international specialist recruitment group placing high quality professional staff into clients on a permanent and contract basis. Currently there are seven consultancies: Project Partners, Target Partners, Finance Professionals, Law Professionals, HR Professionals, Darwin Park and Reflect, a human resources outsourcing consultancy. Publicly listed on AIM since 2006, Hydrogen has a diverse portfolio of blue chip and smaller corporate clients including UBS, BBC, BNP Paribas and Carphone Warehouse.

Company Culture

Established in 1997, Hydrogen achieved market-beating, wholly organic growth in the UK. Revenues at the end of 2007 stood at £103.4m, up from £82.9m in 2006, with pre-tax profits (before exceptional costs) of £8m, up from £6.1m. However, difficult trading conditions hit profits in 2008, with the half-year figure at £3.3m, and the group's share price took a plunge. And with the current economic slump adversely affecting a number of the group's specialist markets 2009 promises to be a challenging year for the business.

Within Hydrogen however there is a firm belief that the long-term future for the business is healthy – that real shareholder value arises due to sustainability of earnings from the diverse client and service portfolio. According to Tim Smeaton, CEO, having achieved very rapid growth in the UK the focus of the group now is increasingly international. It aims to provide the staffing that will be required to meet new client commercial objectives and capture the migratory flows of a new generation of globally minded professionals. He says, "We have a very simple strategy – to keep doing what we've been doing within the UK and build greater market share; to transfer it into western and central Europe; then take what we've done in the northern hemisphere and replicate it in the southern hemisphere."

Company Culture

Hydrogen is not for the faint-hearted. It's a fast-paced work environment where people are coached in their respective roles and in return are expected to deliver. Yet for those who do thrive here it is intensely rewarding. There are real opportunities for involvement in business strategy and genuine scope for career development. Arguably its most distinctive feature is the number of different branded businesses that co-exist under one roof.

Smeaton says, "Our culture is that we have numerous sub-cultures – and the values that exist at a corporate level need to be adopted within those sub-cultures. If you ask people what they consider to be the culture of Hydrogen they say, 'it's acceptable to be a little bit different'."

"Everyone in the business has a career plan that demonstrates what they need to do to get promoted and what behaviours are required of them"
(Tim Smeaton, CEO)

In practice this means you'll notice a difference depending on which part of the business you're employed in. Law Professionals, for example, reflect a close alignment with the culture of the legal profession in the way its consultants deal with candidates and clients. At the same time an overarching Hydrogen identity is apparent in some areas, for example, in the company's leadership development programme.

The business is currently expanding globally and this is creating both opportunities and challenges. The opportunities are to be found on overseas assignments, where different teams of employees work to establish their brand in sometimes less sophisticated markets and use local knowledge to communicate effectively with candidates. The challenge for the business is in managing this growth and the processes that underpin it. The Hydrogen 'family' is more scattered than in previous years and video conferencing, focus groups and HR surgeries are used widely in order to maintain the links that connect all staff.

Though hard work is certainly expected of staff this doesn't mean long hours are necessarily the norm. "We've always been an output-focused company," says Andrea Marshall, the group's marketing director. "We're very clear with people as to what they are expected to do so that allows them to manage their working time accordingly."

Innovation and Creativity

Hydrogen is proud of its extremely high client retention rate. Yet its success in this area doesn't breed complacency; on the contrary, there is an ongoing effort to ensure that existing relationships are strengthened still further. One of the tools used to achieve this is a 'best of breed' account management system. Designed in-house the application provides clients with greater transparency, more detailed information and improved communication throughout the recruitment process. It also enables account managers to cross-sell services between the branded businesses to different clients. It is initiatives such as this that have helped ensure that more than three-quarters of Hydrogen's top 50 clients have worked with them for over three years.

Candidate placement is another area in which the business has gone the extra mile. Notably it has had success in relationship-building with high-calibre people who are not actively seeking to switch jobs using a service called Market Watch. Users sign up to receive regular updates on subjects of interest in their industry, such as employment trends, salary surveys, as well as suitable job vacancies. "We find the candidates in the first place through advertising or contact made by our researchers," says Marshall. "Legal professionals have proved to be particularly keen on this service."

Hydrogen has also improved its internal operations across the group to help galvanise staff. It has installed an electronic management system that provides comprehensive information on key commercial activity within the business. So developments such as new client acquisitions or candidate placements are relayed in graphical form to all employees. To add a fun element, each brand has its own theme song, which plays in celebration at good news.

Pay and Benefits

One of the key values underpinning the business culture is recognition of achievement. Consequently every member of staff is on some form of performance-related salary. The size of the bonus is determined through the performance review process with each payment graded against pre-agreed objectives. For sales staff, who make up around two-thirds of the workforce, the main criteria are customer satisfaction and delivery. High-performers have the potential to earn up to half their salary in bonuses, and can be earning a six-figure salary four years after joining. To ensure they can see how they're performing on an ongoing basis everyone is provided with a commission calculator. Variable pay may increase further depending on the company's performance over a set time period.

Recognition for significant business contribution also takes the form of sales incentives. Team incentives include lunches at exclusive restaurants, cash prizes, sports events and trips away. The ten highest billing individuals are recognised each year – previous prizes have included weekends in Las Vegas and Monte Carlo, and Rolex watches. Staff in operational functions can also be recognised through the award of cash prizes or vouchers.

There is an extensive range of benefits on offer. All staff qualify for 23 days' holiday (rising to 28 based on service), private health insurance (after a year's service), travel loans, an interest-free travel loan, childcare vouchers, subsidised on-site massages and free eye tests. Team leaders can join a tax-efficient share option scheme. There's even help with loans for first-time home buyers – particularly handy in a slow housing market. Subsidised corporate gym membership is popular too.

»

"We're very clear with people as to what they are expected to do so that allows them to manage their working time accordingly" (Andrea Marshall, marketing director)

"If you ask people what they consider to be the culture of Hydrogen they say, 'it's acceptable to be a little bit different'"
(Tim Smeaton, CEO)

Career Development

"Everyone in the business has a career plan that demonstrates what they need to do to get promoted and what behaviours are required of them," says Smeaton, "We then review each individual's progress on a quarterly basis to see what value they've added to the business."

It's a competitive environment in every sense of the word so a premium is placed on good leadership. Team leaders shape the design of much of training provided and are continually encouraged to grow their own leadership skills. As part of its development strategy Hydrogen holds a number of workshops that focus on team leaders acquiring a deeper understanding of how different marketplaces operate. As Smeaton puts it, "on understanding the 'why' as well as the 'how'." The training uses situational leadership tools to better inform staff at each stage of the market cycle.

The internationalisation of Hydrogen is bringing significant change to every aspect of its business and nowhere more so than in people development. Now that the number of career options available to staff is considerably greater, a formal international development plan is taking shape to meet these changes. Individuals can signal their interest in overseas work at roadshows that are held every three months. After discussions about where they would like to be based they are given work objectives and help to achieve them. According to Smeaton, "In order to prepare people properly we give 'stretch projects' to get them used to having to deal with problems at a place where a process or back-office system doesn't exist. So they have to think outside the box a little bit."

As a people business a lot of the training provided at Hydrogen centres on soft skills. This is not simply to interact better with clients and candidates but also to make the work environment more productive. For example, facilitation training has helped operational staff to run meetings more efficiently, while mentorship training provides inspiration for individuals to both work with mentors and to become a mentor themselves.

Corporate Social Responsibility

Hydrogen is a long-standing supporter of Young Enterprise, a national education charity that exists to forge links between schools and industry. Its extensive client base means the company is able to provide facilities for events organised by the charity. It also enables those on whose behalf the charity operates to have access to important

figures from different business sectors. Hydrogen mainly works with local schools in east London: staff have given talks, provided mentoring services and hosted business innovation awards to help young people acquire entrepreneurial skills.

"We are aware of our impact on the environment and it is relatively minimal," says Smeaton. As a knowledge-based organisation the main area of potential environmental impact is in travel arrangements – particularly as the business expands globally. Despite its presence on three continents, company car usage at Hydrogen has remained low, with a maximum of 16 vehicles currently in use. In the UK, the company has a policy of only reimbursing taxi fares for three or more employees per car. Within the work environment there is a real focus on recycling – of paper, cartridges and other stationery products - and the wide distribution of waste disposal facilities reflects this.

In the field of corporate governance, Hydrogen is scrupulous in meeting all regulatory standards. Accordingly, it has a balance of executives and non-executives on its board of directors and employs a senior independent advisor on its audit committee. A member of the Quoted Companies Alliance, Hydrogen distributes compliance guidance published by the association to staff. It represents the interests of shareholders through regular investor reviews and by hosting City analyst hospitality events. Protection of candidate confidentiality is ensured through robust adherence to the Data Protection Act.

Facts and figures

Total number of staff: 325
Office location: London (230), Sydney (16), UAE (40), Benelux (32)
Industry sector: Recruitment
Turnover: £100m

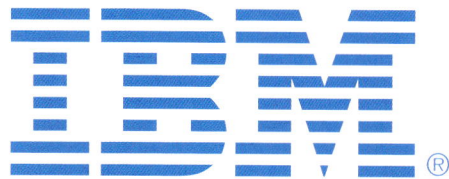

IBM United Kingdom Ltd

76 Upper Ground
South Bank
London SE1 9PZ

Telephone: 020 7202 3000
www.ibm.com/uk
www.ibm.com/employment/uk

Pay and Benefits	★ ★ ★ ★ ☆
Training and Development	★ ★ ★ ★ ★
Career Development	★ ★ ★ ★ ★
Working Conditions	★ ★ ★ ★ ⯪
Company Culture	★ ★ ★ ★ ⯪

Biggest plus
A globally integrated enterprise that allows employees a huge degree of flexibility in choosing when and where they work.

Greatest challenge
Nurturing and retaining its talent, and equipping them to work with clients anywhere in the world.

Discover why IBM is a critical player at the world's best tennis tournaments.

Summary

A world leader in information technology and services, IBM characterises itself as a globally integrated enterprise, with its workforce of 386,000 people serving clients in 174 countries. Around 20,000 employees are based in the UK. The company's technology and services portfolio is built on networked, modularised and embedded technologies, including service-oriented architecture, information on demand, virtualisation and open, modular systems. In 2007, software constituted 40% of its income, with 37% from services and the remainder from hardware and financing. In 2007, the company made US$14.5bn pre-tax earnings on turnover of US$98.7bn. For the 15th consecutive year, it was issued more US patents than any other company.

About the organisation

IBM has been in the information-handling business for nearly 100 years. With roots from the 1880s, it was incorporated in 1911 in New York City as the Computing-Tabulating-Recording Company, and in 1924, having established manufacturing operations in Europe, became International Business Machines (IBM) Corporation.

Since 2000, the company has expanded and integrated its global operations while adapting to a new model of computing and to changes in how businesses apply technology. It has invested in emerging markets, with more than 60 acquisitions since 2003 and the creation of a new growth markets organisation, based in Shanghai; conversely, it exited commoditising businesses such as PCs and hard disc drives. Pre-tax income jumped from US$9.4bn in 2003 to US$14.5bn in 2007, with revenues increasing by 26% in Brazil, Russia, India and China during 2007.

"IBM is a different company today," says Samuel J Palmisano, chairman, president and chief executive. "We have excellent opportunities in an environment that presents significant challenges for our competitors. They are not as global, as strong in high-growth segments or as able to deliver complete solutions, nor do many have the experience and discipline to adjust their economic models as conditions require."

In the UK, IBM's activities are hugely diverse: its technology underpins the global foreign exchange network that has been able to eliminate settlement risk on over £1trillion worth of trades a day, the DVLA's online tax disc renewal facility and London's congestion charge zone from late 2009. Its supercomputers are used to compute figures for work on HIV/AIDS and the formation and dissolution of glaciers. "We are at the leading edge in defining how technology is integrated globally," says Jonathan Ferrar, UK and Ireland HR director. "IBM is ever evolving. In that sense, it's a beautiful company to work for."

»

"We are at the leading edge in defining how technology is integrated globally. IBM is ever evolving. In that sense, it's a beautiful company to work for"
(Jonathan Ferrar, UK and Ireland HR director)

Company Culture

IBM recruits up to 300 graduates in the UK annually, and hundreds of experienced professionals. It hires people 'from all walks of life' who relish a challenge and are passionate about the use of technology in business and global markets. Employees who flourish are those who collaborate, think strategically, and above all, adapt. "We want people who are constantly inquisitive, who ask 'why?' and challenge the status quo, who look for better ways of doing things," says Andy McFarlane, UK and Ireland director of marketing.

Flexibility is key to IBM's concept of 'the new world of work,' and arrangements such as part-time working, job-sharing, and compressed weeks are commonplace. McFarlane cites his own circumstances as a case study: "I have three young children, and I try to ensure I am home for breakfast with the family 3 days a week. It's really important to me to be flexible, and this organisation enables me to do that, so long as I can deliver the value needed." Up to 70% of employees work from home at least one day a week and a number of people each year take an unpaid sabbatical.

Management aims to be 'as diverse and flexible as employees' and in 2008 the company tripled its investment on training for managers in acknowledgement of the complexities of managing a remote workforce effectively. IBM surveys its workforce every three years to gauge working patterns and levels of satisfaction about work-life balance among employees; it also wants to offer 'lighter moments' such as company social events and training that involves business games.

Investment in community activities provides employees with opportunities to contribute and find meaning, as well as fun. "Fun means different things to different people," says Ferrar. "For instance, for the scientists working at our research and development facility in Hursley, near Winchester, fun comes from the fact that they are given total flexibility to innovate."

Innovation and Creativity

IBM's industry dominance over many years demonstrates its flair for innovation. The approach is characterised by the company's chairman as "ambidextrous – seizing the new opportunities that the external marketplace presents while never ceasing to re-examine our own operations or to transform our organisation." Its annual worldwide survey of more than 1,000 chief executive officers reflects IBM's leadership in strategic thinking.

The value of 'bottom-up' contribution is recognised through regular 'ideas jams.' This follows the success of the original 72-hour 'WorldJam' in 2001, in which more than 52,000 employees, and others participated in generating thousands

of suggestions for how IBM could do things better; the most compelling ideas were backed by US$100m of development funds. The most recent jam in 2008 also elicited suggestions from community groups and clients.

Among hundreds of examples of innovation, IBM is proud of its World Community Card Grid, a piece of technology launched in 2004 which enables researchers to tap into the unused computing power of employee laptops to benefit good causes, through speeding research work on cancer, AIDS and climate modelling for Africa. The company is also using its technology and workforce to benefit society at large through the Genographic Project, a five-year study with National Geographic, which will use one of the largest ever collections of DNA samples to map how the earth was populated.

Pay and Benefits

One benefit of working for IBM is the fact that employees are treated well. In 2008, for the second year running, IBM UK beat off competition from the likes of Marks & Spencer, GlaxoSmithKline and Barclays to win Graduate Employer of the Year in the annual TARGETjobs awards. "Two things set us apart," says Ferrar. "One is that we deliver on our message. We have a very well established graduate programme and we put in a lot of management support to help them through. The second is that we offer a remarkable breadth of opportunity: we work with every kind of profession."

The company's policy is to reward performance through differentiation, and although bonuses are paid according to the overall performance of the company, here too there is flexibility to reward individual contribution.

All employees can invest monthly in an equity share programme, while those in more senior positions have access to a stock option programme.

Three years ago, IBM overhauled its benefits system to give employees access to a range of benefits including a 'vacation marketplace,' which allows them to sell up to five days of leave, or buy an additional ten. "The reason we offer fewer days to sell is that we really want people to take a break," explains Ferrar. "Even though we offer such flexibility in working hours, we believe in taking that physical period of time away from the office." »

"The biggest aspect of our culture is that we are truly globally integrated. We don't look at ourselves as country entities. We look at ourselves as a global company" (Jonathan Ferrar, UK and Ireland HR director)

"Giving to communities
is not just about signing a
cheque. We have some
great passion and skills,
and we can make a
bigger difference"
(Andy McFarlane, UK
and Ireland director
of marketing)

The company is looking at changing its existing car policy with a greener scheme, and has an emergency care programme to offer employees help in caring for older relatives or children. Other recognition for effort comes in many forms, from special events for outstanding salespeople to a 'thanks' scheme that allows employees to nominate colleagues for an immediate gift.

Career Development

Graduates joining IBM enter a structured foundation programme that includes work with major clients, and may involve travel. "We don't say to graduates, 'there are 200 opportunities here in London.' Instead, we expect them to relish the opportunity to be flexible and mobile. The great thing about IBM is that no one ever asks where you are: it's about what you achieve," says Ferrar.

Every employee constructs a personal development plan to form the basis of an annual discussion about aspirations. It's common for employees to progress from one function within IBM to another: for example, the UK's head of diversity Elizabeth Loker was previously with the company's consulting arm. "We want you to deepen your skills in your current area but also broaden your skills," says Ferrar. "We are very committed to talent progression and have a number of global programmes looking at how people can get to different levels of the organisation."

In the UK, IBM in 2008 invested heavily in equipping managers to deal with a more mobile workforce. Those with high potential might attend the company's US-based management centre, or participate in a development programme managed by the senior leadership team.

The Corporate Service Corps, now in its second phase, develops future leaders by allowing them to step away from their day jobs for up to eight weeks to work on short-term projects, usually in countries where business is growing rapidly and where skills are applied to support small companies or government agencies. "We develop people in a very rounded way: they have a core job, to deliver client and shareholder value, but outside of that, we give people a lot of trust and open doors so they can develop themselves," says McFarlane.

Corporate Social Responsibility

A commitment to making the world a better place is one of IBM's core values. Some of its main programmes and initiatives aim to improve the environment and reduce carbon emissions; to increase diversity within the company; and to work for the good of communities both locally and overseas.

IBM established a corporate policy on environmental protection in 1971, and has reduced carbon dioxide emissions by 40% since 1990. Energy and climate-related issues still top the agenda, with the company working to make existing products and processes more efficient while accelerating the adoption of products and services that are less environmentally damaging.

Project Big Green, launched in 2007, will see IBM redirect US$1bn per year to mobilise resources to increase energy efficiency, in particular by reducing data centre energy consumption; some 3,900 computer servers will be consolidated onto about 30 mainframes running the Linux operating system. The new server environment will consume about 80% less energy than the current set-up. In addition, IBM is working with local government and the private sector to help reduce carbon emissions, and its consulting service Green Sigma helps companies to increase efficiency and reduce costs, focusing on energy and water usage. At its London location, landfill contribution was reduced by 60% by the introduction of sign-posted recycling bins. Worldwide, it wants to reduce greenhouse gas emissions 7% by 2012.

Blue Talent is an 18-month programme that helps women to accelerate progress within the company; a sister programme works with ethnic minority employees. "Our aspiration is to be as inclusive as possible and mirror the marketplace within the UK. We are passionate about diversity, and work really hard to make sure that the concept is pushed out into the business units," says Loker.

The company sponsors Stonewall's Education For All initiative, which helps to tackle homophobic bullying in schools through mentoring. It also works with Premiership League football clubs on Step Ladder, a programme that sees employees mentoring black and Asian teenagers. Meanwhile, its On Demand Community Challenge programme gives employees both current and retired the chance to help local projects: in 2008, some 1,000 UK staff gave 35,000 hours of help to schools, charities and not-for-profit organisations.

Annually, the company contributes cash, equipment and services to charities and educational institutions. McFarlane points out: "It's not just about signing a cheque. We have some great passion and skills, and we can make a bigger difference."

Facts and figures

Total number of staff: 386,000 worldwide
Office location: North Harbour, Portsmouth
Industry sector: Information technology
Turnover: US$98.7bn

Iceland Foods Ltd

Second Avenue
Deeside Industrial Park
Deeside
Flintshire, CH5 2NW

Telephone: 01244 830100
Fax: 01244 814531
www.iceland.co.uk

Pay and Benefits	★ ★ ★ ☆ ☆
Training and Development	★ ★ ★ ★ ☆
Career Development	★ ★ ★ ★ ☆
Working Conditions	★ ★ ★ ☆ ☆
Company Culture	★ ★ ★ ★ ☆

Biggest plus
The 'family' atmosphere among staff.

Greatest challenge
Persuading potential recruits that working for a budget retailer doesn't mean a cut-price employee experience.

Summary

Iceland, the food retail chain, employs 17,000 staff, almost 500 of whom are based at its headquarters near Chester, with the remainder working at more than 660 stores throughout the UK. The company specialises in frozen foods and sees its niche as a value-based, 'top-up' shop for busy mums. After a very rough ride in the early 2000s, the company was returned to private ownership and has bounced back to become highly successful, with turnover rising from £1.45bn in 2004-5 to £1.86bn in 2007-8.

About the organisation

The strap line 'Mum's gone to Iceland' may be tongue-in-cheek, but it's no joke. Iceland specialises in being a 'top-up' shop providing good-value foodstuffs to busy families, and it competes more directly with the likes of Somerfield and the Co-op than Tesco or Sainsbury's. Most of its stores are medium-sized – typically less than 5,000 square feet and employing around 25 staff – and are located in high streets not edge-of-town retail parks.

Founded in 1970 by two managers from Woolworths, Iceland grew steadily in size and reputation and enjoyed a successful Stock Market flotation in 1984. But a merger with a cash-and-carry chain in 2000 was followed by a change of management and an ambitious programme of product diversification and infrastructure investment which left the company on its knees, with falling sales and a demoralised workforce.

The original management team returned in 2005, including co-founder Malcolm Walker who remains the company's chief executive. They took the company back into private ownership with the help of Icelandic investment group Baugur. They implemented root-and-branch changes in stores and the supply chain and almost halved the headcount at HQ, returning Iceland to its core offering of frozen foods rounded out with a limited number of other lines.

The rescue plan worked. "Continued sales growth combined with tight costs and margin control have resulted in the company being more profitable than it's ever been," says Andy Pritchard, who returned with Walker to become Iceland's managing director.

Unlike its namesake in the North Atlantic, Iceland the company is unfazed by the downturn in the economy. "Recessions can actually be good news for a business like ours that's based on value," says the firm's HR director, Sue Yell. "Our sales are growing and we're still opening new stores."

>>

"The most distinctive feature
of the company is that
everybody says it feels like
a family"
(Sue Yell, HR director)

Company Culture

"The most distinctive feature of the company is that everybody says it feels like a family," says Yell. "We have a shared sense of purpose and our staff are extremely loyal." According to the most recent staff survey, more than 80% of people are satisfied with the company overall and with their manager, a remarkably high score for a retailer, according to Yell.

Walker believes that a happy ship is not just a nicer place to work, it also sails faster. He says that staff attitude has been a critical factor in Iceland's recovery, and believes that a store with a highly motivated manager can sell up to 25% more than one whose manager is demoralised.

Walker's attitude permeates the whole company. "He's a very straightforward, Yorkshire guy," says Yell. "Iceland people are very open, honest and direct with one another, we don't stand on ceremony, and people are always willing to roll up their sleeves and help out, whatever their level in the company. We also have a very flat structure."

Asked what qualities make a good Icelander, Yell says, "A can-do attitude, pride in what they do, treating colleagues and customers with equal respect, and a sense of loyalty and commitment.

"We're a very demanding, results-focused culture and we don't tolerate poor performance," she adds. "But we believe it's important to get results in the right way and treat people with fairness and respect."

Iceland tries to be supportive of colleagues who are finding things difficult and works with The Retail Trust to provide an employee assistance programme for all staff. Absence rates are usually below 3%, which is remarkably low for a retailer. Many posts are part-time, especially in the stores, and requests for flexible working hours are considered sympathetically. Trade unions are not recognised, but all stores are represented on various works councils and the company says labour relations are very good.

Innovation and Creativity

The company claims several 'firsts' in the frozen foods sector, including joints of meat that can be roasted from frozen and budget-priced lines of exotic fish such as sea bass, scallops and langoustines. Walker is a long-time advocate of GM-free foods and the removal of colouring and other additives, and in the 1990s Iceland launched what it claims was the world's first completely GM-free own-label range. In 2008 the company created a number of business

improvement groups at head office to consider everything from more efficient layouts in distribution centres to re-usable carrier bags.

A decade ago Walker decided to introduce a free home delivery service – still unique, the company claims – for customers who bought a reasonable amount of goods (currently £25-worth). "A lot of our customers don't have cars and a lot of our stores don't have car parks, so it made perfect sense," says Yell. "Now home deliveries account for 13-14% of our sales."

Staff at all levels are encouraged to put forward ideas via the regular works councils, known as Talking Shops. One cashier had the brilliantly simple idea of printing bar codes on fresh trifles on the bottom of the packet instead of the top, so they don't have to be turned upside down for scanning. "Malcolm loves listening to people who want to do things better," says Yell. "He's a born entrepreneur with an innate ability to ask the right questions."

Pay and Benefits

Iceland is adamant that being a budget retailer does not mean being a cut-price employer. "We want Iceland to be absolutely at the top of the list in terms of pay and job satisfaction," says Walker. Nobody is on the minimum wage and in 2008 the company gave store staff a pay rise of 6%, twice the sector average. While salaries don't match those of the 'big four' supermarkets, they are good by high street standards, says Yell.

Iceland regards store managers as crucial to its success and their average salaries have risen from £25,000 in 2005 to £31,700 in 2008. Managers and headquarters staff are all paid by results, with annual salary rises of up to 15% for top performers and nothing for slackers. The company deliberately sets tough targets for both personal development and commercial performance. "People know and accept that we're going to keep raising the bar," says Yell.

"We're a very demanding, results-focused culture and we don't tolerate poor performance" (Sue Yell, HR director)

"We want Iceland to be absolutely at the top of the list in terms of pay and job satisfaction"
(Sue Yell, HR director)

The company does not pay bonuses but is keen to reward success. It took all its store managers to Disneyland Paris in 2007 to celebrate the remarkable turnaround in the company's fortunes, and top performing area managers or professional staff may find themselves jetting off to New York or the Seychelles. Twice a year the top performing store in each of Iceland's three regions receives a £10,000 prize to share between staff, plus a new Mini for the manager, and there's a cash prize for the peer-nominated employee of the month in each area. Walker often visits stores in person to hand out cash bonuses and bottles of champagne.

Employee benefits include 10% staff discount on food purchases, Christmas vouchers worth up to £50, health insurance for senior managers and their families, life insurance of five times salary for senior managers, and periodic discount offers from other retailers. The pension is stakeholder-only and take-up is low. Holiday allowance is 22 days a year, rising to 30 days.

Career Development

"We like to grow our own talent and train and develop people to realise their full potential," says Yell. Although Iceland has a graduate recruitment scheme (eight joined in 2008, three in retail, two each in buying and finance, and one on marketing), this is a business where you can literally work your way up from the shop floor. The company's supply chain director started as a warehouse lad, and one of the three regional managers began with a Saturday job. Although annual staff turnover is quite low for the retail sector at below 13%, there are always vacancies for store managers, of which around 60% are filled internally.

Store management is a demanding, fast-paced job with the twin challenges of managing a team of people and meeting tough commercial targets, and Iceland accepts that store managers need a lot of support. It runs a one-year trainee manager programme involving more than 100 people, and all store managers receive at least five days training a year. The latest initiative is a programme called Tough Talk to help them manage their staff's performance better. "It's very hands-on with lots of role-playing involving actors," says Yell. "Our people don't like dry, theoretical lectures – they like to touch it and feel it."

There are separate training programmes for senior supervisors and for professional staff at HQ, which include buying, supply chain management, marketing, accounts, HR, payroll and a large IT department. The VIP (Very Iceland Person) scheme is designed to identify and support talented and ambitious people at all levels by creating personal development plans and providing guidance on how to realise their dreams. "We want to identify a pipeline of talent, and whether your ambition is to be a director or a delivery driver, we want to support you," says Yell.

Corporate Social Responsibility

Most of Iceland's staff work close to home so the diversity of the workforce mirrors communities throughout the UK. The average age is early thirties for store managers and mid-forties for senior managers, but the age range across the company is huge, from 16-year-olds to octogenarians ("We're very flexible about retirement," says Yell). The gender balance among managers is less even, with women accounting for fewer than 20% of store managers, three out of 48 area managers and just one of the 12-person trading board (Yell herself). "I'd like to see more female managers, but retail is quite a tough environment, especially if you've got a family," Yell admits.

Charitable work had to take a back seat while the new management team sorted out the core business, but Iceland is determined to increase this area of activity. Its first major charity project was a series of events on behalf of Alder Hey children's hospital in Liverpool, which raised £1m in donations and match funding by the company. Iceland also supports charities such as Save the Family, The Retail Trust and Missing People, including placing appeals for information about vulnerable missing people onto millions of milk cartons. Some individual stores also do charitable work locally.

Frozen food can have environmental benefits (less wastage, less elaborate packaging etc), but refrigeration and air conditioning make Iceland a big consumer of electricity, so the company is busy analysing its electricity use and upgrading where necessary. For example, new air conditioning controllers have cut consumption by up to 8% at 200 sites, while refits of refrigeration units at 60 sites per year are saving an average 14% each. All 30 of Iceland's Northern Ireland stores are powered by renewable wind energy.

The company is committed to minimising packaging and has signed up to WRAP (the Waste and Resources Action Programme), and every year collects 24,000 tonnes of cardboard and 1,500 tonnes of plastic from its stores and depots for recycling. Its delivery vehicles are fitted with speed-limiters and automatic engine shut-off when idling to reduce fuel consumption, and the company is trialling more efficient technologies such as LPG (liquid petroleum gas).

Iceland has been a long-time and vociferous opponent of commercial whaling and insists that all appropriate suppliers adhere to its animal welfare policy and to its fish and seafood sustainability policy, which aims to avoid over-fishing and depletion of exploited populations.

Facts and figures

Total number of staff: 17,000
Locations: UK-wide
Industry sector: Retail
Turnover: £1.86bn

IG Group Holdings plc

Friars House
157-168 Blackfriars Road
London SE1 8EZ

Telephone: 020 7896 0011
Fax: 020 7896 0010
Email: iggrads@igindex.co.uk
www.iggroup.com

Pay and Benefits	★ ★ ★ ⯨ ☆
Training and Development	★ ★ ★ ☆ ☆
Career Development	★ ★ ★ ☆ ☆
Working Conditions	★ ★ ★ ☆ ☆
Company Culture	★ ★ ★ ☆ ☆

Biggest plus
A supportive culture with a real passion for success.

Greatest challenge
Growing the market – the client base that understands spread betting is relatively small and niche.

Summary

IG Group Holdings plc is a world leader in financial derivatives trading and sports betting. IG Index is Britain's leading financial spread betting firm, offering prices in a huge range of indices, currencies, commodities and options, as well as thousands of individual shares and sports markets. IG Markets is the IG brand for its worldwide businesses and for trading Contracts for Difference (CFDs). IG has grown rapidly and now operates in nine countries worldwide. Over 750 employees work for IG worldwide, 550 in the UK. IG Group is currently ranked #136 in the FTSE-100 and is regulated by the FSA.

About the organisation

IG has travelled a long way from the niche business founded by entrepreneur Stuart Wheeler in 1974. IG remained small until 1998, when things really kicked off. Then, sports comprised 50% of IG's business – it's now just 5%. While sports spread betting has increased fourfold in this time, financial has grown by a factor of 60. This adds up to ten years of uninterrupted growth for IG. Revenue increased by 51% to £180m in 2008 while profit before tax rose by 41% to £97m.

Chief Executive Tim Howkins puts this down to a conflux of events. "First, spread betting on individual shares was created. Then the dot.com boom got more people interested in the stock market, while the Internet allowed private individuals to access research more easily. Even the competition helped, by advertising and growing the overall market."

An initial London Stock Exchange listing in 2000 was followed by a management buyout in 2003 when the founder sold his shares. IG Group re-listed in 2005. Many employees have done very nicely out of this – at the time of the MBO some 100 held an equity interest and employee share ownership is still a strong characteristic of this successful business.

Financial spread betting has grown exponentially over the past decade because it offers traders and investors a unique combination of flexibility, speed of execution and tax-free profits. It's all about leverage. Indices are derivative based – you don't need to own the underlying share – instead you buy and sell an index at a market price and profit or lose by any movements in these indices.

More than 28,000 IG clients log on every day to trade the financial markets. The 24-hour market is covered by 15 hours from London and nine hours from Melbourne. Around 90% of transactions are made online, using IG's browser-based trading platforms.

Company Culture

"Clients get one price, one book, wherever they are in the world," says Howkins. That also means there is one IG employer culture worldwide in the US, Singapore, Australia, Japan, India, Germany, France, Italy and Spain, as well as the head office in Southwark, London.

The four board directors are very much hands-on, without any aura of 'I'm in charge.' Ideas can come from anyone. And they do. "Our culture, and the way in which we have managed and brought on our people, have driven our success," says Howkins.

"There's a great deal of empowerment," says Jackie Bornor, head of HR. "It's more a case of 'what can you do for IG?' rather than what IG can do for you." So don't expect a graduate training programme where you're not allowed to touch anything until you're 30. The green light is on here the moment you pass through the door.

There are possibly misconceptions about IG being a 'traditional' City trading culture of City boys and wheeler dealers. IG's clients are just retail, or private investors who might have some wealth to gamble in backing their opinion on the markets. That's mirrored in the employee culture – IT specialists and customer services are just as important as dealers and probably more numerous. The IT function is critical to IG. While it has quadrupled in size it has retained the culture of an IT department.

IG is a meritocracy without a hierarchy. "Investment banks have a dog-eat-dog reputation. Here we're much more supportive," says Howkins. "The IG way is to be thoughtful – not brash and shouting."

IG is seen as the market leader, an innovator, and the one to aspire to. "We're known for integrity," says Howkins. "We're not as arrogant as we could be, but we are arrogant at being the best."

IG people have grown up together over 10 years and that has generated a common purpose of learning, building and a passion for the business and for success. "I've never worked for a company that cares so much about being successful," says Bornor.

"I've never worked for a company that cares so much about being successful" (Jackie Bornor, head of HR)

"Investment banks have a dog-eat-dog reputation. Here we're much more supportive"
(Tim Howkins, chief executive)

Innovation and Creativity

If you've seen an IG advertisement anywhere then you've seen the words 'Innovation as standard.' IG has a culture of encouraging employees to suggest innovations – and are rewarded for the best ones. IG was the first to introduce dealing from an i-Phone and the first to create dealing directly from technical charts. IG Index also introduced the innovative and highly popular 'Bungee Bet,' a unique limited risk bet that stays 'alive' even when a customer's stop-loss safety level is breached, giving them the chance to bounce back into profit. The member of staff who invented it won an Innovation Award (as did another employee, who dreamed up the name).

"Our trading platform 'PureDeal' is the best in the business," claims Howkins. "It's robust – IG was the only one of the large firms not to have outage in October." PureDeal is intuitive to use and designed so that users can get cracking without needing to read a manual or call customer service.

Most of the innovations in spread betting are down to IG. It was the first to offer spreads on individual shares, out-of-hour indices, binary trades, and guaranteed stop-loss limits. "We're good at turning on and off what is working and what is not," says Howkins.

Pay and Benefits

Apart from senior executives, IG had not traditionally benchmarked pay until 2007. It now compares packages with other financial institutions. At board level IG pays bottom quartile salary but top quartile bonus. For others, recognising that salary is important, it's median to upper quartile.

Bonus is based on a communal pool driven by the overall profitability of the company. The pool is first apportioned by department, and then distributed to individuals on a discretionary basis by department heads. "Some companies carve out individual performance bonuses, but that's why we're different from an investment bank," says Howkins. It's not 'you eat what you kill' here."

A graduate would start on £25,000 in year one, and a 'token' bonus could be 10%. After three years it might be 25%, and 100% has been known.

»

"Our culture, and the
way in which we have
managed and brought on
our people, have driven
our success"
(Tim Howkins,
chief executive)

There's a share incentive plan awarded each year to all UK staff. The company matches shares one-to-one up to £1,500. There's a healthy 30-35% take-up. A smaller number (around 30 across the Group) get long-term share options.

IG contributes 10% into the pension if the employee contributes 5%. "We do it as a salary sacrifice with Inland Revenue approved tax benefits, so it's effectively 17.5%, which is generous," says Bornor.

Other benefits include permanent health insurance for everyone and £500 towards gymnasium or sports club membership. Softer benefits include free fruit every day, free 'coffee bar standard' coffee, and 100 pizzas were recently couriered in during a particularly busy trading week. There's champagne all round when the company enjoys a record month, and ad hoc cash rewards for little things done well. All expenses paid parties in summer and at Christmas are notable events, while client entertaining includes financial dinners in the City, race evenings at Sandown and Corinthian seats at the new Wembley Stadium.

Career Development

Of IG's 750 employees, 200 work in IT, 90 in financial dealing and 70 in customer services. There are also business managers who interface with specific projects, and professional and administrative support functions, including plenty of lawyers. The major recruitment traffic is graduates, with IG looking for a further 25 this year. "Markets respond to volatility, and our customer services and dealers have been very busy of late," says Howkins.

IG offers good development routes in trading and finance. "It's a complicated business and you need to spend 12-18 months immersed in it to contemplate a wider management role," says Bornor. A six-month probationary period is intended to find out if a new joiner enjoys it at IG. These months are intensive, with dealers and department heads role playing with 'bet tests' to make sure new hires can cope and have the right judgment. After 12-18 months a graduate is appointed to a desk.

A growing business is good for career opportunity. Recent graduates have gone from London to Singapore and Australia, and another helped set up the customer services operation in Chicago. Peter Hetherington was the company's first ever graduate trainee employee; he's now chief operating officer.

IG runs training lectures given by heads of desks, on the market and on specific products. Some members of staff have full-time training roles. But the best training is on the job. "The trading demo is sophisticated but only takes you

so far in dealing with the client," says Bornor. "There's no substitute for sitting next to an experienced person." IT people need specialised skills, such as Java, and so specific training is provided. Progress is through your line manager and the annual appraisal. "But often it's about looking for the right person for the right role at the right time, rather than defined career paths," says Bornor. "We're still small enough to do this."

People who do well at IG are academically bright (including strong numeracy skills), proactive, team players, and not afraid to throw their hat into the ring. They 'own' problems, pick an issue up, and run with it.

Corporate Social Responsibility

"At the core of IG is a commitment to treat clients fairly," says Howkins. "There's an FSA obligation to do so, but some competitors only pay lip service to this." IG introduced 'price improvement,' where if a price moves in the fractions of a second between the client clicking a trade and it being executed, and they could have got a better price, then IG gives it to them. "It's symbolic, and applies to perhaps 1% of trades, but others reject a client's trade if the price moves in favour of the client," says Howkins.

Spread betting is not for everyone and there are risks involved. IG does turn away clients, and assesses the appropriateness of a product for a client based on their previous trading experience. IG scores every new client. Low scores means a client has to join the Trade Sense education programme (a six-week module to trial the dealing products with pseudo money) and need to have defined stop loss limits so that they can never lose more money than they have on account.

IG is an equal opportunity employer but 'doesn't do targets.' Graduate intakes are a very diverse group while the IT 'department,' often made up of second, third or fourth jobbers from all over the globe, is the most diverse in terms of age, background and colour.

'Respect for Others' was an initiative launched through workshops, focusing on what that meant to each individual employee. Jokes and emails were used to highlight potential dangers and bring the subject alive.

IG employees asked about recycling so now there are bins for everything strewn around the offices. Bottled water was replaced with filtered tap water. All lights are switched off five minutes after leaving, and PC screens power down automatically. IG's offices were refurbished to be environmentally and ergonomically efficient.

There is an IG charity budget and employees get involved in a spate of charity and sponsored events. The company gives people time off for volunteer work. "We never turn anything down and we match what they raise," says Bornor. "We're a very practical company."

Facts and figures

Total number of staff: 750
Office location: London head office, plus in seven countries worldwide
Industry sector: Financial
Turnover: £180m

informa

Informa plc

Mortimer House
27 Mortimer Street
London
W1T 3JH

Telephone: 020 7017 5000
Fax: 020 7017 4286
www.informa.com

Pay and Benefits	★ ★ ★ ★ ★
Training and Development	★ ★ ★ ⯨ ☆
Career Development	★ ★ ★ ★ ⯨
Working Conditions	★ ★ ★ ★ ☆
Company Culture	★ ★ ★ ★ ☆

Biggest plus
A company full of fantastic team players.

Greatest challenge
Attracting and retaining talent – because the business is only as good as its people.

Informa plc

Summary

Informa provides specialist, high value information to the global academic, scientific, professional and commercial markets through publishing, events and performance improvement. It operates in 70 countries, has over 150 offices in more than 40 countries and employs 10,000 staff. For the year ending 31 December 2007 revenue was £1.3bn and adjusted operating profit was £261m – up 9% and 19% respectively on the previous year. Operating profit for the year ending December 2008 was £305.8m.

About the organisation

The roots of Informa go back to 1734 when the first issue of the maritime publication *Lloyd's List* was pinned to the wall of Edward Lloyd's City of London coffee shop. Its other brands include some of the oldest-established names in world publishing, including the leading physics and material science journal *The Philosophical Magazine*, the first issue of which was printed in 1798.

Informa as it exists today was created when IBC Group plc and LLP Group plc merged in December 1998. LLP Group plc was the publishing division of the Lloyds insurance market until a management buy-out in 1995.

In July 2005, Informa announced the acquisition of IIR Holdings. Not only did this bring together the two largest events businesses in the world to create an undisputed powerhouse, it also meant that Informa acquired seven robust, market-leading Performance Improvement businesses.

Of Informa's three operational strands, Publishing accounts for around 46% of the Group's revenue and 57% of the adjusted operating profit. It publishes over 40,000 magazines and journals and owns Datamonitor, the market intelligence provider. Academic titles amount to 40% of this sector, but it also has market-leading products in the healthcare, financial, maritime and professional areas. Over 60% of its publishing revenues are delivered through annual subscriptions. As chief executive Peter Rigby says, this gives Informa "high visibility of earnings, which have a strong degree of predictability."

The second strand is events businesses, which account for 37% of revenues and 33% of operating profit. Informa is the world's largest publicly owned organiser of conferences and courses, running over 12,000 every year.

Performance Improvement is the smallest of Informa's three activities, accounting for 17% of revenues and 10% of operating profit, but it is growing fast. Its businesses here include Omega, the market leader in credit and commercial training.

Company Culture

The Group has a light touch, and individual businesses are not constrained. Instead, they have a high degree of autonomy. Furthermore, the systems in place are designed to minimise bureaucracy: staff can ask their manager or indeed the executive anything in this organisation. "The way we operate across our businesses and brands is highly entrepreneurial," says Group HR director Keith Brownlie, "and we want to ensure it stays that way."

A good insight to the corporate culture is the values formed by the acronym of the Group's name: Innovative, Non-bureaucratic, For profit, Open, Rewarding, Market-focused, About quality. Despite its size, in terms of operations and staff, the Group manages to remain fast moving, decisive and able to act quickly.

Informa is not for the faint-hearted. It comprises a real hive of activity wherever it operates – as its revenue figure of £1.3bn attests - and lots of people are working very hard for this organisation. However, it is also full of people who really enjoy what they do – and get a real sense of achievement in doing so. The pace of change at the Group is challenging, but it's also exhilarating.

The company that works hard and plays hard must be the biggest cliché in the book, but here at least this statement is true. Where else would your chief executive dress up as a banana and allow himself to be chased over Regents Park? As with everything else the Group does, this exercise was not just a fun way to raise money for charity, but designed to make a point: a healthy workforce makes for a healthy company. And perhaps an executive that doesn't take itself too seriously all the time helps too.

Innovation and Creativity

As the corporate acronym underlines, innovation is one of the core values at Informa. This is especially true of training and internal staff transfers. For example, each employee has an Informa 'passport' which is completed with a line manager at the end of the probationary period. This document contains all the information necessary to apply for an internal vacancy with ease. The Group also uses some innovative training formats, including 'webinars.' Informa uses the virtual world of Second Life as a way to help its employees meet their colleagues from around

the world – and also to develop their own careers. Using this system they can wander around 'Transformed Careers Island' and encounter information presented in a way that matches our memories and experiences from everyday life.

Touring the Island makes it possible to meet career ambassadors from around the global business. Staff members can adopt avatars and participate in a range of games, from playing football to tackling an assault course.

Play is used elsewhere too – the Group pioneered business strategy games to boost the sense of corporate identity and cross-divisional involvement. It also challenges employees to work in teams to find new business ideas for the company, incentivised by financial rewards as well as the chance to develop the concept.

Pay and Benefits

As the company's Corporate Responsibility Report puts it, "Informa's staff is its most vital asset – and we know it." It is under no illusion that its future growth and prosperity depends on recruiting and holding onto the most talented people, not only in the UK but increasingly overseas as the Group continues to build its global operation.

In the competitive markets in which it operates, the Group's leadership knows that it has to offer a compelling benefits package. Brownlie: "We've taken a hard look at remuneration across the Group, linking performance to the bottom line." Following a major survey recently, Informa changed the way it remunerated all its staff. Salaries are still benchmarked against other publishing companies and reviewed each year, but now everyone in the organisation receives a profit-related incentive of some type.

Performance is also rewarded through various schemes on a team basis. Achievements are recognised by giving out prizes at the annual company conference.

Informa Invest is the Group's share incentive plan. UK employees can buy shares each month and make tax and National Insurance savings when doing so. This is being rolled out to the rest of the Group. »

"Informa's staff is its most vital asset – and we know it"
(Informa Corporate Responsibility Report)

"The way we operate across our businesses and brands is highly entrepreneurial and we want to ensure it stays that way"
(Keith Brownlie, HR director)

A contributory pension scheme is available for UK staff. Informa matches employee contributions up to 5% of salary after 18 months' service. Basic annual holiday is 25 days. The Group also offers a flexible benefits scheme. This includes private medical insurance, critical illness cover, dental insurance, travel insurance, gym membership, childcare vouchers, health screening, bike loans and charitable giving. Employees can change their benefit choices (for example, by buying two more days of holiday), and can see the effects of their decisions using a calculator available on the intranet.

Career Development

Informa can be a hard place to join. It currently receives around over 1,000 applications for its graduate openings each year. Once on board, however, there is a raft of development opportunities. The Informa Media Academy, based in London, provides an extensive 12-month rotational programme in areas such as Conference Research, Editorial, Marketing and Data & Analysis.

Says Brownlie: "The Media Academy gives you a very broad scope of roles: you get to spend three months as an analyst, three as a journalist, three as a marketer, as so on. People often leave university without knowing exactly what route to pursue, and this type of programme can help them decide." The usefulness of this route is shown by the fact that those attending the Academy are often business managers five years later.

The Sales Academy offers similar exposure and early experience in sales. It too is a 12-month fast track programme, with challenges to develop and stretch skills every day. Successful applicants work within one of the Group's divisions with their own clients, targets and the opportunity to earn uncapped commission.

There is also a talent management agenda, aligned to the Group's business strategy. The Group grooms future leaders for business-critical roles, invests in opportunities to bring those high-fliers together and supports them to work on strategic issues. It pools the leaders across its businesses, helping to ensure that talent is matched to opportunity wherever possible.

As a global company, Informa offers plenty of openings to travel the world, particularly in the Gulf and in the Far East where growth is strongest currently. Employees in some divisions spend much of their time working with customers overseas.

Corporate Social Responsibility

All the Group's activities impact on the environment, especially in publishing: it publishes over 2,000 subscription-based information products and over 45,000 books. Its approach is to share best practice around the Group, train key staff, offer incentives to suppliers to improve their operations and to exploit new technologies which improve process efficiency. It also uses 'green' stationery where this is practicable.

One way forward is to make its publications paper-free. Some of these titles are pushing technologies to offer their readers a highly experiential online reading environment. This trend is likely to increase, although in some cases readers still demand both digital and print runs.

Events also have environmental consequences. In association with the CarbonNeutral Company, Informa has its own CarbonNeutral events scheme. This helps each events team to calculate an event's carbon footprint by taking into account travel, energy use and waste production. They can then offset this by contributing to high-value carbon offset projects around the world. This service has also been bundled into a green sponsorship package. In total, Informa offset 3,455 tonnes of carbon dioxide equivalent in 2007 using the scheme.

Informa has a policy of giving back to the communities in which it operates. This can be through its own products: for example, the Map of Medicine is a web-based visual representation of evidence-based patient care journeys, subsequently sold. It works with the World Health Organisation to reduce AIDs, malaria, tuberculosis and death in childbirth in Africa by providing up to date, accessible clinical information through the Map.

It works with the World Cancer Research Fund, which provides research and education programmes on the role of diet and physical activity in the prevention of cancer. Other initiatives include its staff working with Habitat for Humanity to refurbish the homes of people near their places of work unable to afford or perform much needed repairs on their houses. And its employees support Book Aid, which provides books to libraries, hospitals, refugee camps and schools in over 40 countries.

Corporate governance is controlled at board level, with four independent non-executive directors acting as watchdogs. An Audit Committee checks the integrity of the Group's financial statements and announcements.

Facts and figures

Total number of staff: 10,000
Office location: London and 169 others in over 40 countries
Industry sector: Publishing, events and performance improvement
Operating profit: £305.8m for 2008

innocent

Innocent drinks

1 The Goldhawk Estate
Brackenbury Rd
London W6 0BA

Telephone: 020 8600 3939
Email: jobs@innocentdrinks.co.uk
www.innocentdrinks.co.uk

Pay and Benefits	★ ★ ★ ★ ☆
Training and Development	★ ★ ★ ★ ★
Career Development	★ ★ ★ ★ ☆
Working Conditions	★ ★ ★ ⯪ ☆
Company Culture	★ ★ ★ ★ ☆

Biggest plus
An employer that's genuinely different – and strives to make a difference.

Greatest challenge
"Making the world a little bit healthier" – Richard Reed, founder

Summary

Innocent is the UK's leading manufacturer of smoothies (drinks made from whole crushed fruit and juice), and is expanding into other healthy fruit and vegetable products. Founded in 1999, the company has grown rapidly and now employs around 200 people at its west London headquarters, plus a further 60 in sales and marketing in Austria, Denmark, France, Germany, Ireland, the Netherlands and Sweden. The company is privately owned and turned over £113m in 2007, up from £76m in 2006. Innocent takes pride in its ethical stance and a remarkable 10% of profits are donated to charity.

About the organisation

A visit to the offices of innocent drinks will leave your arm black and blue – from pinching yourself. But eventually you have to accept that you're not dreaming after all. The delivery vans really are smothered in fake grass. The switchboard operator really does answer with, "Hello, innocent banana phone!" The office notice board really does feature baby pictures of all the staff.

But don't be fooled. Beneath the cutesy exterior is a thoroughly professional business that pursues its aims rigorously in a fast changing and highly competitive market. That is what has propelled the company in less than a decade from a personal enthusiasm – the three founders took £500-worth of crushed fruit to a jazz festival and asked people whether they should give up their day jobs and make smoothies – to a £113m business employing nearly 300 people in eight countries, with more than 60% of the country's smoothie sales.

Innocent knows it must diversify to maintain its growth, so in 2008 it launched two new product lines: an orange juice made from the best oranges from around the world, and veg pots, healthy microwaveable ready meals. Both were developed and brought to market very quickly, evidence that the company has retained the agility of a small start-up business despite its increasing size.

Nor has it abandoned its core principles: to produce convenient food that is natural, healthy and sustainable, and that benefits the people who grow it as well as those who consume it. The company »

gives at least 10% of its profits to its own charitable foundation, the innocent foundation, and was the first drinks manufacturer in the world to use bottles made from 100% recycled plastic.

Company Culture

Innocent tries to be as natural as its products. "We're very informal yet professional and we expect people to be warm and friendly and to come to work as themselves," says Karen Callaghan, the company's head of People. This is reflected in the informal working environment, which is complete with beanbags, picnic tables and a lot of trailing greenery (it's easy to forget that the building is actually an industrial warehouse).

"We like bright, engaging people with a track record of success who want to make things happen," says Tom Fraine, innocent's recruitment specialist. "Most people who work here don't just see it as a job – they want to be part of something special. When we do exit interviews, people say how much fun they've had and how much they'll miss their colleagues."

Not only are the offices open plan, but most people don't sit in teams. "You don't live in your own little bubble," says Tom. "One thing people say they really like about working here is the breadth of stuff you get involved in."

Responsibility comes quickly – startlingly so at times – but this is backed up by a lot of feedback and support. "Feedback is a big cultural thing for us," says Karen. "We see it as a responsibility of everyone. Giving feedback is part of our value of 'generosity' as it's a key way to develop people."

A flat structure and entrepreneurial attitude mean that decisions are taken quickly, and everyone is expected to contribute. "We're not soft and fluffy," insists Karen. "If you make a commitment we expect you to deliver on it. And we're quite tough commercially. We'll always work hard to get the best possible deal."

A year or two ago innocent set up a wellbeing committee, organised lunch-time 'chatwiches' with external experts on a range of subjects from sleep to diet and fitness. They also appointed a number of staff to act as wellbeing champions. People can work flexible hours or work from home sometimes as long as it doesn't adversely affect their team, and some work part-time.

Innovation and Creativity

Despite its growing stature as a member of the food and drink establishment, innocent works hard to retain its small-company ethos. If you have a good idea you are encouraged to run with it. The company's famous Big Knit

campaign, for example, was one individual's idea; now people all over the UK knit hundreds of thousands of miniature woolly hats to raise money for Age Concern.

Innocent prides itself on its ability to move rapidly. "With veg pots it took us less than 12 months to develop and market a completely new product, because everybody in the business got behind it," says the company's UK managing director, Jamie Mitchell. "In most other companies that would have taken two years at least."

Some innovations are ground-breaking, such as the world's first all-recycled plastic bottle. Others are beautifully simple, like putting chocolate coins in the bottom of smoothie crates at Christmas to encourage supermarket shelf-stackers to unpack them as fast as possible.

Everyone is encouraged to exercise their creative abilities, whether it's writing the quirky copy on the company's packaging or photographing vegetables for the veg pots, and lateral thinking is encouraged: the head of Products recently spent a three-month sabbatical at Heston Blumenthal's restaurant, The Fat Duck.

Pay and Benefits

Innocent reckons to pay competitive salaries– with each individual's remuneration driven by their personal contribution, which is regularly and formally assessed. "We pay people according to the value they bring to the company," says Karen. An element of the package, profit related pay, is dependent on the company's profitability and the sales people earn commission on top.

The company is privately owned, mostly by its three founders – who remain closely involved in the business – and one original backer. But 10% of shares are reserved for staff, who can buy them at discounted rates. High achievers may receive share options or a gift of one, or even two, innocent shares for every one they buy, and everyone receives some share options at the end of their first year.

The benefits package includes private health care for all staff, interest-free loans of up to a few thousand pounds to help with life's little surprises, subsidised gym membership, childcare vouchers, »

"People really like the breadth of stuff they get involved in here" (Tom Fraine, recruitment specialist)

"For us CSR isn't the icing on the cake. It is the cake" (Karen Callaghan, head of People)

free breakfasts, and all the smoothies you can drink. Staff can also apply for £1,000 scholarships that can be spent on anything from driving or dancing lessons to trips abroad; the company awards three such scholarships every quarter, decided by popular vote. There is a pension but it's a stakeholder scheme only (i.e. with minimal contributions from the company).

The standard working week is longer than average, at 40 hours, but staff get 25 days' annual holiday, plus a one-off extra fortnight after five years' service, a week if they get married, and four months on full pay for maternity leave.

Career Development

Innocent occasionally hires a few newly qualified graduates and it offers a handful of student placements, but most permanent recruits are experienced graduates in their twenties; current employees can earn a bonus of up to £4,000 for recommending successful candidates. Manufacturing is contracted out, so innocent's own people are responsible for innovation, product development, sourcing ingredients, sales, marketing, supply chain, plus the usual range of support functions such as accounts, IT, Finance and HR.

The company worked closely with the London Business School to develop personal and management training for all staff, in the form of its Academies. The latest programmes include a course to develop team-leading skills, and a 2½ day 'business academy' programme that uses a sophisticated game to teach advanced business skills like making a watertight business case, using financial concepts, advanced negotiation, and project management. Additionally, the company will spend up to £1,000 per person per year on developing skills relevant to their job function. Staff are also supported in gaining professional qualifications.

As the business expands, innocent needs its staff to expand with it. "Roles are getting bigger and more complex by the day," says Mitchell. "This isn't a business of status quo." To ensure people get the support and skills development they need, everyone has a 'development chat' with their manager at least four times a year, and the company likes to stretch good performers with more responsibility. Because the business is relatively flat career development is less about climbing a rigid ladder and more about people developing, professionally and personally through taking on more and different responsibilities, says Karen.

Innocent has offices in seven other European countries and its buyers travel the world to source fruit and other fresh ingredients, so there are opportunities to travel. Every year two people are selected to visit international projects run by innocent's charitable foundation.

Corporate Social Responsibility

Innocent's philanthropic and environmental credentials are scarcely in doubt. The company donates a whopping 10% of profits to charity, mostly to the innocent foundation, established in 2004 to help build a sustainable future for some of the world's poorest people. The foundation mostly operates in countries where innocent sources its fruit, with projects ranging from supporting prickly pear farmers in Ecuador to helping Indian women set up a brick factory to rebuild flood-damaged homes. Back home, all staff can take a day's paid leave each year to do voluntary work, the company runs The Big Knit to support older people (see above), and participates in the FareShare programme, which distributes unsold food to vulnerable people.

In its products the company promises not to use any artificial additives, flavourings or concentrates, and it says it takes the responsibilities of sourcing ethical and healthy ingredients very seriously. "According to our suppliers our standards are the most exacting in the industry," says Jamie. All the company's fruit suppliers must work the company's own minimum standards which cover social and environmental issues.

Around 60% of staff and more than 40% of senior managers are female. The average age of staff is just 28, with most senior managers aged under 40. People from ethnic minorities account for 5-10% of staff, although the company has grown so rapidly that the focus has been on getting the best people and skills regardless of ethnic background.

At head office the company does all it can to reduce its environmental footprint, from eschewing photocopying to composting food waste, but it knows that much bigger impacts are to be achieved in manufacturing and distribution. It has cut the carbon footprint of a smoothie by 15% and is encouraging its suppliers to go greener, with promising results. A notable coup was the introduction in 2007 of the world's first drink bottle made entirely from recycled plastic.

"CSR is very significant for us and it's one of the reasons people join us," says Karen. "It's the way we've chosen to do business and forms part of everybody's job. For us it's not the icing on the cake. It is the cake."

Facts and figures

Total number of staff: Around 280
Office location: Mostly west London, plus seven European cities
Industry sector: Food and drink
Turnover: £113m

Irwell Valley Housing Association

5th floor, Paragon House
48 Seymour Grove
Manchester M16 0LN

Telephone: 0161 610 1000
Fax: 0161 877 0660
Email lizatk@irwellvalleyha.co.ik
www.irwellvalleyha.co.uk

Pay and Benefits	★ ★ ★ ★ ☆
Training and Development	★ ★ ★ ★ ☆
Career Development	★ ★ ★ ★ ☆
Working Conditions	★ ★ ★ ★ ☆
Company Culture	★ ★ ★ ★ ☆

Biggest plus
Its people and dynamic leader.

Greatest challenge
Growing in size but not losing its touch.

Summary

Irwell Valley is a medium-sized registered social landlord providing homes and services to 30,000 people across Greater Manchester. There are 2,000 such housing associations in England and Wales and Irwell Valley stands out among them for its innovation and pioneering approach. It provides a wide range of housing – affordable properties for rent and outright sale, supported and sheltered housing and key worker, first-time buyer and retirement homes. It is at the forefront of delivering the Government's agenda for sustainable communities and it also manages and supports education, training and employment and local business initiatives, community and social activities and events.

About the organisation

As a registered social landlord regulated by the Government Irwell Valley, set up in 1972, does not make a profit. It makes a surplus and re-invests that surplus into new housing.

Its housing stock is around 8,000, it has assets of £300m and a turnover of £37m. It also has a property building business.

A charitable organisation it might well be but that does not stop it from being run like a successful company with a social heart. Chief executive Dr Tom Manion says they are "ethical capitalists, entrepreneurs". He is a man who is regarded as a pivotal and fundamental driver in the success of the company, an inspirational figure leading a nationally and internationally recognised business.

Irwell Valley's raison d'etre is to provide good quality homes, maintain them and bring in the rents, and this means providing incentives and an improved environment for tenants. It has pioneered a Gold Service scheme that rewards tenants who behave responsibly and pay their rent on time with cash and a better service than those who default.

It also gives education grants, discounts at major retailers and a whole range of entitlements to residents who pay their rent on time and meet their responsibilities. More than 90% of the tenants are on Gold Service which the Irwell Valley chair, Nigel Neary, says is now regarded as a beacon of delivery of social housing into the 21st century.

It is a system which has been copied and replicated by many other companies in the sector in the UK and Europe under the consultancy of Irwell Valley personnel. Irwell Valley knows full well that to be »

"We are ethical capitalists"
(Tom Manion,
chief executive)

successful it has a responsibility to improve the lifestyle of the community in which it operates so it is at the fore in initiating award-winning health, crime reduction and environment projects.

Company Culture

Chief Executive Tom Manion puts in a full day and each one includes swimming for about a mile. He does not, of course, think that the workforce of 208 should take a lengthy daily dip but he believes in setting an example. He explains: "You have to be in shape mentally because things happen that test you on a regular basis. You have to retain your stamina and energy and get the best out of yourself."

Manion says the association's mission is to revolutionise customer service delivery and public sector employment. The company's whole purpose is based on its sound principles of social responsibility.

From the top the policy is to treat people with dignity and respect, to learn from mistakes, work with passion and fun, be pioneering and free thinking and "believe in tough rights and responsibilities". Its visions include reaching unprecedented levels of service performance in letting its homes, maintaining them and collecting income. Also 'To be the best organisation to work for where people exceed their potential and create a buzzing working environment.' Adds Manion: "We want to grow in size, but size is not the be all and end all – we will grow without compromising our mission. And we want to create fantastic neighbourhoods."

The chief executive and senior management hold informal seminars with colleagues to discuss any proposed company changes and to hear suggestions and ideas for the improvement of services. They also work in open plan offices and operate an open-door policy. There is a free flow in communication and cross-fertilisation of ideas because that is the way the company wishes to operate.

Because there are discrete roles and areas of expertise the association encourages regular departmental and inter-departmental question and answer workshops to develop a corporate understanding of the business.

Innovation and Creativity

You might think that building houses, repairing them and collecting rents does not leave much scope for innovation and creativity but that would be wrong. For a start, the Gold Service scheme, which rewards good tenants, is a big first.

Irwell Valley's Chorlton Park development has been hailed as a showcase in futuristic energy efficiency and sophisticated planning and it is now trialing ecologically developed construction at several other developments. It has taken delivery of a micro compact sustainable energy efficient home – the first registered social landlord to do so.

Two projects are being developed to build affordable homes without the need for grant funding to help people trying to get on the housing ladder and older people moving into their own purpose-designed retirement home on a shared ownership basis.

Internally Irwell Valley has developed Your Mind Your Business (YMYB), a two-day programme to help people think differently about the way they work and open minds to different ideas and ways of doing things for the benefit of themselves, residents and the association as a whole. These courses have been so successful that the Association has made them available to 15 external companies that tailor them to their own cultural work environment.

Pay and Benefits

There are 40 other housing organisations in Greater Manchester so there is no shortage of housing jobs but Irwell Valley easily matches the competition. Tom Manion does not mince his words: "Our four-tier performance-related pay structure with escalating levels of benefits ranks amongst the best in the world."

This four-tier system was introduced in 2008. Irwell Valley claims it is revolutionary in its sector and is a move from service to performance-related pay, directly linking pay and access to benefits with performance, which is measured on a competency-based appraisal system.

The scheme enables Irwell Valley to become more competitive in attracting high-calibre job seekers from the private sector whilst at the same time retaining its own highest performers. It used to be a three-tier system but a fourth tier has been added – the Platinum tier – for the top 5% of the highest performers. They are deemed to have gone that extra mile and as a result receive a 10% bonus on top of their salary increase plus a range of personally tailored additional benefits.

Tom Manion explains: "In most public sector organisations you can move up as long as you don't punch the manager or get caught with your fingers in the till. Here, pay is linked to performance. We can't afford to have anybody not believing in what we do – a bad attitude becomes bad performance and attendance. And there is no benefit a director gets which the cleaner does not."

High performers get the chance to represent the company at awards dinners and other corporate events; one-off ex-gratia payments or gifts for those who 'unlock their discretionary effort;' birthday cake; away days; and a Christmas party paid for by the association.

"Our escalating levels of benefits rank among the best in the world"
(Tom Manion, chief executive)

"There is no benefit a
director gets which a
cleaner does not"
(Tom Manion,
chief executive)

There is a defined contribution stakeholder pension scheme, a wellness programme of health and fitness classes, private healthcare, dental care, family friendly benefits, and interest-free loans in times of need.

Career Development

Every colleague has a personal development plan that incorporates his or her tailored training requirements, targets, methods of achievement and schedule. This is used as a record for the Colleague Development department and the colleague involved to ensure that all training requirements are met.

Compulsory in-house corporate training is run on a three-year rolling programme. Many of the sessions are health and safety requirements that ensure the safety and well-being of colleagues. Work Buddy is a scheme that supports and mentors juniors and apprentices to ensure they receive the best training and development and understand the culture of the Association. Internal promotion is encouraged through succession planning and during 2008, 25 colleagues progressed through internal promotions. Continuing professional development is encouraged and supported. Management development training includes leadership development and skills based on a coaching/mentoring approach reflecting the company culture, goals and visions.

The HR philosophy is to attract and retain people who want to contribute to and enjoy the company success and help drive the company forward. Tom Manion states: "We want people who are passionate about our approach and culture and who want to develop themselves personally and professionally. We offer more than just a job with excellent wages."

The association rewards people who are motivated and constantly reaching for their full potential – with more than a little help from the association. Clearly one way to catch the eye and move up the promotional ladder is to embrace the corporate culture that says 'if you see it, do something about it.' As Manion says: "We want people to sort it out for themselves. We don't believe in emails to cover your back and all that rubbish. People don't like change but all the time we are trying to get people to embrace change."

Corporate Social Responsibility

Social responsibility is right at the top of the Irwell Valley agenda. Its development and investment work focuses not only on building and maintaining attractive homes but also includes a clear commitment to investing in neighbourhoods and it supports Government priorities for promoting efficiency and value for money.

At an organisational level it has established high standards in the procurement of new products and services as they impact upon the environment, sustainability, local employment and training and this is demanded of the supply chain. At Haughton Green in Tameside, for example, it has initiated a regeneration works contractor partnership that stipulates apprentice employment once the turnover target has been met and it also contributes to a trust fund that looks at developing local skills and training initiatives.

Irwell is committed to exceeding the Housing Corporation's minimum standard of sustainability in its new-build schemes and is active in researching and promoting modern methods of construction. It has a diverse workforce and assists ethnic organisations. It produces all of its information in a score of languages and Braille.

Colleagues are encouraged to find efficiencies such as turning off lights and equipment, using recycled paper – it made a point of changing its stationery supplier – and it also encourages recycling cans and plastic by having recycling centres at its offices. Its Neighbourhood Managers and Project Workers, as part of their role, educate residents in ways of recycling household waste.

Irwell's award-winning Sunshine Community Café recruits employees locally and through its sister catering company delivers healthy buffets that include supplying locally grown produce and Fairtrade beverages to local businesses.

Through donations to Oxfam Irwell Valley has supported educational and welfare programmes in developing countries and has provided enough to build a classroom, provide clean water for 1,000 people, maintain a well and provide eight desks and chairs.

To encourage residents at its Haughton Green development to maintain regeneration and promote the all-round benefits it provides, it has launched an annual gardening competition for the best window boxes and hanging baskets as well as conventional gardens.

And there are even special awards for young residents or people who just show a commitment to the environment.

Tom Manion states: "We are committed to social responsibility to reduce our carbon footprint. We also encourage initiatives that benefit local communities and wider society. Colleagues frequently take part in charitable work, raising money and giving time to help people in need."

Facts and figures

Total number of staff: 208
Office location: Manchester
Industry sector: Housing
Turnover: £37m (assets £300m)

J D Wetherspoon plc

Wetherspoon House
Central Park, Reeds Crescent
Watford, Herts WD2 4QL

Telephone: 01923 477702
Fax: 01923 247961
www.jdwetherspoon.co.uk

Pay and Benefits	★ ★ ★ ★ ⯪
Training and Development	★ ★ ★ ☆ ☆
Career Development	★ ★ ★ ★ ⯪
Working Conditions	★ ★ ★ ⯪ ☆
Company Culture	★ ★ ★ ★ ☆

Biggest plus
A fast-paced business environment with plenty of opportunities for career development.

Greatest challenge
The need for continued evolution to ensure all aspects of our offer remains attractive to our customers.

Summary

J D Wetherspoon (Wetherspoon) owns and operates more than 700 pubs throughout the UK. It aims to provide a friendly and comfortable drinking atmosphere in its pubs, serving good-quality, competitively priced food all day. Based in Watford, the company employs around 21,000 staff across the business.

About the organisation

Wetherspoon was launched in 1979 by Tim Martin, who remains the company's chairman to this day. The company's name has become a familiar presence on many of Britain's high streets as the size of the pub estate has grown – almost all of it organically.

Expansion accelerated after 1992 when Wetherspoon floated on the London Stock Exchange as a public limited company. In recent years the company has opened an annual average of 40 new pubs, bucking an overall trend of pub closures.

Last year was arguably the most challenging yet for the pub trade: operators having to cope with a smoking ban in public places, rising commodity prices and the biggest beer duty increase in a decade. These factors combined to hit profits, which fell by 4.3% (having grown by 20% and 12% in 2006 and 2007). Yet the company continued to grow sales – just as in the previous two years – with overall revenue rising by 2.1%. And in the five weeks to the end of August, like-for-like sales grew 1.1%.

The company's strategy in such a testing environment is based on growing its property portfolio for increased revenues, and on continuously refining and improving its pub offering. Ironically the economic slowdown is to the benefit of the first objective as new sites are cheaper to acquire. A good example of the second aspect is the recent £15m investment in cooling technology to ensure drinks are served at the right temperature.

Looking to the future Tim Martin says, "As a result of our strong cash flow, our dedicated management team and our efforts to improve every area of the business, we remain confident of our prospects."

Company Culture

The expression work-in-progress might almost have been coined for Wetherspoon. Not so much because it is unfinished but because the company is relentless in its quest for business improvement. »

According to Su Cacioppo, personnel and legal director, "It's an incredibly fast-moving, driven company – both in terms of sales growth and high standards. We believe in constant evolution and to thrive here you need a positive, can-do attitude and shouldn't be afraid to get your hands dirty."

The company's strategy has two key elements: firstly, to draw upon the talents and knowledge of its people and second, to incentivise and reward as much as possible.

A useful source of ideas for continuous business improvement is the employee suggestion scheme, known as 'Tell Tim' (Martin). Remarkably the company receives around 20 suggestions a day, all of which are individually reviewed by senior managers. Suggestions with merit receive a £5 prize and are passed onto the relevant business area to see if they should be actioned. As an example, it was through this scheme that Wetherspoon decided to retail the popular Kopparberg Swedish cider.

The hard work that staff put in throughout the year is rewarded at an annual party and awards ceremony. An award goes to the individual who is judged to have made the best overall contribution to the business that year. Other notable awards are for sales performance, people development and pub manager of the year. In all about 15 awards are made, with cash prizes of up to £2,000 among them.

It hardly needs saying that for many Wetherspoon employees a conventional nine-to-five day does not exist. "We often work when other people are out to play so you have to be a certain type of person to enjoy the pub industry," says Cacioppo. "If you don't mind the anti-social hours it's a phenomenally fun environment."

Innovation and Creativity

Over the past two decades there has been a transformation in the way pubs market themselves to the wider public. It is no exaggeration to say that Wetherspoon has been at the forefront of many of these changes, pioneering new products and ways of service. Food offer innovations such as the curry club, the steak night and beer and burger all originated with the company and were duplicated elsewhere. So too the use of dedicated coffee machines and the siting of cash machines on pub premises.

"It's an incredibly fast-moving, driven company – both in terms of sales growth and high standards" (Su Cacioppo, personnel and legal director)

"We did these things because we quickly realised it's very expensive running a pub," says Cacioppo. "So we aimed to make our pubs as attractive as possible to as many people as possible for as long as possible." This determination to maximise the revenue-making potential of pubs saw some of the company's pubs opening in the morning to provide breakfast and host coffee mornings for (amongst others) toddler groups.

Food provision has been a key driver of Wetherspoon's growth in the face of the smoking ban and greater industry regulation. Direct food sales alone constitute around one-third of all business and the focus now is to ensure standards and quality rise in line with customer expectations. The company manages all its own sourcing and distribution and where necessary works with international producers who can guarantee the desired quality and volume of food supply.

Pay and Benefits

"Our overall reward strategy is to be an upper quartile payer within the pub industry," explains Cacioppo. "To ensure this is the case we benchmark ourselves not only against the pub industry but also the licensed retail industry generally. We also carry out an annual pay and benefits survey."

Excluding senior executives at head office, the highest earners are found in the pub estate. An experienced pub manager can expect to earn a base salary worth £35,000-£65,000 depending on the size of the operation. At head office a middle manager will receive £35,000-£50,000 as well an annual car allowance of around £7,000. Salary levels rise at least in line with inflation, sometimes more.

Performance–related pay is a significant component of reward. Pub managers and area managers can earn up to half their base salary again depending on the success of their operation, while head office employees can earn up to 30% of base salary.

Like the career development opportunities on offer Wetherspoon's share incentive plan is an important employee retention tool. Under the terms of the plan – which is available to all staff with at least 18 months' »

"We have a phenomenal reputation for stability but also internal promotion and for the length of time people stay with us"
(Su Cacioppo, personnel and legal director)

service – shares worth between 5% and 20% of gross earnings, depending on job grade, are awarded twice per year to each individual. The shares are held in trust for three years before being released to the employee.

Other non-flexible benefits include a stakeholder pension scheme, private healthcare and life insurance. Flexible benefits include holiday time and childcare vouchers.

Career Development

"We have a phenomenal reputation for stability but also internal promotion and for the length of time people stay with us. This really embeds in the company a knowledge of the business and its operations," says Cacioppo.

In demonstration of this internal renewal all present pub managers were previously assistant managers, over half of all area managers were pub managers and all general (regional) managers were area managers. There are formal and informal fast-track programmes for star performers. Overall turnover runs at 30% – about half the market level.

The emphasis on good training provision spans all the way from hygiene awareness for the entry-level employee doing hourly-paid kitchen work to a bespoke diploma in leisure retail management which the company operates with Nottingham Trent University. Every year more than 50 managers graduate with this diploma and around a dozen more receive support for degree-level study in the same subject.

Most formal training is provided by the personnel department. However there's also support for employees studying for professional qualifications, for example in law and finance. Another feature of the business is encouraging employees to see movement across the business as an important part of their development. "Running a pub is like running a baby business," observes Cacioppo. "The skills people acquire there are very transferable – financial management, people management, team coordination and so on."

The strength of Wetherspoon's training has been regularly recognised over the years in the form of various awards. To date it has been recognised five times at the National Innkeeping Training Awards, including "Best Training in Managed Estates" and twice receiving the "Supreme Award for Best Overall Training". Other awards were for catering training and most recently the Diploma programme was considered "Best training in conjunction with a college of further & higher education".

Corporate Social Responsibility

Wetherspoon has adopted a Corporate Social Responsibility (CSR) Plan in recognition of the need to link business growth to socially and ethically aware practices. The plan targets five activity areas: people; community and charity; energy and the environment; ethical working; and health.

An important element of the company's CSR profile is its support for CLIC Sargeant, a charity which helps children suffering with cancer and leukaemia and their families. In the last six years £2m has been donated, partly through fundraising activities such as football tournaments and raffles, and the company aims to increase its support to £500,000 annually. A charity committee exists to handle all national charitable requests, and pubs have decision-making powers in respect of local community causes they may wish to support.

The company takes seriously its role as a responsible alcoholic drinks retailer. It has published a policy on the subject and is a member of National Pubwatch, which promotes a safer social drinking environment in pubs, and The Drinkaware Trust. "We always work with local police to ensure our pubs are safe places," says Cacioppo. "If a troublemaker is barred from one pub they are automatically barred from the rest of them."

In order to source the quality of food it wants to serve in its pubs Wetherspoon has to work with international suppliers. A number of these suppliers are in less developed countries and the company strives to be ethical in its dealings with them. As well as carrying out formal audits of prospective partners it visits suppliers annually to check that required standards of management, hygiene and employment practices are being maintained. To reinforce its awareness of these issues the company only serves Rainforest Alliance coffee in its pubs.

From a diversity perspective, the company is notable for the advancement of women in the business. Forty per cent of all pub managers are female as are three of the eight executive board members.

In the area of energy and environment a number of steps have been taken. Specialist fridge controls and new high-tech taps have helped cut energy and water waste respectively, while smart electricity meters were installed in 327 pubs during 2007-08. Ambitious recycling targets have also been set; for example, last year nearly a quarter of all glass used was recycled, next year this proportion is planned to increase to three-quarters.

Facts and figures

Total number of staff: 21,000
Office location: Watford (head office) plus 700 pubs throughout the UK
Industry sector: Pubs and restaurants
Annual turnover: £907.5m

John Lewis Partnership

John Lewis Partnership plc

171 Victoria Street
London
SW1E 5NN

Telephone: 020 7828 1000
www.johnlewispartnership.co.uk

Pay and Benefits	★ ★ ★ ☆ ☆
Training and Development	★ ★ ★ ☆ ☆
Career Development	★ ★ ★ ★ ☆
Working Conditions	★ ★ ★ ★ ☆
Company Culture	★ ★ ★ ★ ☆

Biggest plus
A strong brand that offers worthwhile and satisfying employment in a successful business through a model of co-ownership that harnesses employee loyalty.

Greatest challenge
Maintaining quality, commitment, sales and a distinct company culture and values.

Summary

John Lewis Partnership is known for its chain of 27 UK-based department stores. In addition, it operates 193 Waitrose food shops, an online and catalogue business (John Lewis Direct) and a direct services company (Greenbee). New John Lewis stores are planned in locations including Cardiff, Oxford and Stratford, while Waitrose recently opened its first supermarket in Dubai. In 2007, group sales increased by 6.3% (in 2006) to £6.8bn, with operating profits (excluding property) up 17.1% to £402m. The partnership's 69,000 permanent employees, known as partners, entirely own the business and have a share in its profits.

About the organisation

John Lewis has, in recent years, become a high street star. In 2008, Verdict named it Britain's favourite retailer, while *Which?* magazine awarded its sister company Waitrose a similar accolade. The partnership maintains ambitious plans to double turnover over the next decade, employing more than 100,000 partners.

The first John Lewis draper's shop opened on London's Oxford Street in 1864. The founder's son, John Spedan Lewis, placed ownership in the hands of partners, holding shares for them in trust rather than owning them privately or trading them on the stock market. This was followed by the introduction of a profit-sharing scheme and formed the basis for the modern partnership, established in 1940.

Looking after partners is fundamental to business strategy, according to director of personnel Tracey Killen. "Trust is at the heart of the organisation, and that starts with our partners. In the current climate, they are feeling the impact [of economic downturn] just as much as big businesses. Our commitment to supporting the people who work here becomes more important and a stronger indicator of the values we hold."

In 2007-2008, John Lewis increased its number of product lines and gained market share in fashion, holding ground in its 'backbone' market of home technology and electrical goods. Meanwhile, Waitrose modernised in-store communications, continued to innovate with product ranges, and invested to improve customer service and price perception. It is also trialling a convenience store format.

In the half-year to July 2008, the group's sales rose 3.6% to £3.27bn, though operating profit fell. "The outlook for 2009 is challenging," says partnership chairman Charlie Mayfield. "However, our product and service offers are well differentiated, our partners are highly committed, and with our long-term approach we are well positioned to take advantage of the recovery in confidence when it comes."

"Trust is right at the heart of the organisation, and that starts with our partners" (Tracey Killen, personnel director)

Company Culture

In tightening times, John Lewis Partnership believes its longstanding ethos and values will help it outperform other retailers. With the group's emphasis on durability, responsibility and a longer-term view, "the zeitgeist has moved in our favour," says Killen.

Values such as respect, honesty, recognition and working together remain constant. "We create a sense of community in the business at a very local level," says Killen. "Partners bring a level of discretionary energy that is hard for other businesses to replicate. That's the magic of co-ownership: our partners don't like to let their colleagues down."

Good communication is an important part of the partnership's approach. In addition to a weekly magazine and an intranet, there are weekly 'communication half-hours' for managers to keep partners informed. In 2007, 62,000 partners gave feedback in the annual partner survey, on issues from job satisfaction to management.

The recent replacement of the old system of branch councils with informal forums, to which partners elect their peers, has been tremendously successful. "Partners feel really able to tackle local issues," says Killen. "What matters is what happens at your branch. These forums help partners to feel they can engage, and gives them confidence to contribute. It's also about management being prepared to listen."

The ability to work flexibly is an attraction, since many partners are part-time. A carer's leave policy allows anyone with a year's service up to a year off in unpaid leave, and all partners with 25 years' service can take up to six months' paid leave. "What today's workforce wants is more flexibility – our life stages are much more complicated. We need to recognise that and have an adult conversation about it," says Killen.

Innovation and Creativity

In certain areas, such as sustainable construction and green IT, the partnership has recently been so successful that other businesses have come to ask for advice.

Its new Leicester store, for which more than 90% of building waste was recycled, has a glass frontage that resembles a roll of fabric to celebrate the city's textile heritage, while its Portsmouth store will commemorate the port's history by including sails in the design. "John Lewis is often mistakenly perceived as being quite safe, but our designs are extraordinary," says Killen. "It's about being respectful of where we are, and trying to put into that community a building that respects the environment but also respects the heritage of the environment."

The partnership has helped to found a cross-industry group to develop more sustainable IT strategies, and internally it has initiated measures such as reducing the need for new servers by increasing the processing power performed per unit of energy consumed; ensuring all new desktop and laptop computers conform to the highest energy efficiency standards; using software that powers down computers overnight; and reducing the energy used for air conditioning.

Pay and Benefits

John Lewis Partnership pays its partners at a mid-market rate, rewarding exceptional performance with pay that goes into the upper quartile. It also offers partners an attractive range of benefits, together with a significant annual bonus when trade thrives. In 2007-2008, for example, partners were paid a partnership bonus worth 20% of salary, or 10 weeks' pay.

"When times are good, the bonus is good; but there's a sense of responsibility when times are tough," says Killen. "Partners understand, because they see fewer people in the shops, and they will work with the organisation to manage costs and increase productivity. It's a two-way deal: we offer partners that level of support when times are tougher, and in return, we get an engagement and a willingness to understand." Partners can subscribe to the group's Bonus Save scheme, which allows them to retrieve their partnership bonus tax-free after five years.

Other benefits include a final salary non-contributory pension scheme, now available to partners with three, rather than five, years' service. Partners also enjoy a 25% reduction on John Lewis goods, 12% off at Waitrose, and access to services including free legal advice. In addition, the partnership operates several recognition schemes such as its 'good work' initiative, which rewards 20 partners with a luxury holiday abroad; partners also nominate colleagues for spontaneous 'thank you' vouchers.

>>

"In this business, you can develop yourself in the most holistic sense"
(Tracey Killen, director of personnel)

"People are attracted by the brand... They trust our products and our people."
(Tracey Killen, director of personnel)

The partnership employs some 50 people to organise social events. These have included an expedition to Thorpe Park, and inter-branch activities such as bowling and evenings out. Partners can take advantage of cheap breaks at the group's hotels around the country which are for the exclusive use of partners and their families, and in 2008, partners voted to spend £3m on a new hotel in North Wales, bringing the UK total to five.

Career Development

At John Lewis Partnership, roles are divided into management and non-management. Its Horizons programme enables any partner to progress into management through a competency-based modular route. "We want that to be open and transparent, but it is a partner's responsibility to act on it," says Killen.

Despite putting the onus on partners, the partnership takes talent management seriously. A head of talent development oversees succession planning, and using new technology the partnership has increased capacity for transferring talent between parts of the business. Candidates for promotion are assessed both for capability and readiness to enter a role. "Partners will tell you that their experience of being a partner is only as good as the person managing them," says Killen. "We put a lot of energy into leadership and general management. If you get that right for partners, the customers feel it."

Each year, the partnership recruits 50 graduates to a general management programme, and employs dozens more who leave school after A Levels. Senior managers receive coaching, and the group's top 200 partners participate in an academy scheme, in conjunction with business schools. As the vast majority of the business is UK-based, there is limited chance for international travel.

The partnership believes in developing its workforce holistically, offering a year's career break after five years of service, and access to Once in a Lifetime, a fund to help partners fulfil their dreams. "The more opportunities you have, the more confident and fulfilled a person you will be," says Killen. "The founder believed that if you care for the individual, the individual cares for the organisation. If partners want to do something, the business will try support them."

Corporate Social Responsibility

CSR is integral to the way in which the partnership does business – and always has been. According to Andy Street, managing director of John Lewis, "because we don't have external shareholders, we can make long-term decisions about how we source products, run operations and support local communities for the best interests of all our stakeholders."

The partnership sets itself specific targets for change. It has vowed to lower its carbon impact by using green sources of energy and reducing energy-related transport emissions from store deliveries. Its new national distribution centre, Magna Park, will "play a key role in avoiding unnecessary mileage and reducing journey times," and incorporates innovations such as movement-activated lighting, solar thermal energy to heat water, and rainwater in the low-flush toilets.

John Lewis aims to recycle 50% of waste by 2010, and has an 'old for new' mattress recycling scheme. It uses the Supplier Ethical Data Exchange (Sedex) to ensure suppliers comply with its Responsible Sourcing code of practice, and plans to work with the Environmental Justice Foundation to make the cotton supply chain more transparent. Its timber policy helps it source goods "with the least possible damage to the natural environment," and it has started an annual promotion of Fairtrade, organic and energy-efficient products. Meanwhile, Waitrose gives increasingly in-depth information about the provenance and quality of products.

The partnership aims to make 'a positive contribution' to communities by investing in local initiatives and encouraging partner involvement. It gives away at least 1% of pre-tax profits and in 2007 donated £6.2m to charities and community groups, including £316,000 raised during its charities week. It also sponsored more than 75,000 hours of partner time given to charity; under its Golden Jubilee Trust scheme, partners can go to work for a charity for up to six months.

As the partnership looks to take on more partners, it has started to work with external consultants to consider diversity issues such as ageing and migration. Currently, its diversity strategy group helps under-represented groups to move into management by raising awareness and finding role models.

Because of its equity-owning structure, the partnership is not subject to external public scrutiny. Instead, its system of checks and balances includes an elected partnership council comprising some 90 members, which votes five directors onto the partnership board. There is also a partners' 'counsellor' who sits on the management committee and acts as an ombudsman to the partnership.

Facts and figures

Total number of staff: 69,000
Office location: London (head office); 27 UK department stores and 193 Waitrose food stores
Industry sector: Retail
Annual turnover: £6.8bn

John Wood Group plc

John Wood House
Greenwell Road
Aberdeen AB12 3AX

Telephone: 01224 851000
www.woodgroup.com

Pay and Benefits	★ ★ ★ ☆ ☆
Training and Development	★ ★ ★ ☆ ☆
Career Development	★ ★ ★ ☆ ☆
Working Conditions	★ ★ ★ ☆ ☆
Company Culture	★ ★ ★ ⯪ ☆

Biggest plus
FTSE 100 business with a light touch in managing its individual group companies.

Greatest challenge
Finding the capable and experience people it needs for growth.

Summary

Aberdeen-based Wood Group is a leading global contractor for onshore and offshore oil and gas facilities and the world-leading independent provider of integrated maintenance solutions for industrial gas turbines. Over 27,500 people support its operations worldwide, across 48 countries, working for most of the major oil and gas and power producers. Wood Group is a market leader in engineering design, production enhancement and support and industrial gas turbine services. Global sales are now more than US$4.4bn and its last interim results showed pre-tax profit up by 46% to US$181.3m.

About the organisation

In 1983 a number of Scottish institutions bought a 10% stake in Wood Group. Even then it was one of Scotland's largest and most profitable companies but until then the Wood family had kept a tight hold on the shares.

This move was rightly seen as a prelude to further expansion and acquisition and as was said at the time by one of its investors: "The Wood Group has demonstrated what can be achieved by strong leadership and intelligent strategy in a competitive international industry. We believe that the company has excellent prospects for sustainable growth in the 1980s."

How prophetic. The company, transformed from a fishing repair business in the 1970s into an oil and gas services giant, just continues to grow and acquire, keeping its investors more than happy.

It is regarded as a North Sea icon yet the North Sea, which was the company's platform for success, now accounts for only 20% of the business with about half of it in the United States of America. Canada, Venezuela, Colombia, Brazil, North and West Africa, Russia, Asia Pacific and the Middle East make up the rest. There are three umbrella businesses – engineering and production facilities, well support and gas turbine services, and they are all growing.

CEO Allister Langlands says one of the key areas of focus is to extend the company's engineering presence in the Eastern Hemisphere. He explains: "That's where we see the growth in the next three to five years – focused on areas like the Middle East. We're working to organically build the resources we have on the ground out there – we'd also love to do acquisitions."

〉〉

He continues: "We really do feel we're an international group. That's how we behave and think. If you look at our 27,500 people, 75-80% of them are based overseas. You must have an international mentality, not a UK one, to succeed."

Company Culture

Scotland might have a devolved parliament but the Wood Group pioneered devolution worldwide. Peter Nicholson, group head of Human Resources, describes it as "limited bureaucracy". Its companies in different parts of the world have considerable autonomy, doing it their way without having to check back with base. The view is that they know their local markets and customers better and as long as they maintain the Group's high ethical values, they can get on with it.

Allister Langlands puts it thus: "We run the business in a relatively decentralised way and we think that's been a significant strength. We attract high quality management and we give them a reasonable degree of autonomy for them to work in and deliver the results within an agreed framework and strategy."

The company strives to be an employer of choice and to attract, develop and retain the best talent available. That means competitive pay – sometimes over the market odds when the right people are in short supply – while adhering to the now-established practice of work/life balance. It has what it calls a whole range of "successful people initiatives" which include using its internationally mobile workforce to support new market opportunities.

One example is that its highly skilled South American managers are involved in projects around the world, including in Algeria, Dubai, Malaysia and Trinidad. The potential for work experience is considerable. One graduate said: "I want to be involved in the deepest oil well or the biggest oil platform and that is the chance I get."

But beware! Chairman Sir John Wood says: "Future growth will not be achieved without risks and challenges. The global oil and gas industry needs to develop reserves in harsher locations and geopolitical uncertainty in some of the world's key oil and gas provinces is a fact of life."

Innovation and Creativity

As the worldwide search for oil and gas is stepped up the demand for new products and services intensifies. For the Wood Group this requires a constant flow of innovative solutions. The company meets this challenge and prides itself on providing solutions, products and services to enhance production rates and efficiency from oil and gas reservoirs.

"If you look at our 27,500 employees 75-80% of them are based overseas. You must have an international mentality, not a UK one, to succeed."
(Allister Langlands, CEO)

"We invest very heavily in training and development and career prospects in the industry are very good" (Peter Nicholson, group head of Human Resources)

The operators need help in maintaining and enhancing production from existing fields and exploring new reserves while reducing greenhouse gases and being cost effective.

For example, with much of the Arctic region's hydrocarbon reserves lying under seasonal or year-round ice the company has developed new software technology that is designed to help operators achieve significant savings in exploring this untapped region.

This is what the company calls New Horizons – continually developing new solutions to meet the needs of global clients as they enter new territories and face new challenges.

On the engineering front it provides solutions across the board based on what it calls the expertise, ingenuity and experience of its people and the GTS (Gas Turbine Services) side of the business delivers solutions that are right for each individual customer with gas turbine operators the world over benefiting from innovative processes.

Pay and Benefits

The global oil and gas industry continues to be hit by a significant shortage of experienced and qualified people. To maintain the constant inflow of people of calibre the company tops the table with pay and benefits – graduates, for example, around the early stages of their careers can command a salary in the high twenties.

Allister Langlands says: "The international scale of our operations means that our graduates enjoy many opportunities to share their experiences, participate in international exchanges and secondments and learn from the experience of their senior colleagues. We also recognise the need to attract engineers from other industries and have a number of successful initiatives in this area."

Wood Group has increased its apprenticeship programmes worldwide and recently invested in a new apprentice training school in Aberdeen at its Rolls Wood Group joint venture business. Wood Group's flagship management development programme continues to be highly valued by its people.

The company's brief statement on compensation and benefits: "Our business units offer competitive pay and benefits packages in line with your ability and performance. Wood Group companies also provide opportunities for continuing training and education."

»

One of the areas of current focus is on benefits that support health and wellbeing and that includes everything from free fruit, sports club membership and advice on weight loss and giving up smoking. In Aberdeen there is a cycle-to-work scheme – one person asked for it, only about a dozen cyclists use it, but the request was made and it was granted.

It all comes under the heading of PeoplePlus and its popularity was shown when more that 300 staff turned up for a Wood Group Health and Fitness Fair when they were given free health checks and advice, were able to try out a new dance or exercise class and take part in a Steve Redgrave rowing challenge. Life in the Wood Group is all about challenges.

Career Development

The Wood Group message is clear enough: "It you're the best in the oil and gas industry, the Wood Group is looking for you."

Time was when it was not difficult to get the people it wanted. It benefited from the downsizing in other industries, such as shipbuilding, but now that has dried up. Many new people are moving into the industry but there is an experience gap. Peter Nicholson describes it as a demographic time bomb but the upshot is that career opportunities and advancement abound. Nicholson adds: "We invest very heavily in training and development and career prospects in the industry are very good."

The Wood Group plug to those seeking a career in the industry: "Our corporate culture values innovation, integrity, hard work and ethical business practices and gives employees scope to use their skills. We are a truly global business with operations in more than 48 countries and an approach which allows each of our businesses a high degree of autonomy and independence."

The result is many different cultures and destinations gathered under a single corporate umbrella. It makes for exciting opportunities for people who desire to experiment and innovate. "If you're after the advantages a global company can offer but don't want to be hemmed in by a heavily bureaucratic approach the Wood Group might just be the place for you."

An extra plus, according to Nicholson, is the company's elevation to the FTSE100. He explains: "Progressive people want to be part of something which is successful and we are a success story." That story can be told in many languages and accents, with graduates pouring in worldwide and career ladders beckoning. In Houston, for example, our Mustang graduates development programme called Young Guns, promises to acclimatise, expose, encourage, empower and motive the company's future leaders.

Corporate Social Responsibility

Being a quoted company and a member of the FTSE100 the John Wood Group is squeaky clean on the corporate governance front. It is led by CEO Allister Langlands who took over in January 1 2007 from Sir Ian Wood, who remains as chairman of the board. An accountant and former partner in Deloitte's, Langlands has a firm grip on the business having served previously as group director for the GTS division and as deputy chief executive.

Wood Group is committed to treating all employees fairly, responsibly and with dignity, respecting their individual differences and helping them achieve their full potential. Wood Group's Ethics Policy sets minimum acceptable standards of conduct and best practice and provides resolution procedures when questions arise.

Wood Group's policy on charitable and community sponsorship is to support causes in the regions in which they do business through long term covenants and targeted donations. With particular focus on organisations that contribute to education, health, the environment and community needs, the Group also supports charities that Wood Group employees are themselves connected with and matches employee contributions through the Wood Group's Employee Community Fund (ECF).

Being in the oil and gas sector health and safety are paramount and it is particularly proud of its Vision for HSE Excellence, which sets down its policies and procedures. The key way that the Group makes a positive contribution to lessening the negative environmental impacts of the oil and gas sector is to use its expertise and innovation to help clients find environmentally better ways of doing things.

Examples of these initiatives include helping clients in measuring the efficiency of their hydrocarbon processing systems and the integrity of pipelines and environmental feasibility projects.

The annual report states: "Our employees' health and wellbeing is a priority wherever they operate in the world. Education and raising awareness of key health issues play an important part in our initiatives, which include employee health fairs. We also focus on initiatives that address local health needs such as malaria prevention and clean water in Africa."

Les Thomas, director with Group responsibility for HSE, states: "We have won awards for our performance in many of our companies across the world. But we cannot be complacent. People are still being hurt and we must continue to be alert and committed to further improvements in HSE performance. We will be successful when no one is hurt and when others copy us." Wood Group continuously strives for further improvement and is a strong advocate of sharing best practice across the industry worldwide.

Facts and figures

Total number of staff: 27,500
Office location: Aberdeen, and operations in 48 countries
Industry sector: Oil and Gas
Annual turnover: US$4.4bn

Lloyds Banking Group

25 Gresham Street
London
EC2V 7HN

Telephone: 020 7626 1500
www.lloydstsbjobs.co.uk/talent

Pay and Benefits	★ ★ ★ ★ ★
Training and Development	★ ★ ★ ★ ★
Career Development	★ ★ ★ ★ ⯪
Working Conditions	★ ★ ★ ★ ☆
Company Culture	★ ★ ★ ★ ★

Biggest plus
As part of Lloyds Banking Group, the Board (formed on 19th January 2009 following the acquisition of HBOS plc) wants to become the UK's leading financial services company and has more than 30 million customers across the UK.

Greatest challenge
The acquisition and integration of HBOS.

Summary

Lloyds Banking Group is undergoing a fundamental reorganisation in 2009, following the announcement in September 2008 of Lloyds TSB's plan to acquire Halifax Bank of Scotland (HBOS), thereby creating the UK's largest retail bank. The merger has doubled the company's current 65,000-strong global workforce, and created a network of more than 3,000 branches across the UK. Lloyds TSB was the UK's fourth largest retail savings bank at the time the deal was announced, while HBOS was the market leader. The recent acquisition means that the new Group is now number one in terms of market share in a number of areas, including current accounts, retail savings and mortgages.

About the organisation

As Lloyds TSB, the bank faced criticism in the boom times pre-2007 for its conservative, long-term approach to business, but has reaped the rewards as markets have turned. It was relatively sheltered from the worst of the recent market turmoil because it was well-funded and had limited exposure to the more complex financial products that precipitated the credit crunch.

Lloyds TSB ranked sixth in the 2008 league table of the 'World's Safest Banks,' published by *Global Finance*, making it Britain's safest bank, and has been voted 'Britain's Most Trusted Bank' for eight successive years by *Reader's Digest*. The bank has also won the Real FD/CBI FD's Bank of the Year Award every year since 2005.

This strong position allowed the bank to acquire HBOS, the UK's biggest savings bank, announced in September 2008. The newly enlarged group has already announced that it will maintain the existing high street brands of Lloyds TSB, Halifax and Bank of Scotland.

The newly formed Lloyds Banking Group comprises five divisions: Retail, Insurance, Wholesale, Wealth and International, and IT and Operations, and a number of group executive functions, such as Risk and Human Resources. It has operations in more than 30 countries around the world.

When the acquisition of HBOS was announced, Sir Victor Blank, then chairman of Lloyds TSB, said: "This will be a unique opportunity to accelerate and extend our strategy and create the UK's leading financial services group. Lloyds TSB/HBOS's outstanding franchise will enable it to service more of its customer needs with the balance sheet strength to prosper in challenging markets."

"Lloyds TSB/HBOS's outstanding franchise will enable it to service more of its customer needs with the balance sheet strength to prosper in challenging markets"
(Sir Victor Blank, chairman)

The new Group's vision is to be recognised as the best financial company by its customers, colleagues and shareholders, by building lasting customers relationships.

Company Culture

Lloyds TSB takes considerable pride in its 250-year history, having been founded in 1765 as a private banking business in Birmingham. The merger in 1995 of TSB and Lloyds Bank created one of the largest forces in domestic banking, and then the acquisition of Scottish Widows in 2000 created one of the UK's largest providers of life, pensions and unit trust products.

The Board has described the acquisition of HBOS as an opportunity to create a great British Bank: the UK's leading financial services company. Today's management wants to build on the bank's reputation for relationship-based banking and create lasting relationships with the new Group's 30 million customers.

A great organisation is defined by its people and at Lloyds Banking Group, the people is what sets them apart from other leading organisations, with David Littlechild of Group Engagement, saying: "We are a people business. The creation of Lloyds Banking Group provides us with a great opportunity to be the best. We are committed to providing our people with opportunities to develop new skills and supporting their performance throughout their time with the organisation."

The result is a very meritocratic environment, where those who wish to work hard are able to reap the rewards and rise quickly through the organisation. Andrew Harley, the HR director for the Retail Division, says: "The Group is driven by performance, with a set of measures in place that everyone is clear about. It's all about a consistent framework for assessment, based on clarity, simplicity, employee engagement and getting the extra discretionary effort from every employee."

In practice, creating a good working environment means employees will give their best for customers, but it cannot easily be dictated from the top. For most employees, Harley recognises that the perception of the bank's culture is based on their relationship with their line manager, and as a result a lot of work goes into making sure every manager across the business is portraying the right message.

Harley says: "People that do well here are people that have a customer orientation. The days of it being about who you know are long gone – it's about results and customers."

Innovation and Creativity

Innovation at every level of the business is positively encouraged at Lloyds Banking Group, and within the retail banking division in particular, group executive director Helen Weir has an online blog inviting ideas, queries and comments from staff members. "If you ask her a question, you will get an answer," says Harley.

A recent example of the blog in action saw a branch manager in Halifax write in to express concern about the way in which the merger was being communicated in his area, that being the centre of operations for the Halifax bank, a large part of HBOS. Weir's response was to visit the branch and meet with staff members to explain the plans for integration.

Innovation also forms a key feature of the career development programmes, by which those people who regularly put forward ideas on how things might be improved are quickly identified as senior executives of the future.

The bank as a whole maintains a position at the cutting edge of its industry. Harley says: "As a bank, we are fairly restless. If you look at new store design or mobile internet banking on your phone we are pretty much up there at the forefront of developments."

Pay and Benefits

Lloyds Banking Group has introduced a Total Reward package and a flexible benefits arrangement that ranks among the most developed of any FTSE 100 company.

The Total Reward programme has won awards, and is designed to be attractive to all employees, regardless of age, role or lifestyle. Littlechild says: "It allows colleagues to benefit from competitive pensions, savings and share schemes, health and wellbeing initiatives, and insurance packages. It even provides financial support for people who want to learn in their own time a new skill."

The entire scheme is online so that colleagues can study it in their own time and in the comfort of their own home should they choose to do so. Harley says: "Up until a year ago it was very complicated, but we have done an awful lot of work on communications so that people can make a choice of what's right for them."

»

"We are committed to building a great place for our people to work and believe this will help to create a great place for customers to bank." (David Littlechild of Group Engagement)

"There are examples of stratospheric promotion, but equally there are people who joined 20 years ago and have gone through at their own pace and achieved the same results."
(Andrew Harley, HR director, Retail)

The 140 graduates a year who join Lloyds TSB are offered a competitive salary and benefits package. The deal at the end of 2008 was a starting salary of £28,000 (£31,000 in Corporate Markets), plus a London weighting of £3,450 where applicable. Additionally there are benefits including 25 days' holiday, rising to 30 days on completion of the graduate programme. There are Sharesave schemes and a contributory pension scheme, plus preferential rates on a whole range of services from car hire to mortgages.

Career Development

Harley describes the bank's approach to career development as "a meritocracy – if you want to do something, you can pretty much do it if you're prepared to work."

Graduates begin their journey with a week-long induction programme, at which they hear from guest speakers, meet with senior management, and get a welcome to the business. The graduate programme includes three six-month secondments into the business, with everyone having to spend time in the branches working with customers before progressing to the senior ranks.

A full menu of learning and development materials allows individuals wishing to stretch their abilities to do so, and all employees are encouraged to change and grow. Littlechild says: "If online learning is what an individual needs, we can provide that. If they want a mentor, we will find a suitable candidate, and if they require a specific qualification we can provide access to some of the best external suppliers."

The Lloyds Banking Group has one of the largest corporate universities in Europe and it is effectively a full bank of tutors and courses available online. It is regularly updated so that colleagues can quickly access information on developments in the financial world and other training resources.

Those who work hard can progress quickly, with Harley pointing out that he is currently interviewing to fill a very senior post, for which three of the four applicants are former graduate trainees who have been with the group less than three years. Harley says: "There are examples of stratospheric promotion, but there are equally people who joined 20 years ago and have gone through at their own pace and achieved the same results."

Corporate Social Responsibility

With a business strategy focused around building long-term customer relationships, corporate responsibility is a serious priority. Chief executive Eric Daniels says: "By investing in the communities where we operate, we not only create economic value, but also make a positive social contribution."

Colleagues are encouraged to support a wide range of community organisations, both through volunteering and fundraising. Colleagues chose the British Heart Foundation as the Lloyds TSB charity for 2008-2010, and over this two-year period the aim is to raise in excess of £2m to fund 15 new British Heart Foundation nurses in local communities. The previous chosen charity was Barnardos, for which staff raised £1.3m, exceeding the £1m target by some margin.

Furthermore, there are four Lloyds TSB Foundations throughout the UK, as well as an HBOS Foundation. Collectively they are one of the country's largest grant-making bodies. The Lloyds TSB Foundations alone received £37m from Lloyds TSB in 2007 and contributing over £360m to thousands of charities over the last 13 years.

The company has worked over the last five years to reduce its carbon footprint by almost 36,000 tonnes, and has set a demanding target of a further 30% reduction in emissions by 2012.

That year is significant because Lloyds TSB was the first organisation to sign up as a domestic partner to the 2012 Olympic and Paralympic Games. The vision for the partnership is "to inspire and support young people, communities and businesses all over Britain on their journey to the Olympic and Paralympic Games and beyond." Internally, the company has already begun a raft of initiatives including inviting both aspiring and established athletes to talk to staff about achieving goals, and an Olympic torch has been on display in the group's head office in Central London.

The company has excellent diversity within the workforce. Lloyds TSB ranks number one in the Female FTSE Index, based on the number of women on its executive committee, and tops the Employers' Forum on Disability benchmark. It was awarded first place in the Race for Opportunity benchmark in 2008 thanks to its progress on race equality, and ranks first in Stonewall's Workplace Equality Index, which rates the UK's top 100 employers of lesbian, gay and bisexual staff.

Facts and figures

Total number of staff: 70,000
Office location: Central London head office, plus 2,100 branches in the UK and operations in 27 countries
Industry sector: Financial services
Annual turnover: Total income for 2007 was £18bn

L&Q

HOUSING TRUST

London & Quadrant Housing Trust

Osborn House
Osborn Terrace
London SE3 9DR

Telephone: 020 8552 9181
Fax: 020 8852 1517
Email: humanresources@lqgroup.org.uk
www.lqgroup.org.uk

Pay and Benefits	★ ★ ★ ⯪ ☆
Training and Development	★ ★ ★ ★ ⯪
Career Development	★ ★ ★ ★ ★
Working Conditions	★ ★ ★ ★ ☆
Company Culture	★ ★ ★ ★ ⯪

Biggest plus
The product L&Q is delivering – affordable housing – and working in a fun, ever changing, challenging environment with great people.

Greatest challenge
As one of the Top 50 European workplaces, there can be no resting on one's laurels. The key will be to keep up the game with strong leadership.

Summary

London & Quadrant Housing Trust (L&Q) is a housing trust providing affordable housing in London and the South East. Residents include families, couples, single people, key workers, the elderly and those with special needs. L&Q is continually creating places where people want to live, some 60,000 homes to date. In the process it has become one of the UK's largest providers of affordable housing. There's a good degree of financial strength and a record of merging with other companies to the tune of one per year for the past four. Annual turnover for 2007/08 rose to £230m on which it made a surplus of £44m. Headcount is 1,070.

About the organisation

L&Q was started in 1963, at a time when a television programme called 'Cathy come home' stirred up the country's emotions regarding deprived people and accommodation problems. As a response many small housing associations were created. L&Q itself was the product of a merger of two associations and saw steady growth from 1987 under the direction of a chief executive who retired in 2008. "We now have our former group finance director David Montague as group chief executive," says Tom Nicholls, group director, Human Resources. "Since we were founded and had relatively few houses, we have grown through taking on local authorities' portfolios, stock transfers and building our own homes. We are now one of the largest housing association developers in the UK."

Over the past eight years L&Q has been focusing heavily on its people – it was the first housing association in London to obtain Investors in People (IIP) accreditation. Now there is continuous learning development underway. Eight years ago L&Q put a business plan in place across four areas, one of which focused on the development of people in support of other strategic objectives. Meeting customers' needs, financial health and adding value make up the remaining areas. "We look to develop responses in the areas," says Nicholls. "We examine training and development, and opportunities, and how we reward and recognise people, making things clearer. Development and training schemes focus across a range of areas in response to what we're told by managers and the marketplace."

The employment practices must be doing something well – L&Q continues to win awards, such as Personnel Today recognising its employer branding, moving up *The Sunday Times Best 100 Companies to Work For* ranks over five years, featuring in the *FT Top 50 Great Places to Work* – even the *FT Top 50 in Europe*.

Company Culture

"A large part of our corporate plan is dedicated to people issues – how, what and why – and staff surveys, all of which is used to competitive advantage," says Chris Gillam, assistant director, Human »

Resources. Feedback from staff surveys is wrapped together with a focus on leadership. A focus group with staff looks at the three areas of leadership, a competency framework and values within the business. The key question asked is "what do we need to do to improve?" All managers meet annually in April for a day. This year the morning was led by HR, to focus on leadership asking where the organisation is in the three areas and how to progress.

This year the results have seen a management competency framework put in place across the organisation and a new five-year corporate plan introduced by the chief executive of which people are a fundamental part. "As a result – as work in progress – we are developing new values, which will be launched by year-end [2008]," says Nicholls. "We will look at the new competency framework and what we expect in behaviours and styles, and how to help people to develop."

"Feedback from everyone in the organisation has never been so forthcoming," says Gillam. In November it is planned to launch the L&Q Leadership Academy which is currently being researched and developed by two of the UK's most prestigious business schools. "It's an opportunity to bring our people managers on," says Nicholls. "We will look at other areas of leadership and how to link values with customer service." Taking a lead from the 2008 Olympics, there is also likely to be more of an emphasis on coaching than managing.

L&Q aims to be a family-friendly employer, with great arrangements in place for flexible working (note, not flexi-time). Over 70% of the workforce is female, many being part-time workers.

Innovation and Creativity

"We are always trying to get people to come up with ideas," says Gillam. "There is a staff suggestions scheme for innovations and ideas, plus the L&Q intranet. Generally we try to avoid unnecessary bureaucracy. With 14 offices across our territory we aim for local input and making decisions locally wherever possible. Successes are shared within the organisation." The annual staff conference is also a place to share values, tell of successes and learn what the future holds in store. "Ideas to improve the structure of the organisation can be put forward and implemented," says Gillam.

Economic difficulties in the UK have led to a housing slowdown and L&Q has been looking at how and when it sells houses. "We are looking at offering more flexibility to customers," says Nicholls. "That includes the mix of rentals, tenant support needs, purchasers and how we can be flexible in marrying what people like and want, and can afford."

"The key point about working for L&Q is the people and what they stand for" (employee comment)

"We are now one of the largest housing association developers in the UK"
(Tom Nicholls, Human Resources group director)

To bolster recruitment activity, L&Q offers its own trainee schemes, with training for different parts of the business, e.g. surveyor training. Motivation in customer service capabilities is available, as are communications and customer care skills training, to name but a few. "It is more about attitude," says Nicholls.

Pay and Benefits

While the housing sector is fiercely competitive, it is necessary to keep the salary structure under constant review through monitoring of trade journals, internet sites and annual salary surveys. "We have looked at reward mechanisms and award schemes," says Nicholls. "Six years ago, the annual bonus scheme was not perceived to have been truly transparent. Staff satisfaction surveys showed more transparency was required." The result is a set of People Awards. The outstanding achiever award is given to those going the extra mile while demonstrating they have lived L&Q's values and given great customer service, and is up to 2.5% of salary as a bonus. "It's all public now and awarded at the annual staff conference – 150 people received one this year," says Nicholls. There are opportunities to reward teams and individuals throughout the year with meals, wine, chocolates, etc. There are performance quality achievement awards (money plus certificates) given at the staff conference. Outstanding achievers receive a certificate and gold badge as well as money. There's a category of special awards e.g. individual customer service, team customer service, living L&Q's values.

At the core of the benefits package is basic pay with annual increments and the potential to gain an award. Annual leave allowance starts at 26 days plus 8 Bank Holidays, rising after five years to 31 days plus Bank Holidays. There's a defined contribution pension scheme, with L&Q doubling employee contributions up to 12% of salary. "Long" service awards kick in at five years' service with £250 to be used for training (e.g. in golf, languages and wine tasting) rising to £500 at 25 years. After 10 years service it's possible to have a career break with a year's sabbatical. Other benefits include buy-back of up to five days holiday and one day extra leave if no sick leave is taken. Company cars/allowances are given where relevant.

Career Development

"The formal apparatus we have in place is for annual and half-yearly appraisals with needs and suggestions ›

"A large part of our corporate plan is dedicated to people issues – how, what and why – and staff surveys, all of which is used to competitive advantage" (Chris Gillam, Human Resources assistant director)

fed through to the training and development team," says Nicholls. "Informally there are discussions about learning and development and training needs every four to six weeks."

Corporate training needs will be met through the L&Q Leadership Academy. Today 150 people are undertaking professional qualifications with L&Q (15% of the workforce). Applications are received from all over the organisation for different courses, all relevant to L&Q's business. L&Q will develop its own schemes if no suitable course exists. There are secondment opportunities from time to time and shadowing where possible.

As a manager, people benefit from managing the L&Q way, learning skills such as how appraisals work, how performance management works, how to manage recruitment – all delivered in-house by people offering total support. Managers and team leaders can achieve a diploma in management and team leadership delivered with Oxford Brookes University.

Graduates (some eight per year) join a structured two-year training programme, supported by their own mentor. Graduates have four six-month positions with the opportunity to acquire in-depth experience and a relevant professional qualification. "We've been running this programme for six years," says Gillam. "There's a 100% success rate with those having a permanent job with us at the end of the programme." L&Q has won a National Training Award for its graduate training programme.

Some training is compulsory. The local induction is attended by David Montague, who meets every joiner. Everyone attends a two-day course on customer service provided by US guru Mary Gober. L&Q grows its own talent. Most promotions are internally-sourced (one in 10 is an external appointment at manager level), and 42% of managers are female, with 32% of managers from a BME background.

Corporate Social Responsibility
There is a governing board of 12 people, including David Montague, which ensures that all relevant laws and regulations

are complied with. L&Q actively encourages resident participation in its governance and many residents sit on committees of operating divisions. Indeed residents state that 'integrity' is an attribute they strongly associate with L&Q.

L&Q invests heavily in its people, not only because of the statement that satisfied staff have satisfied customers. There is a formal policy to ensure its communications procedures are totally compliant with the Information and Communication with Employees (ICE) legislation.

Equal emphasis is placed on health and safety issues, while a quality manager ensures L&Q adheres to all its business promises. The organisation complies with the National Housing Federation's code of governance, "Competence and Accountability," and has implemented measures to meet the six core principles of good governance set out in Public Services standards.

On environmental issues, there are green champions in L&Q's offices and on its house building side. In the offices, the green champions raise the profile. There are recycling bins, low energy light bulbs (plus staff are given them to use at home), energy-efficient toilets, no-plastic-cup policy, etc. Anyone caught leaving their monitors switched on overnight is 'named and shamed.' There's a cycle-to-work scheme and allowance, car sharing, and blogs on the intranet to share experiences of what's been learned. Procurement is London-wide with ethical sourcing as a key driver, particularly in packaging and stationery. Staff are encouraged to use public transport wherever possible when travelling on business.

"Every home we build will be to an eco standard," says Nicholls. "Indeed we strive to go beyond the standard. We have three objectives of maximising customer satisfaction, growing the business and building greater communities with CSR guidelines." L&Q aims to provide more opportunities through youth, elderly, job creation and educational programmes. L&Q is the developer employing consultants to design, and contractors to build, all its homes.

Time off is granted for volunteering purposes. Staff were in the 2008 Sunday Times Leadership Challenge, a competition where volunteers helped communities in Africa. L&Q was one of four teams that travelled to Africa to help build a schoolhouse and raise funds. Staff have also worked with the Remploy organisation which assists those with disabilities back into work – four offices are helping out by offering work experience (e.g. in administration, telephone answering and using technology).

Facts and figures

Total number of staff: 1,070
Office location: London, and 14 offices spread across L&Q's territory
Industry sector: Housing Trust, providing affordable homes in London and South East
Annual turnover: £230m with a surplus of £44m

LIVERPOOL VICTORIA

LV=

County Gates
Bournemouth
BH1 2NF

Telephone: 01202 292 333
Email: recruit@lv.com
www.lv.com

Pay and Benefits	★ ★ ★ ★ ★
Training and Development	★ ★ ★ ⯪ ☆
Career Development	★ ★ ★ ★ ☆
Working Conditions	★ ★ ★ ★ ★
Company Culture	★ ★ ★ ★ ☆

Biggest plus
Everyone is happy to work here – and it shows.

Greatest challenge
Keeping up with the company's pace of growth.

Summary

LV= is the UK's largest Friendly Society, providing insurance, protection, retirement, savings and investment products and advice. Group profit before tax in the year ended 31 December 2007 was £56.4m (2006: £113.7m) reflecting weaker investment markets in 2007. However, Group operating profit, which reflects long-term investment returns, recovered to £49.6m in 2007 from a loss of £20.1m in 2006.

About the organisation

The roots of the Group go back to 1843 when it was founded by William Fenton. The organisation has changed out of all recognition since then, of course, but one thing remains the same: it is still a mutual organisation. As such, it has no external shareholders to appease. It exists solely for the benefit of its members and customers – all 2.5 million of them.

In 2007, the Group changed its name from Liverpool Victoria to LV=. This was much more than a cosmetic rebrand. The newly appointed senior management team wanted to ensure that, while remaining a Friendly Society, it would operate with all the efficiency and business rigour of a quoted company. This spirit underlines the Group's internal ambition to be "Sharp with a heart." As Group chief executive Mike Rogers puts it, "We combine the trusted behaviours of a mutual with the competitiveness you'd expect from a successful plc."

Since Rogers's appointment in 2006, he has taken strides to position the Group as a consistently relevant and effective provider of financial services, better harnessing the advantages of its attractive customer base and its financial strength. This has meant exiting some poorly performing areas such as credit cards and its whole of market business. The turnaround in Group operating profit underlines the effectiveness of this strategy.

The Group has also pursued an aggressive expansion policy. It acquired Britannia Rescue in Huddersfield; Tomorrow, a retirement solutions business in Hitchin; and Highway Insurance plc in Essex, all in recent months. As a result, in the year to November 2008, it employed around 4,000 people in 14 UK locations compared to 3,000 in seven locations at the same time in 2007.

Corporate governance is well to the fore at LV=. As an insurance company the society is governed by the FSA and all of its board members are approved by it.

»

Every member of staff involved in transactions is given some sort of compliance training. The company is noted for its good customer service – it has consistently been voted in the top three for this quality in independent surveys.

Company Culture

There is a strikingly distinct feeling about this company. For a large organisation, it has a small, almost family feel. People definitely seem to enjoy working here. This is no doubt partly due to its Friendly Society ethos, as well as its air of building success and sharpening its focus. In 2007, employee engagement rose from 64% to 75% as measured by an independent researcher, close to its target of 80% which it feels is appropriate for a high-performance company.

The senior management is keen to ensure that the rapid and significant expansion does not change the company's culture. Enormous efforts are made to integrate the new people into the LV= fold. Whenever a company is acquired, the CEO and senior leaders are always on hand at the relaunch to welcome them.

Having no external shareholders to pander to does seem to foster a different air. As head of internal communications Karen Sharpe puts it, "While we are responsible to our members to get the best value for them, it is not a business where we have to squeeze short-term profit from everything. This enables us to behave in a more transparent way."

This has often been endorsed by independent observers. For example, the *Sunday Express* scored its life assurance call centre very highly when it investigated it in October 2007. "We felt it was more concerned with putting the customer before trying to sell its products," it wrote.

This is clearly a company which knows where it's going – and it's not wasting time getting there. This means that there is a real buzz about its offices. It also means that the work is both exciting and demanding. "If you're not willing to take personal responsibility, you won't get on here. But if you care and want to make a difference, you will succeed," says Sharpe.

Innovation and Creativity

The first thing that's different about LV= is its new brand and identity, the result of a great deal of research and planning. It won the Best Brand in Financial Services in the 2007 Design Week Benchmarks Awards. The judge commented that "this new, well-applied identity breathes fresh life into this brand."

"We combine the trusted behaviours of a mutual with the competitiveness you'd expect from a successful plc"
(Mike Rogers, Group chief executive)

"If you care and want to make a difference, you will succeed here" (Karen Sharpe, head of internal communications)

The company's internal communications reflect this energy and vibrancy. Its stylish and state-of-the-art Intranet, 'Heartbeat,' allows staff to see video clips of the CEO and his team using their broadcast-quality video equipment. The Intranet also carries information about new TV ads and much more to help people feel part of the Group wherever they are in the UK.

A recently launched recognition scheme allows anyone to nominate a colleague (or themselves!) for an extra-special behaviour award. The nominations state what the nominee did, why it was special and which of the company's values this behaviour embodies. The nominations are assessed and points are allocated to the successful person, which can be redeemed for vouchers. There is also a suggestion scheme, and the best ideas submitted to this also receive points as well as feedback on use.

Pay and Benefits

LV= has now benchmarked all its core staff salaries, ensuring there are no anomalies within its rapidly expanding group. The company is a mid-market payer in terms of salary, but is continuing to increase its other benefits.

For instance, it has recently launched its 'Your Choice' flexible benefits package. This has all the benefits one would expect of a modern programme, including shop vouchers that can be used in an array of high street stores and gives them an extra 10% buying power. During a three-week period in December, employees can change any or all of the benefits: buy or sell holidays, buy more PMI or dental insurance and so on, at better rates.

The company regularly consults its people through its 'Engage' programme. Last year, for instance, it asked them what they would like to see: they answered, more part-time working, and training during normal working hours. These requests and others have since been implemented.

Bonuses have continued to improve. In 2008 there was a greater bonus payment than in previous years, rising from £3.1m in 2007 to £5.5m. This is now part of the review process, and it looks not just at what employees did but how they did it. The bonus can be worth up to 30% of salary.

"Our growth has led to huge opportunities and immense prospects" (Karen Sharpe, head of internal communications)

Other benefits include Healthy Steps, an online health and well-being programme; a healthcare plan; and 'Workmates,' a scheme which rewards people who refer friends to join LV= with up to £1,000. There is also a well-funded sports and social club which arranges evenings out such as theatre trips and other events. Milestones and successes are always noted and celebrated at LV=, adding to the 'wow' factor that comes from working here.

Career Development

At LV= career development begins on day one with a well-planned induction process. The whole welcome programme has been revamped and updated: new recruits will definitely meet members of senior management, be shown videos and generally be given an excellent introduction to the company and its culture.

New joiners also receive a presentation from one of the staff. This looks at their career trajectory and shows how it is possible to move across disciplines within the organisation. Having doubled its UK locations in little over a year, this is even truer today.

Training has been realigned. Following the appointment of a new HR director in 2008, a whole raft of developments has been introduced. A key part of this was to bring a lot of previously outsourced training back in house, allowing the company to do it 'their way.'

There are more opportunities now than ever before for ambitious people to succeed at LV=. Sharpe: "Our growth has led to huge opportunities and immense prospects. In a growing organisation, everyone has more opportunities – and we always recruit from within if possible. What's essential is to have the right attitude and approach. We can provide skills, but we can't change attitudes."

A new course, 'Becoming a Leader,' fosters talent management, with over 65 people attending to date. Four additional leadership programmes are in the pipeline, each one being sponsored by a member of the Executive team. While LV= hires graduates, it does not yet have a formal graduate recruitment programme. This is expected during the next year.

Appraisals take place three times a year. Personal development is very much a value of the company, and there is a lot of scope for managing your own career. LV= will fund people through the entire range of insurance exams, and has been known to put an entire ten-person team through CII qualification.

Corporate Social Responsibility

CSR is taken seriously at LV=, as demonstrated by its creating the role of Corporate Social Responsibility manager. There are many examples of this policy in action, including £17,000 worth of matching charitable donations.

LV= was an official call centre for Sport Relief. It took nearly 3,000 calls, which led to a total of £100,000 being pledged. Its Heart of Business charity prize draw encouraged IFAs to donate £60,000 to their chosen charities. The company continues to sponsor Streetwise and Kidzone, and gives financial support to the Croydon Opportunity Pre-School Group that takes care of disabled children. It also sponsors the Studyflex management course at local schools in Bournemouth, Croydon and Bristol.

In 2008 it promised to donate 50p to charity for each proxy form received from its members. This raised £15,000. LV= also donated its old PCs to Oxfam, which cleaned and reused them. Following the corporate rebrand, the company sent its redundant stock – including items such as t-shirts, umbrellas and stationary that carried the old branding – to an orphanage in Africa.

LV= plays its part in the green revolution. In 2007 the company recycled 169 tonnes of paper and cardboard – the equivalent weight to over 30 African elephants! It has also introduced binless offices, encouraging people to use less packaging and disposable bags.

Individual units often contribute directly to the community. Recently its Bournemouth Group Risk Management team armed itself with paint brushes and scaffolding and renovated the interior of a local church that runs many community-based activities. Altogether, volunteer projects across the Group have involved 180 employees.

The company has 'cycle days,' on which it encourages people to cycle to work in return for a small reward like a free bacon sandwich. There are also walk to work days, and the Bournemouth head office operates a park and ride scheme.

Facts and figures

Total number of staff: 4,000
Office location: Bournemouth, Croydon, Exeter, Bristol, Hitchin and others
Industry sector: Financial services
Group pre-tax profit: £56.4m

MᴄCᴀɴɴ Eʀɪᴄᴋsᴏɴ

● ● ● ● ● ● ●

McCann Erickson Advertising

7-11 Herbrand Street
London
WC1N 1EX

Telephone: 020 7837 3737
Fax: 020 7837 3773
Email: contact.us@europe.mccann.com
www.mccann.co.uk

Pay and Benefits	★ ★ ★ ★ ☆
Training and Development	★ ★ ★ ★ ★
Career Development	★ ★ ★ ★ ⯪
Working Conditions	★ ★ ★ ★ ☆
Company Culture	★ ★ ★ ⯪ ☆

Biggest plus
A top advertising agency with real heart and soul.

Greatest challenge
Delivering on the raised expectations it now has as a people manager.

Summary

McCann Erickson London offers creative and development services for broadcast, digital, print and outdoor advertising, as well as campaign planning and management services. McCann Erickson Advertising is the second largest agency in the UK ranked by billings. It has 270 employees in the London office. McCann Erickson is part of McCann Worldgroup, with agencies in 160 cities in 111 countries, offering expertise in Public Relations, Brand Identity, Relationship Marketing, Events and Promotions, Media Services and Advertising.

About the organisation

McCann Erickson is a powerhouse in advertising. Flush with awards, it has a UK client list that speaks for itself: MasterCard, Intel, L'Oreal, Microsoft, Nestle, Sony Ericsson and Hewlett Packard to name but a few. McCann says it aims to create the perfect blend of creativity, effectiveness and innovation to help grow the brands in its care. The London agency annual billings amount to around £100m.

McCann has departments dedicated to Planning, Account Management, Digital, Creative, Project Management, Art Buying and TV Production. It also has some specialist services in-house, including Pulse (insights and analysis on trends, culture and future projecting); Loveurope (print and production): Chrome (audiovisual content); and McCann Business (integrated marketing solutions to clients).

Management changes at the beginning of 2008 saw the introduction of a flat management structure. In addition to chief executive Chris Macdonald, the Management Team comprises Nikki Crumpton as the chief strategy officer, the two creative directors, Simon Learman and Brian Fraser, and Alex White as chief financial officer.

McCann London states two objectives: to set new standards for the industry and to be one of the best places to work. One should follow the other. McCann has put a lot of work into culture, trends and insights, exploiting the latest communications channels including digital media, and articulating and delivering a clear vision. "We believe an idea is only as good as the demand it creates and to create that demand the idea must plug the brand into the culture that it needs to connect with," says Crumpton. "That's why we believe in the power of cultural connections."

Company Culture

As you would expect, the culture at McCann is vibrant, buzzing and fun. But it has been taking great strides to make itself an even better people manager. McCann conducted an 'Climate Survey' early in 2008 through quantitative and qualitative employee surveys. The highest ratings came back on confidence in the new management and the future of the agency; the value of the open approach to communications and the effective transmission of information; and clarity that each individual knew how they could pay a bigger part in the company.

"This led to a complete re-engineering of our HR practices and revitalised how we shaped our internal environment," says Barry Richards, head of HR. A new logo and new website were outward expressions but the agency never lacked confidence in its creative work. But now it felt energised internally. "It's how we communicate and instil our culture that has really changed." says Macdonald. "We've created a real cultural democracy. Everyone who works here knows why they are here and what they are here to do."

The 'Welcome' experience for new joiners was revised: 'McCann Do' days were created to stimulate teamworking and generate great thinking; a mentoring and buddy programme was introduced; and a new Intranet was developed to boost communication. Monthly meetings are looked forward to, where people can stand up and describe their 'three favourite ads.' There are creative collaboration workshops involving the whole agency. The appraisal system was reviewed to incorporate the agency's vision and objectives.

The Human Resource function at McCann plays a vital role, and glues the Agency together. Richards suggests that this role includes making sure that people are happy, are well looked after, and have a strong moral code.

The nature of being a local agency in a global network is that each has its own local flavour, "or particular flavour of McCann-ness." The London agency has that. The creative and stimulating environment is tangible from the moment you enter the West End office with creative scribblings adorning the walls and ceilings.

"When people join McCann, they've made a conscious decision to come to a big agency. And they want to get trained."
(Barry Richards, head of HR)

"...the HR department here is celebrated as somewhere you can always go to"
(Chris Macdonald, chief executive)

Innovation and Creativity

You don't become the second largest advertising agency in Britain without creativity being lifeblood. McCann works hard to nourish its creative culture and keep it cutting edge.

Words are an inadequate way to describe creative advertisements. But some of the following recent campaigns, which follow the approach of 'cultural connections,' may be familiar: 'Good with food' (the Co-operative); 'Aah! night' (Bisto); 'We know why you fly' (American Airlines); 'No one grows ketchup like Heinz'; and 'There are some things money can't buy. For everything else there's Mastercard.'

McCann drives the cultural debate to spawn ideas that consistently connect with consumers and their cultural context. In 2007 it revealed a 'Moody Nation.' From that it developed the ways of thinking that would increase a brand's success – or ARK brands – and then tracked the impact of a change of Prime Minister and how that would affect issues pertinent to its clients. This exercise has been extended further as McCann monitors the mood of the nation this year in 'Moodier Britain.' It is also 'agitating' the Obesity Debate, examining ways that brands can be part of the solution, not feeders of the problem.

To sharpen staff members' digital skills further, 'Digital Evangelists' volunteer to take on and learn about one aspect of digital (for example display advertising, search, virals or digital planning) and then act as evangelists and knowledge distributors to the rest of the Agency; They write, star in and produce their own little information films to get their findings across.

Pay and Benefits

Remuneration is benchmarked against the industry standard based on information gathered by the Institute of Practitioners in Advertising (IPA) from leading agencies. Head-hunters and recruitment companies also provide market information on pay and benefits.

McCann then aims to hit the upper quartile, along with agencies of similar stature. Advertising agencies are always under close scrutiny from clients in terms of pay, rations and overhead ratios. There is not usually much fat in these businesses.

A management incentive programme operates on various performance criteria, with an annual pool of »

"We've created a real cultural democracy" (Nikki Crumpton, chief strategy officer)

(from left to right) Brian Fraser, executive creative director; Nikki Crumpton, chief strategy officer; Simon Learman, executive creative director; and Chris Macdonald, chief executive

cash lying in wait. Once the pool has been filled, usually determined by revenue and profit growth, local management recommend how it is emptied to each individual. Long-term incentives in the form of restricted stock units are granted to senior management. "Because of the success of the agency, the pool has become big enough to offer to more people," says Richards. More than 25% of staff had a share of the pool last year. "It's a meritocracy," adds Richards. "You always get the chance of jumping in the pool next year."

A flexible benefits scheme was set up two years ago and McCann encourages employees to create their own perfect combination. Core benefits might include pension – the company matches contributions up to 6% – group income protection and medical insurance. The comprehensive range of flexible benefits includes additional holidays, additional life cover, the cycle to work scheme, and childcare vouchers.

There is a raft of fringe benefits including free breakfasts in the agency, free fruit bowls, a 'Looks Good Naked' running club (but no need to be alarmed), discounts on the local gymnasium, bars and shops, and on-site massage and reflexology. Friday afternoon tea and cakes has become an institution, while less sober events include the legendary seasonal parties. The summer party has seen the McCann High School recreate an entire fairground, while at Christmas a Soho Club is taken over, with black tie and an ice sculpture of the McCann building the order of the day.

Career Development

"When people join McCann, they've made a conscious decision to come to a big agency," says Richards. "And they want to get trained." So early on there's a lot of dialogue about aspirations, the job specification, what training people have had to date or feel is still missing.

McCann Erickson won an IPA distinction award for its training. It celebrated by increasing its training budget by 25% in the current year. McCann employs an in-house trainer and training begins from the day that you join, when a bespoke programme is put together for each individual. "It's now a two-way street," says Richards. "We want you to enjoy your job and what you're doing and both sides must input." Regular 360 degree appraisals lead to inputs and outputs and you meet the trainer again within 14 days of each appraisal.

If you've got talent, progress can be quick. There is also the opportunity to do a three-month placement at another advertising agency on an exchange programme. "It's a very good programme for someone who is fast-tracking to go off somewhere else, learn, and bring things back," suggests Richards. However, as Fraser and Learman explain, Creatives don't live by the same rules. Effectively they are building their own 'book' or portfolio of work. They don't move from junior creative to senior creative; creatives don't need job titles. Instead it's all about delivery, fighting for the best briefs, and delivering great creative work while training might be more like a day off to see a great exhibition. The one critical step would be from creative to creative director.

What types of people does McCann Erickson look for then? According to Tara Howell, Client Services director: "A good people person in terms of managing relationships; the intelligence that comes with original and diagonal thinking and marketing nous, to understand instinctively how to sell things, that brands have emotions and passions attached to them. They also need to be people who we all enjoy having at the pub at the end of the day!"

Corporate Social Responsibility

The agency has been ratcheting up what it can contribute to good CSR. First there are the little green things like turning off the office lights at 9pm instead of 11; photocopying on both sides of paper; and asking (and answering) "why don't we use tap water instead of bottled?" Initiatives are driven by the Agency's 'Green Team,' which is also responsible for all recycling, sourcing eco-cars instead of gas guzzlers, and tending to the agency's (legal) herb rooftop garden. An annual 'Green Day' captures achievements to date and discusses what more can be done.

McCann does much for charity. It has been contributing to the National Advertising Benevolent Fund for many years and does a lot of work supporting its favoured charity, Great Ormond Street Hospital for Children. It also helps vicariously through its clients, for example donating a day at a TV advert shoot as a prize for a client's charity auction. McCann does pro bono work in the form of free advertising for organisations such as Médecins Sans Frontières and sends planning staff to work on other charity projects.

In its staff survey, the highest score (98%) was for 'no restriction on any type, colour, creed, age, sexual orientation or religion.' "It was very compelling," says Macdonald. "People just don't see any differences."

Over 53% of the Agency is female. Meanwhile, advertising will always attract young people in droves, with the highest proportion at McCann being in the range 26-30. There is no ageism here. Barry Richards himself has been with McCann for no fewer than 25 years, providing extraordinary consistency in an industry not particularly renowned for high profile HR functions (or even an HR department at all).

HR is of course the custodian of guidelines, policies and entitlements but it is much more proactive than that. It plays a pivotal role in helping the agency get things done, such as its Green Team, the Digital Evangelists and of course the staff survey. It's also very much about how the agency deals with staff. "We want to support people, not leave them to sink or swim," says Macdonald. "And the HR department here is celebrated as somewhere you can always go to."

Facts and figures

Total number of staff: 270
Office location: London West End (with three regional offices in the UK)
Industry sector: Advertising
Annual turnover: £100m

i'm lovin' it®

McDonald's

11-15 High Street
East Finchley
London N2 8AW

Telephone: 020 8700 7000
www.mcdonalds.co.uk

Pay and Benefits	★ ★ ★ ★ ★
Training and Development	★ ★ ★ ★ ☆
Career Development	★ ★ ★ ★ ⯨
Working Conditions	★ ★ ★ ★ ⯨
Company Culture	★ ★ ★ ★ ★

Biggest plus
Real opportunities, real career progression that you can easily work around your life.

Greatest challenge
Doing a better job of showing and sharing the good work it is doing.

Summary

McDonald's has operated in the UK since 1974 and now has nearly 1,200 restaurants nationwide, including 700 drive-through outlets. Many restaurants are run by franchisees, which now account for 50-55% of the total. Restaurant locations range from high streets to airports, roadhouses to bowling alleys. McDonald's UK has around 72,000 staff, the majority of whom are paid hourly or work part time. They serve more than two million customers each day. The UK company is a wholly owned subsidiary of the McDonald's Corporation, one of the world's best-known brands, with over 30,000 restaurants around the globe.

About the organisation

McDonald's continues to grow at a tremendous rate in the UK. In the last financial year, sales reached £1.8bn, representing a comparable annual increase of 10%. August 2008 has just been recorded as its busiest month on record.

The company has spent considerable time and money reinvesting in and re-imaging restaurants to improve their look and décor, with staff even wearing smart Bruce Oldfield-designed uniforms as part of the revamp. It's doing this at a rate of 200 a year. A lot of work has also gone into extending opening hours.

The operating platforms in the kitchens have changed too, allowing McDonald's to offer customers a wider variety of food. Renowned for its burgers, the extension of menu choice has included salads and new breakfast items. Since their launch, McDonald's has sold over 25 million salads and 21 million fruit bags. In a year, it sold nearly 400,000 bags of carrot sticks and 1.6 million servings of porridge.

These initiatives have all contributed to a very healthy performance of the business, creating 4,000 new jobs as a result and defying the credit crunch.

"The past year has been a tricky one for any business involved in food retail but we're delighted that consumer confidence in the great value food you get in McDonald's restaurants has meant that our business performance has remained buoyant," says Steve Easterbrook, chief executive officer, McDonald's UK.

Franchising has also been on an upward trend. "We've identified the top performing franchises over the past five or six years to help us decide who we want to grow with," says Richard Forte, director of operations . A franchisee typically has 4-5 restaurants and one franchisee in Central London has 24. "This increasing size also increases the ability to invest over the long term. We're seeing all business performance indicators improve," adds Forte.

Company Culture

Key senior management changes, which in addition to Steve Easterbrook include chief people officer David Fairhurst, have coincided with an accelerated business performance and a more formal approach to talent management.

It's not unusual for employees to stay with McDonald's long term. The average length of service for a manager exceeds 10 years and even for part-time workers is a remarkable two-and-a-half years. "People can see opportunity," says Forte. "Even if you are working part-time over weekends, it's quite likely that your manager started the very same way." People with ambition can progress all the way – and quickly.

McDonald's values include open communication, respect, honesty, teamwork and integrity. These values are articulated and lived out by the leadership and cascaded down. Of course its values are rooted in the US but McDonald's UK sees itself very much as a modern, progressive burger company, a British organisation working in its local communities with distinct local characteristics.

This is an integrated company. Almost half the executive team started on the restaurant floor, and frequently visit the restaurants to meet the teams. One day each year, all head office staff visit the restaurants to live and breathe the operation. All new office recruits spend around two weeks training in-store.

McDonald's is open, communicative and invites feedback. The recent opinion survey had an 80% response rate – particularly high for hourly-paid staff. "The level of pride in the company highlighted in these surveys is overwhelming," says Forte.

Work-life balance is fundamental to McDonald's and indeed, 'flexibility' is one of the four key elements of the Employee Value Proposition. Workers can swap shifts, choose their hours, work around family or study commitments, and even choose to work with friends and family members. This focus on staff has brought rewards and awards, including *Caterer and Hotelkeeper's* 'Best Places to Work in Hospitality' in 2008.

Innovation and Creativity

McDonald's 'Plan to Win' framework embraces Place, Product, Promotion, People and Price. It's how the organisation engages strategic idea formulation among leadership, franchisees and others to flag ideas 2-3 years out. "The process engages stakeholders and gets buy-in so that ideas are executable and have a positive effect on the business," says Forte.

A 'Place Team' is charged with looking at the store of the future, supported by a dedicated laboratory in the US that performs time and motion studies. Much work goes into both sides of the restaurant counter, including using technology to order food and redesigning the traditional queue-order-food model as customers often say 'it doesn't need to be that fast.' Meanwhile free Wi-Fi access in all restaurants explains why you see many laptops in McDonald's.

The 'McPassport' initiative verifies training and core skills and enables hourly-paid employees to work abroad in 26 participating countries, often when English speakers are needed. At the 2008 Beijing Olympics, a crew of five experienced the working holiday of a lifetime.

Reflecting increasing confidence of the brand, McDonald's set up www.makeupyourownmind.co.uk for the public to query anything about McDonald's food, business, people and practices. 'Quality Scouts' (independent members of the public) go behind the scenes at McDonald's and its suppliers to find out for themselves and then report back on the site.

Pay and Benefits

"Rewarding performance is a key driver of our business," says Nicky Ivory, Reputation and Resourcing consultant. "We're

"Consumer confidence in the great value food you get in McDonald's restaurants has meant that our business performance has remained buoyant" (Steve Easterbrook, chief executive officer)

competitive within our market but we urge employees to assess the whole package." Little wonder – many benefits are offered to even the most junior employees. Benchmarking against competitors means retailers as well as restaurants, including Marks & Spencer and Tesco. "We pay what we believe is right and benefits are an enhancement," says Ivory. "The length of service makes us confident we are getting this right."

An annual pay rise is based upon performance, plus any standard raises across the board. Performance generally monitors personal competencies; individual restaurant business results; and restaurant managers also have their own goals, including training, environment, food safety, recruitment, and so on. Management might have up to 35-40% of salary paid as a bonus. The guiding principles are the overall performance of the (UK) company, plus individual performance variables.

Hourly-paid staff can also earn a monthly bonus, based on a mystery shopper programme with each restaurant visited twice a month to evaluate service, quality of food, and cleanliness.

A sabbatical programme after 10 years' service entitles that person to eight weeks' paid holiday in addition to the six weeks granted annually. A pro rata calculation on holiday is made for part-time workers, based on 24 days a year.

A stakeholder pension scheme is offered to all, with 3-10% staff contributions matched by the company. There is free life insurance and private medical cover is extended to spouse and children. Other benefits include assistance with home telephone calls, free food whilst at work and an employee discount card. Restaurant managers receive a company car (or cash option). All benefits can be viewed on McDonald's 'Our Lounge' employee website, which also covers areas such as advice, support and assessing learning needs.

Career Development

"Around 80% of restaurant managers started as crew, and almost half the executive team and franchisees started out by working in restaurants," says Forte. It's fair to say that McDonald's training system facilitates progress through the organisation. "The culture here is based around spotting talent and working with it," adds Ivory. Indeed, the company assumes anyone can reach the top.

>>

"Around 80% of restaurant managers started as crew, and nearly half the executive team and franchisees started out working in restaurants" (Richard Forte, director of operations)

The structured training programme runs from the first day you join to when you first run your own restaurant – which could be within a year and leave you accounting for annual turnover of £1.5m. "Things happen quickly here," says Ivory. Restaurant managers find themselves responsible for all areas of business: an average of 60 work colleagues, budgets and P&L's, equipment, recruitment and local marketing. In a very busy environment that requires high energy levels, commitment and a customer-facing attitude, managers also need to spot emerging talent on the shop floor.

The trainee business manager programme lasts 20 weeks. "It's high investment – you need a lot of experience to run a multi-million pound restaurant," says Forte. And as you scale the management ladder, there is always a more senior manager responsible for identifying and delivering your next development needs.

Performance reviews feed into a personal development plan, which identifies next career steps. The in-house Hamburger University is the conduit that allows potential to progress. Its broad range of courses include project management, strategic presentation, and computing, as well as the bread and butter skills needed to run a restaurant.

There's flexibility to switch locations within the UK and many heads of business lines are spread across UK regional offices. There are also opportunities to work in Europe and on secondment to the US.

Which qualities thrive in this culture of progress and self-fulfilment? Ambition; a desire to assume positions of leadership and influence; and alignment with the values of the organisation, including teamwork. "It's an energetic job, and you can be on the shop floor for hours at a time. It's natural that you should want to be around people," says Ivory.

Corporate Social Responsibility

As a food business it's quite right that McDonald's puts good food provenance high on the bill. And dialogue with its customers shows that trust is building.

McDonald's works closely with its suppliers. Nearly everything is sourced locally, with McDonald's proud to support over 17,000 British and Irish farmers, all of whom work closely with McDonald's to ensure high standards of food quality and animal welfare,

whilst still enabling McDonald's to offer its food at competitive prices. Indeed, McDonald's was named best restaurant chain for animal welfare by the RSPCA in October 2008.

The obesity debate has encouraged McDonald's to be open and up-front in reducing salt, sugar and fat content of its foods, "We've done this because it's the right thing to do," says Forte.

Ray Kroc, the founder of McDonald's, has always said that if a business is profiting from a community it should put something back. Every restaurant is involved in a host of local schemes as well as supporting the company's global charity, Ronald McDonald House Charity, which provides nearby accommodation for the families of sick children who are in hospital.

McDonald's has for five years now been running a grass roots scheme in conjunction with the Football Association. Under the auspices of its Director of Football, the legendary Geoff Hurst, McDonald's has helped to train 11,200 youth football coaches in the community.

Flexibility of work attracts people at both ends of the age spectrum and McDonald's employees range from 16 to 80! A significant number of older workers come to McDonald's after retirement and often play a valuable 'grandfather' role in the restaurants. The gender split across the company, including managers, is roughly 50:50. Ethnicity is reflective of communities, providing local jobs for local people. McDonald's was the first high street brand to achieve the new Investors in People enhanced standard.

Employees asked the company to tackle the negative way in which the word 'McJob' is portrayed in the media. Within McDonald's you will only find McJob used in a positive way, enhancing the qualities that employees say they really value.

McDonald's has converted about two-thirds of its transport fleet in the UK to run on biodiesel, made from recycled restaurant cooking oil, with a view to converting the whole fleet by 2009. The company also invests heavily in energy efficiency of cooking equipment and heat exchangers, and is currently engaged on a trial to assess the feasibility of composting its packaging as part of its goal to have 0% waste to landfill. When it changed to designer uniforms the old fabric was even recycled into fuel pellets. These represent real environmental initiatives rather than statements.

Facts and figures

Total number of staff: 72,000 staff in the UK spread throughout the country
Office location: Head office in London and regional offices throughout the UK.
1,200 restaurants nationwide, including 700 drive-through operations
Industry sector: Restaurants
Annual turnover: Sales of £1.8bn

MemeryCrystal

Memery Crystal LLP

44 Southampton Buildings
London WC2A 1AP

Telephone: 020 7242 5905
Fax: 020 7242 2058
Email: info@memerycrystal.com
www.memerycrystal.com

Pay and Benefits	★ ★ ★ ★ ☆
Training and Development	★ ★ ★ ★ ☆
Career Development	★ ★ ★ ★ ☆
Working Conditions	★ ★ ★ ★ ★
Company Culture	★ ★ ★ ★ ★

Biggest plus
An inclusive culture, helping its people build successful and challenging careers through tackling complex work for strong clients.

Greatest challenge
Maintaining its high standards and friendly working environment as it expands and develops its business.

Summary

Memery Crystal was established in London 30 years ago, and has grown to become a highly respected independent firm that is known for a commercial practice that punches above its weight. With 22 partners and a total of 103 employees, Memery Crystal operates from a single site in London, thereby embodying a spirit of cohesiveness, collegiality and ease of management amongst its staff. The firm's main practice areas are corporate and commercial, real estate, dispute resolution, intellectual property and employment. In 2008, Memery Crystal's revenues increased by 7% to reach £14.9m.

About the organisation

One of Memery Crystal's founding partners, Peter Crystal, continues to work at the firm, giving this mid-sized London outfit a sense of identity and continuity. The practice has grown organically since its foundation in 1978, and has made its name in the crowded London legal market thanks to first-class expertise in corporate finance, real estate, tax, litigation, intellectual property and employment.

Best-known for its work advising small and mid-cap companies listing on the public markets, and also for mid-market mergers and acquisitions, a niche education practice and a top-rate commercial property team, Memery Crystal is built on a belief in strong and enduring relationships with both clients and staff.

The future retirement of Peter Crystal has led, in the last couple of years, to a period of navel-gazing and a handover of responsibility to the next generation. A new management team, under the leadership of managing partner Harvey Rands, was put in place in 2007, along with a more corporate-style board complete with new directors of human resources, marketing and finance.

Together, and following extensive consultation with staff, this team has worked in its first 12 months to draw up a list of visions and values for the business, and to fix strategic objectives. Managing partner Rands says the vision is now "to be a highly respected and profitable independent law firm". The values promise clients "Trusted business-focused advisers," "Individuality and Personal Responsibility," and a "Friendly and Supportive Approach."

In the summer of 2008 Memery Crystal published its first Career Development Programme, given to all employees and outlining three main areas of commitment: development of people, business-led training, and career and personal development. Director of Human Resources Michael Jones says: "This firm relies ›

"Our vision is to be a highly respected and profitable independent law firm"
(Harvey Rands, managing partner)

on the quality of its people for its success, and devotes substantial time and resources to training, mentoring and providing for the development of lawyers and support staff as contributing business partners."

Company Culture

With the introduction of a set of core values at Memery Crystal in 2007, the firm is now intent on incorporating those guiding principles into behaviour, both internally and externally. The values are reinforced and integrated into many aspects of the day-to-day business, being central to both individual performance reviews and new business pitches, for example.

One element that emerged from the consultative process that went into the values statement was a desire on the part of staff members for stronger internal communication. Management has therefore led a drive towards transparency and ownership of ideas and processes, and now uses working groups drawing upon members of staff of all levels in a wide range of activities, including the establishment of the new performance development review system, and the launch of a new Communications team.

In summer 2007, Memery Crystal launched its first internal newsletter, called Memo, distributed monthly with news of goings-on that are both business, social and personnel-related.

There's a commitment to work-life balance that is rarely found in larger law firms. 2007 saw the removal of a chargeable hours target for fee-earners that had required 1,500 hours' client work a year, and replaced by a minimum level of 1,150 hours. Many employees work part time, have flexible start or finish times, or regularly work from home. HR director Jones himself works four days a week.

On the social side, Memery Crystal has devoted serious energies to making the place a fun firm to work for, with the introduction of a bi-monthly office social where staff gather for drinks in a relaxed environment. In 2008, there was a large 30th anniversary party for staff at a venue overlooking the Thames, and there is also an annual Christmas party. A working group manages an allocated social budget, organising quiz nights, pool evenings and 10-pin bowling competitions, among other things.

Innovation and Creativity

Memery Crystal prides itself on remaining at the cutting edge of developments when it comes to issues affecting its clients and their industries, and has taken innovative steps in recent months to foster that mentality amongst its staff.

As an embodiment of one of its values – personal responsibility – the firm has introduced a programme whereby each individual is responsible for capturing information and innovation behaviours, and communicating that to others through team meetings, internal seminars or project reviews. Jones says: "We encourage people to become experts in their own particular fields, and by giving people personal responsibility and making them aware of the benefit of sharing knowledge, we are fostering innovation across the firm."

The firm recently introduced its first Career Development Handbook, which is a clear demonstration of their commitment to their people setting out their policies on Performance Development Reviews, Business-led Training, Career and Personal Development. Also a new induction package for temporary staff which, following a suggestion from a partner, was designed by secretarial co-ordinators to help integrate temporary staff quickly and make the best use of their productivity.

Memery Crystal has worked closely with a charity called Poetry in Wood, which gives opportunities for adults with learning difficulties to design and produce works of art in wood and mosaic, and the artwork is now displayed in the firm's meeting rooms.

Pay and Benefits

Memery Crystal benchmarks its remuneration using a range of survey data, and pays in the upper quartile within its peer group. The firm's salaries fall short of those offered at much larger City of London law firms, but Memery Crystal seeks to offer a balanced package of both financial and non-financial rewards to staff.

In May 2008, the firm introduced a revised Fee Earner Bonus Scheme for lawyers, bringing remuneration in line with the values of the business. The new scheme aims to incentivise and reward exceptional business contribution, and moves away from an hours-based bonus scheme to a much broader evaluation of performance and contribution. Bonus awards are now based on chargeable hours; fees billed; non matter-related contributions; core values; and teamwork. Employees who introduce new clients to the firm receive 10% of all the fees billed to that client in year one as a bonus, and there is a £4,000 bounty for introducing a new member of staff.

Other benefits include a 50% gym subsidy, a pension scheme, life assurance, health cover, travel insurance and enhanced maternity and paternity leave, the last two of which have now been extended »

"It's part of our culture. If someone wants to develop, we are happy to help them. It makes for a more rounded person" (Michael Jones, director of HR)

"This firm devotes substantial time and resources to training, mentoring and providing for the development of lawyers and support staff as contributing business partners"
(Michael Jones, director of HR)

to all staff as well as fee-earners. Holiday entitlements have also been harmonised across lawyers and support staff, with the minimum increasing from 22 days to 25 days a year. The opportunity to accrue extra days based on length of service means the maximum has risen from 28 to 30 days a year.

A career break of up to three months' unpaid leave is offered to those who have worked at the firm for more than five years: "People sometimes need the opportunity to recharge their batteries," says Jones. "The opportunity to take a break seems to us to be quite sensible."

Career Development

With low staff turnover, Memery Crystal seeks to promote from within, and half of its current partners have risen through the ranks.

The firm offers work experience placements and has fostered links with universities across the UK in a bid to attract a diverse array of strong candidates. In 2008 it introduced a vacation scheme for 12 students to spend a fortnight with the firm. On completion, they can opt to apply for training contracts at the practice, which are two years in duration and have around six successful recruits each year.

Graduates spend six months working in four different practice areas at the firm before qualifying as solicitors. Non-lawyers are also encouraged to develop, and the firm has sponsored various secretaries and junior staff in obtaining qualifications, with people passing exams from the Chartered Institute of Personnel and Development, the Institute of Legal Cashiers, and the Association of Accounting Technicians. "It's part of our culture," says Jones. "If someone wants to develop, we are happy to help them. It makes for a more rounded person."

Promotions from associate lawyer to partnership positions are now based on individual ability rather than length of service, and applicants are assessed according to their financial performance, the quality of their work, their values, wider contribution, professionalism, client skills and seniority.

Memery Crystal takes its training responsibilities seriously, not only with respect to legal developments and continuing professional training, but also with regard to business skills. In 2008 the firm launched a programme called Introduction to Corporate Finance, which taught secretaries in the corporate department about the work being undertaken by the lawyers in their team, so that the partners, fee-earners and secretaries could work more closely together on transactions.

In 2008, Memery Crystal spent £441,936 on training of fee-earners, and £15,780 externally on training for support staff. That combined overall investment of £457,716 represented just over 5% of the firm's entire basic salary bill.

Corporate Social Responsibility

Memery Crystal takes its responsibilities to the local community in which it operates very seriously, and traditionally individuals at the firm have raised funds for charity with the firm matching those amounts. In 2007 the firm formalised its approach and set up a charitable trust with an emphasis on supporting young people's development through education and sports, to which it gives a proportion of profits annually.

One outcome of the firm's Values Conference in 2007 was the establishment of a CSR Committee, which consists of pro bono volunteer work and charitable fundraising elements. The firm allows employees to spend up to 30 hours a year doing voluntary work, with two specific projects being the firm's School Volunteer Programme and its pro bono legal advice efforts.

Memery Crystal has linked up with the Globe Primary School in nearby Tower Hamlets, where a high proportion of pupils do not have English as their first language. Once a week a group of Memery Crystal staff, both lawyers and non-lawyers, go to the school to help children with their reading. Lawyers also volunteer at a law centre to give free legal advice to members of the public.

Two charity events a year are designed to raise money, and in 2008 staff took part in the Great City Race to raise funds for breast cancer charities. The firm also supports Poetry in Wood, which gives opportunities for adults with learning difficulties to design and produce works of art in wood and mosaic.

Memery Crystal believes the firm's make-up reflects the population better than many of its competitors: 59% of the workforce and one-third of partners are female, and more than 10% of employees come from ethnic minorities, including a wide range of nationalities from Finnish to American.

The firm has a long-running programme of waste reduction and recycling, and with offices in Central London, employees are encouraged to use public transport through season ticket loans. Photocopying machines are now programmed to print on both sides, and the firm has begun recycling plastic bottles with receptacles around the building.

In 2008 Memery Crystal introduced a Cycle to Work scheme, allowing staff to save 40% on bikes bought through the firm, and providing them with safe storage facilities during office hours.

Facts and figures

Total number of staff: 103 employees, including 22 partners
Office location: London
Industry sector: Legal
Annual turnover: £14.9m

Metro

Northcliffe House
Derry Street
London
W8 5TT

Telephone: 020 7651 5256
Email: talent@ukmetro.co.uk
www.metro.co.uk

Pay and Benefits	★ ★ ★ ☆
Training and Development	★ ★ ★ ★ ⯨
Career Development	★ ★ ★ ★ ⯨
Working Conditions	★ ★ ★ ★ ★
Company Culture	★ ★ ★ ★ ⯨

Biggest plus
An exciting brand, where the buzz, fun and energy are tangible.

Greatest challenge
Balancing the benefits of being a subsidiary of a much larger group.

Summary

Metro is the UK's fourth-largest national newspaper, and the biggest in London. The printed version is distributed free to morning commuters in London and 15 other UK cities, including Birmingham, Bristol, Edinburgh, Glasgow, Leeds, Manchester, Newcastle and Cardiff. It aims to provide a '20-minute read' founded on fact not opinion, to young 'urbanites.' There is also a digital 'e-Edition.' Metro employs around 250 people, of whom 60% are editorial staff. Most work at the London headquarters in Kensington, while smaller regional offices produce lifestyle sections for Scotland and English regions.

About the organisation

Metro hit the streets in 1999 as a free, stapled, colourful daily newspaper. Metro is designed to be a concise read and contains bite-sized national and international news wrapped around local information, including entertainment previews, listings, weather and travel. Metro delivers the key daily news stories of the day to readers in its own quick, politically unbiased and easily digestible format.

Metro is targeted at a unique market – information-hungry morning commuters that it calls 'urbanites.' With this young and affluent readership profile, Metro has developed a valuable niche-advertising proposition.

An immediate success from the outset, Metro has developed its brand and grown circulation rapidly. In just ten years it has raced from a standing to a circulation of 1.36 million nationally (around 750,000 in London). Every single weekday, over three million people up and down the country read Metro. Not surprisingly, this means that Metro is one of the biggest sellers of advertising space in the British newspaper industry.

There has been a big push into the digital age with an e-Edition of Metro and a convergence of other projects. Advertising Space is sold in print, online and on mobile platforms. Journalists write for both the printed and online versions of the newspaper.

Metro.co.uk covers everything you would expect from a national newspaper's website – 24/7 rolling news, sport, entertainment info, reams of video in Metro TV – and a lot more. It also wants visitors to have fun, so it selects the most entertaining stories and writes them in the wittiest way possible – as seen in the Weird, Fame and Metrosexual channels.

»

Metro recently launched MEview and MEmusic – digital platforms based on user-generated content (music and video clips) where people can earn money from their contributions.

Company Culture

"Metro wouldn't be in this strong position if we didn't have a highly talented and motivated team," says managing director Steve Auckland. "Talent and Culture is one of our five key business goals. We believe company performance starts and ends with people."

Employee surveys are taken seriously – and feedback is acted upon. The 2008 survey revealed even better ratings on communication and managers giving feedback. And 91% of employees said they are proud to work for Metro.

"People are here to do a job but there is a real culture of fun," says Karen Wall, assistant managing director. "It's very informal – it really is a lovely atmosphere." Metro has forged a successful formula where it is communicative, consultative and a fun place to work. It's apparent from the moment you enter the office.

The 'Metro Vision' team is tasked with making it a nice place to work and it's often those little things that make the difference: like free smoothies available in the kitchens, food at team meetings, or after-work cocktail parties. All offices are open plan and a 'Success Wall' encourages people to put up storyboards of a job done well. Led by Steve Auckland and editor Kenny Campbell, managers are very open, always accessible and get involved in just about everything.

HR is an active function. Many policies and initiatives are determined at Associated Newspapers Group level, including management development training and employment law issues. "Metro has flexibility in other areas," says Angela Bentley, head of Talent and Culture, "and one role is to keep things moving, listen, communicate, and help to make it a genuinely nice place to work."

"When I joined there were 21 vacancies so I soon got a good idea of the type of person that would fit in," adds Bentley. "I would describe them as 'sparky', proactive, want to develop, and are not afraid to challenge things and suggest ideas."

Innovation and Creativity

An e-Edition of Metro has recently been launched, meaning the paper is now available in both print and electronic media. Furthermore, the paper is created using a system that combines electronic page planning, electronic booking of advertisements, and digital storing of all images for print and web – the first paper in the Associated Newspapers Group to do this.

MEview and MEmusic are user-generated content sites that go well beyond an online version of the newspaper. MEview is a video sharing portal that rewards users financially for viewings of their video clips by sharing advertising revenues. It's a similar model for MEmusic. Both reflect the young urbanite readership of Metro and their inclination towards social networking sites.

"People look to Metro to be quirky," says Bentley. Advertisers never know what to expect next. Metro's media agencies were visited one day by Amy Winehouse and Pete Doherty lookalikes delivering detox juices to reinforce their approach!

'The Hub' does what it says on the tin. Except it's an online tin. The Hub is a web-based information source that allows Metro people to find out whatever they need to know about what's going in the company – news, benefits, training,

"People look to Metro to be quirky"
(Angela Bentley, head of talent and culture)

events, just about anything really. It's intuitive and interactive (on screen you see a busy desk – you need to work out which items on it to click on!).

Meanwhile the Company Soapbox is a twice-yearly communications platform where senior management report on progress across the business, show targets, and encourage new ideas.

Pay and Benefits

"We look to benchmark against our competitors and use agencies for this," says Bentley. Annual salary increases have become more transparent than in previous years with managers empowered, in a spirit of fairness, to explain why they have been given.

Commercial staff tend to have a lower base salary and a higher bonus, based on Group financial targets being met quarterly, but at senior level, this will also include individual targets. Most sales teams can double their salary this way, while for other commercial roles, including administration, marketing, research, distribution and finance, it is nearer 20%. These tend to be above market averages.

Editorial staff are paid salary only, but Metro is looking at introducing bonuses for editorial managers based on performance against their development plans.

The Group provides an increasingly rare phenomenon – a final salary pension scheme. The Group contributes 15% of salary, employees 5%, which can increase by a further 7.5% for those eligible for Pension Plus. There is private medical insurance. Also, health professionals, including nurses and nutritionists, visit the offices on quarterly 'health days' to give free consultations.

Other benefits are centred around work-life balance initiatives requested by employees. These include the cycle-to-work scheme, season ticket loans, childcare vouchers; local gymnasium membership; your birthday given as an extra holiday, and flexible working arrangements. These include home working, organising work around children and families, and sabbaticals. You can also flex your hours on any given day if agreed with your manager 24 hours in advance.

Quarterly Star Achievers are the top sales performers, nominated by their peers, and there are also £500 »

"Talent and Culture is one of our five key business goals" (Steve Auckland, managing director)

awards for Best Small Business and Best Big Business win. Managers have discretion to give an ad hoc 'thank you' for excellent individual performance, be that a £100 voucher or dinner for two at a leading restaurant.

Career Development

People development is one of Metro's top priorities and this starts from the day you join. The joiner's 'Welcome Box' is full of novelties and 'fun things' to accompany the usual company literature.

Induction is a welcoming process designed to give people a good idea of what Metro is about and what is needed to get involved. One-on-ones with your manager happen during weeks one, four and eight, and at the end of your probationary period. This process will identify what training and experience is needed. "We want to make sure that everyone is happy and ready to go," says Bentley.

All vacancies are advertised internally and Metro employees get one week first to apply for vacancies before the company looks externally. "I'd rather promote someone internally even if it's a big jump for them," says Bentley. There is an editorial graduate trainee scheme with three joiners placed onto the News Desk before being given permanent positions.

"Everyone gets a personal development plan," says Bentley. This is written following the appraisal meeting. The annual appraisal is an opportunity to get two-way feedback from employees on how the company is doing. It also assesses an individual's development needs and the roles that they wish to get into. The annual training budget exceeds £200,000 a year. People can indicate their 1-2-3 preferences and then specific training and development needs are worked out between Talent, managers and the individual, and their managers, balancing individual wishes and the interests of the business.

Managers are scored against core competencies and how they communicate with their teams. Talent produces 'skills maps' for each team within Metro. Metro has rolled-out 1-1 coaching sessions for its managers and these have proved to be very successful. Talent has been very astute in knowing how each individual responds to different learning methods to produce the best results.

Corporate Social Responsibility

Employees at Metro are roughly 50:50 male/female. There is a fairly wide spread of ages across Metro from 18 to 60 plus, with the average age around 30.

HR has diversity training and policies are reviewed regularly to ensure there are no barriers. Managers are trained in recruitment techniques and how to treat people from different backgrounds. Metro is very ethical in its business practices. Sales are very much above-board and Metro doesn't negotiate on advertising rates. Metro also has an approved suppliers' list which it sticks to – it doesn't try to 'get things for free.'

Metro's editorial mantra of 'facts not spin' is one that is still upheld rigorously. The emphasis remains on responsible reporting, free of political or campaigning bias. This policy is very effective in keeping the newspaper out of the libel courts.

Shelter is this year's nominated charity and Metro aims to raise £10,000. There's a host of activities to get people involved, including sports days, cake days and pub quizzes. Employees are given a day a year 'out of the office' to do voluntary work.

Metro of course generates paper, and a lot of it. Metro has launched a trial in six Tube stations, one of the main distribution points, to recycle newspapers and if successful the scheme could be extended. Alongside recycling solutions, advertising campaigns encourage readers to recyle their copy.

Metro carries features on its regular 'Green Metro' page to educate people to take their copy of Metro into work and recycle it there. Metro offers free recycling bins to offices – the first day of this initiative saw 250 bins given away.

Metro itself is printed on 80% recycled paper (production reasons limit it to this level).

Metro is part of the Mayor of London's Green Procurement Code, being the first newspaper to sign up, and is also part of London Green 500. Metro supports Trees for Cities – a green charity that works with local communities on tree-planting and landscaping projects.

The business itself is green in its own activities, to cut down on waste. Plastic cups and mobile phones are recycled; Metro uses Green Tomato taxi cabs, and bicycles for couriers instead of motorbikes; low-energy lighting and sensors; green stationery supplies; and energy-saving signs around office premises. There's a dedicated 'Green Day' in the office. "In our business, we have to make sure we do everything we can," says Wall.

Facts and figures

Total number of staff: 250
Office location: London (head office), plus 16 regional offices in the UK
Industry sector: Newspapers
Circulation: 1.36 million daily

Moorfields Eye Hospital
NHS Foundation Trust

Moorfields Eye Hospital NHS Foundation Trust

162 City Road
London EC1V 2PD

Telephone: 020 7253 3411
www.moorfields.nhs.uk

Pay and Benefits	★ ★ ★ ⯪ ☆
Training and Development	★ ★ ★ ⯪ ☆
Career Development	★ ★ ★ ★ ☆
Working Conditions	★ ★ ★ ★ ☆
Company Culture	★ ★ ★ ★ ☆

Biggest plus
A worldwide reputation for excellence in ophthalmic research, treatment and care.

Greatest challenge
Surviving in a world in which eye care would increasingly be delivered in community settings and operating out of buildings that are no longer 'fit for purpose.'

Summary

Moorfields Eye Hospital NHS Foundation Trust was founded in 1804 and opened in 1805. It is the oldest and one of the largest centres for ophthalmic treatment, teaching and research in the world. More patients in the UK come to Moorfields than to any other eye hospital or clinic because of its world-famous reputation, based on the expertise of its clinical staff and the cutting-edge research undertaken. Indeed, over half the ophthalmologists practising in the UK, and many more overseas, have received specialist training at Moorfields. The hospital and clinic offer a comprehensive and seamless internationally renowned ophthalmic service. Last year nearly 25,000 ophthalmic operations were carried out here.

About the organisation

Moorfields became one of the first Foundation Trusts established in the NHS and since then has taken full advantage of its public benefit organisation status. It has increased turnover by 12% on average for eight years running (to £105m in 2008-09) with 66% of its budget deriving from Primary Care Trusts around the UK and 16% from private treatments and commercial sales.

Complex ophthalmic cases (tertiary referrals) come to Moorfields from across the UK and further afield. In partnership with the Institute of Ophthalmology (part of University College London), Moorfields manages the largest ongoing ophthalmic research programme in the world. All this is only possible because of the unique combination of doctors, scientists and a variety of other clinicians, supported by state-of-the-art research at the Institute of Ophthalmology, who work together to provide a dedicated service that is second to none. "The doors are never closed here and everyone who walks through them, be they staff, patients, or friends and family, all are a part of the Moorfields community," says chief executive John Pelly.

Committed to providing the best possible care for patients, Moorfields employs some 1,400 people who work on 12 sites in and around London. Staff include ophthalmologists, ophthalmic nurses, optometrists, orthoptists, medical photographers, ophthalmic technicians, and many other specialists. Also employed are clerical, managerial and other professional staff, scientists and researchers, teachers and lecturers, catering and portering staff, all of whom are equally important in ensuring that high standards of care and treatment are maintained.

Moorfields Pharmaceuticals, the hospital's Pharmaceutical Manufacturing Unit, is typically producing small runs of specialist eye treatments (eye drops and injections) commissioned by clinicians and which large pharmaceutical enterprises find uneconomic to handle. It has also won its first license to actively sell »

"The doors are never closed here and everyone who walks through them, be they staff, patients, or friends and family, all are a part of the Moorfields community" (John Pelly, chief executive)

its first prescription product (preservative-free artificial tears), in the UK. It costs £0.35m to develop a license and takes some years, and there are further products in the pipeline and a sales force working the market. The future looks good.

Company Culture

"An understanding of why we are here constitutes the basis of our culture," says Ken Gold, Moorfields' director of personnel. "People are here to look after patients, to give great ophthalmic care. There is an understanding that we are the best, will carry on being the best and improve on being better." The staff at Moorfields are friendly, helpful and professional in their approach. They aspire to be world class – certainly as far as the patient sees it. There is an almost tangible buoyant and caring atmosphere permeating the hospital, and its satellites.

Communication with the staff is under constant review. There are departmental meetings, which utilise a bottom-up approach for staff to feed through suggestions, a weekly bulletin on the Intranet, a print magazine *Review* which is coincidentally also under review, and an annual staff survey, the outcome of which is passed to all the staff through the Intranet. The CEO is also keen to have more regular open sessions for staff.

"We are introducing email days where staff can email any director on any question and expect a reply within a day or days," says Gold. "We want to hear from the staff who are best placed to say how systems and processes work."

"The key HR message is that we are not just here to provide a slick service," says Gold. "The future of HR is in developing our staff. We ensure we have in place people who are adequately prepared for what they have to do and to develop."

A set of qualities including diligence and integrity makes a Moorfields person. An Employee of the Month award recognises such attributes as going the extra mile, not minding how long they stay for work, etc. "It's difficult to measure but makes it the place it is," says Gold. There is a project on celebrating staff successes now underway.

Innovation and Creativity

Moorfields is keen to keep and attract talented people for all the services it delivers at its sites. In October 2007 it took over Bedford Hospital Eye Unit and now provides ophthalmic services in that region. "We deliver care where the patient is," says Gold. "This continues to be a key plank in our strategy. Some 40% of our work takes place in our outreach units in and around London rather than at the City Road site." The Dubai hospital development continues to make progress and Gold indicates there is likely to be at least one other outreach site up and running

next year. Last year the Department of Health awarded Moorfields and the Institute of Ophthalmology Specialist Biomedical Research Centre Status, recognising its strengths in translational research.

An Academic Health Science Centre has also been established, focusing on research and linking Moorfields with University College, Royal Free, and Great Ormond Street Hospitals, and University College London as its academic partner. All are equal players in the venture which is seen as a model for the future, following developments in the US, Europe and the Far East. Research funding is under strategic review generally, but Moorfields is getting research monies.

Pay and Benefits

Working at Moorfields is in fact its own reward – anyone who wants to specialise in eyes will want to work there. All the staff are motivated by the care and assistance they can offer to patients. Most staff are paid on national NHS rates, including London weighting, which have been enhanced after the NHS Agenda for Change some four years ago. "The pay is around the average for the area," says Gold. "Doctors will progress along an incremental scale whereas non-doctors will progress along a scale not based on performance but on whether they have undertaken an agreed development plan. The theory is to have competency scales with scope for us to vary, as a foundation trust, and include collective bargaining." There are no performance-related pay or bonus schemes here. The strategy is to apply everything properly. "In addition we need to know what to do to deliver the business – good practice, provided it delivers the business, or best practice where there is no detriment," says Gold.

There is a generous benefits package: final salary pension scheme which is contributory; 27 days plus eight days public holidays, rising to 29 days and 33 days plus public holidays after five and 10 years' service respectively; investment in training and development; childcare voucher scheme; maternity and paternity leave – and parental leave; carers leave; adoption leave; flexible working opportunities; childcare voucher scheme; eye care facilities; ride to work scheme; telephone counselling scheme; season ticket loans; social activities; and many more discount opportunities.

However, working at Moorfields will provide something no (City) job ever could – but to appreciate that fact »
you have to have been a patient. The staff care.

"The future of HR is in developing our staff" (Ken Gold, director of personnel)

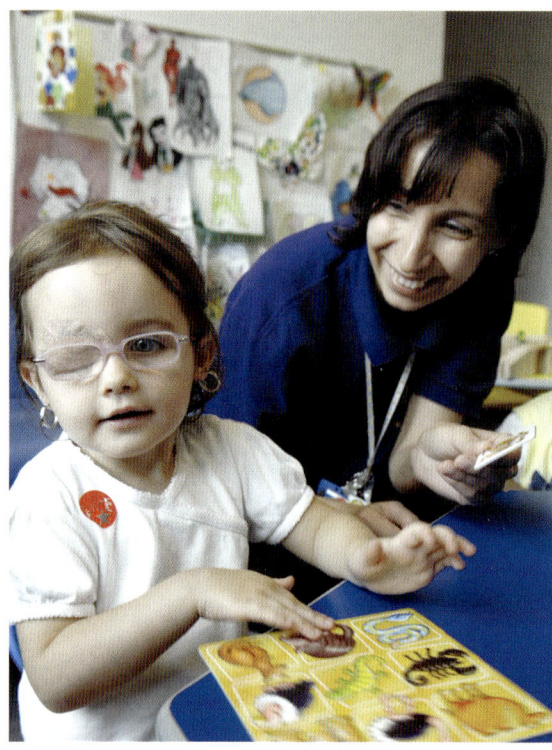

"We deliver care where the
patient is"
(Ken Gold, director
of personnel)

Career Development

"We value learning and development for our staff," says Gold. There are many opportunities to develop, with good representation across all disciplines. At any one time there are 70 junior doctors undertaking a core part of their 4.5 year training programme at Moorfields, plus the hospital supports the training of pharmacists. "The only area we experience any problems is with qualified pharmaceutical posts," says Gold. "It's one of the most difficult positions to fill because of the shortage of people and the fact that District General Hospitals offer a range of ailments to treat other than eyes."

Staff turnover is about 11% which is low for Central London (and lower still in the more senior positions at Moorfields). There are three graduate intake positions (from any background) in finance, HR and general management. A non-graduate trainee in general management would spend one year at the hospital, preceding that with a 20-day induction, and then move on to a 'real' job for a year. Someone with an academic qualification on a two-year programme would move on to another trust. The point to make is that job roles are developed as the hospital modernises the way patient care is provided and managed.

"We look for people who can demonstrate flexible thinking, pragmatism, drive, ambition, creativity and innovation, commitment to public service and, because of the stressful environment we naturally operate under, a keen sense of humour," says Gold.

A learning centre offers classroom and computer-based training, and also provides (mostly IT) training to other NHS organisations and European computer driving licence ECDL training – indeed Moorfields is an examining centre. Anyone studying for professional qualifications is encouraged to have a coach or mentor. Staff here have taken MBAs, other masters degrees, Open University degrees, accountancy and HR qualifications, NVQs, etc.

Corporate Social Responsibility

Moorfields is big on corporate governance and diversity. Over 50% of the staff are non-white, and on average the gender ratio is one-third male to two-thirds female. The biggest age band is 36-45, but there is also a noticeable bulge if one takes an 'over 50' reading, which is similar to the bump of 26-35 year olds. The hospital provides diversity and disability awareness training to all staff. A race equality scheme is in place plus a diversity forum for black and minority ethnic (BME) staff.

Moorfields operates similar corporate governance procedures that apply to any commercial organisation as well as the strictest clinical governance arrangements. The hospital is monitored by over 100 external bodies, most notably the Healthcare Commission, the Audit Commission, the National Audit Office, and the NHS's Foundation Trust Regulator Monitor. There is a director of corporate governance who heads up a department dedicated to ensuring that the highest standards of corporate governance are met.

Hitherto Moorfields has gained the "Improving Working Lives" national accreditation for being a model employer, as well as securing a *Nursing Times* award for being a good employer of nurses. Feedback from staff surveys and suggestion schemes is ongoing and continues to be used to improve conditions for the staff.

A 15-page environmental policy is available to all staff. While most transport is contracted out, many staff and patients arrive by public transport as the area is well served by excellent bus, Tube and train communication links. There are good bicycle parking facilities (there is no car park). An arrangement exists with Evans Cycles to provide bicycles at favourable prices for staff in a salary sacrifice scheme.

As part of compliance with the Disability Discrimination Act, the frontage of the hospital has been rebuilt and the Carbon Trust is to assess the carbon footprint of Moorfields' buildings. The site has been successfully utilising a CHP (combined heat and power) facility as part of its drive to reduce carbon emissions. Elsewhere, paper, printer cartridges, toners, drinking cups, old computer equipment, etc, are recycled, e.g. according to the Waste Electrical and Electronic Equipment (WEEE) directive regulations.

Yet the overriding key investment the hospital makes will remain the one it places in its patients, while a major emphasis will be placed on the continuing development of its staff to enable them to perform to the highest standards to treat the patients.

Facts and figures

Total number of staff: 1,400
Office location: London, and 12 sites in/around London
Industry sector: Healthcare – specifically eyes
Annual turnover: £105m, 66% from Primary Care Trusts, 16% from private treatments and commercial sales

Ofcom

Riverside House
2a Southwark Bridge Road
London SE1 9HA

Telephone: 020 7981 3000
www.ofcom.org.uk

Pay and Benefits	★ ★ ★ ★ ½
Training and Development	★ ★ ★ ★ ½
Career Development	★ ★ ★ ★ ½
Working Conditions	★ ★ ★ ★ ½
Company Culture	★ ★ ★ ★ ½

Biggest plus
The opportunity to work in the communications industry in a genuinely knowledge-sharing organisation.

Greatest challenge
Maintaining pace and energy whilst thinking for the long term: e.g. career paths and talent development.

Summary

Ofcom is an independent organisation responsible for regulating the UK's broadcasting, telecommunications (telecoms) and wireless communications sectors. In order to carry out its work it receives funding from the broadcast industry through licence fees communications providers and from the public purse via grant-in-aid. In 2007-08 it had operating expenditure of £130m.

About the organisation

Ofcom was formed at the end of 2003, inheriting the duties of five different regulatory bodies: the Broadcasting Standards Commission, the Independent Television Commission, the Office of Telecommunications (Oftel), the Radio Authority, and the Radiocommunications Agency.

Independent of Government but accountable to Parliament through the Communications Act 2003, Ofcom has a number of areas of responsibility. In the broadcasting arena it is charged with protecting audiences from offensive or harmful material, maintaining plurality of provision and ensuring the high quality and wide appeal of TV and radio programming. It also ensures optimal use of the airwaves used by a range of spectrum users. In telecoms, Ofcom works to ensure there is a wide range of electronic communication services – including high speed data services.

Ofcom is largely funded by the companies that it regulates; because its own costs are a net cost to its stakeholders it is committed to operating as efficiently as possible. Its budget for 2007/08 of £130.2m was the lowest so far and during the same financial year Ofcom repaid the remainder of the £52.3m loan from Government that covered the cost of its establishment. This year's budget has been set at £133.7m.

Ofcom has enjoyed a high profile since its inception. In the recent past it has heavily fined the BBC, GMTV and ITV over phone-in scandals, received thousands of complaints over the Big Brother/Shilpa Shetty controversy and fined Barclaycard for silent calls.

According to chief executive Ed Richards, "The interests of citizens and consumers are at the heart of everything we do at Ofcom. Whether it is technical spectrum policy or a decision concerning the Broadcasting Code, all of our work is driven by seeking to meet the interests of the UK's citizens and consumers."

>>

"Following a colleague survey we made some changes to our assessment and reward process to introduce greater clarity and transparency"
(Janet Campbell, head of HR)

Company Culture

"People who work for us need to have a real interest in the communications industry," says Janet Campbell, head of HR. "It's a fast-moving, ever-changing environment and that's reflected in the way we work." Campbell is based at Ofcom's London headquarters where the open-plan office layout encourages cross-functional teamwork – indeed, the ergonomic design reflects the knowledge-sharing culture throughout the whole organisation.

This is a genuinely inclusive place to work. All staff are known as 'colleagues,' regardless of their level of seniority – although the structure is in any case relatively flat – and everyone, from the chief executive downwards, can be directly contacted, whether by email or in person. Plainly it's also a customer-oriented environment. Whether taking calls from concerned members of the public or preparing an industry report for publication, colleagues never lose sight of the fact that Ofcom regulates on behalf of citizens and consumers.

A big part of the lifeblood of the organisation is the Colleague Forum. This is made up of elected representatives of the different business areas, and they meet regularly with senior managers for briefings and to work together on issues of collective concern. Another feature is the 'Inside Ofcom' educational events; these take place at lunchtime and can be on any subject of interest to colleagues – internal or external. Video footage from these and other events are often posted on Ofcom's interactive online magazine 'The Loop.'

The nature of the industry means that colleagues don't always work a traditional working day. This is especially true of the hundred or so field workers undertaking radio spectrum enforcement work. According to Campbell, "We've always had really flexible policies around work/life balance. We have a number of people of both sexes with different arrangements running from working compressed hours to part-time work. We can also loan out laptop computers for home working activities."

Innovation and Creativity

Ofcom's remit as a regulator is to set as well as enforce rules governing competition and industry standards. In order to anticipate regulatory changes the organisation produces numerous reports. These are produced by a range of specialist colleagues: sector specialists, economists, lawyers and strategic policy advisors. Each is informed by market research and before any significant changes are made there is a public consultation process.

In 2008 Ofcom embarked on a major report on the future of public service broadcasting. Important issues covered included the status of Channel Four, the licence fee and the digital switchover. In the telecoms sector Ofcom worked closely with companies to ease the difficulty the public faced when moving from one provider to another. The result was the introduction of a migration authorisation code, which enables customers to both make a switch and retain their existing phone number.

From an internal perspective the organisation is particularly proud of its management development programme. Aimed at all managers below senior management level this is accredited through the Charted Management Institute. The year-long programme delivers blended learning to small groups of participants and employs mentors and 360 degree feedback as part of its toolkit. The success of the format means that it will be rolled out to senior management this year.

Pay and Benefits

Regular assessment underpins a performance culture at Ofcom and this in turn links directly to reward. Colleagues are given a set of personal objectives and progress in achieving them is reviewed at twice-yearly appraisal meetings. Alongside the acquisition of technical skills a competency framework is used to measure the degree of alignment with the organisation's values.

Campbell explains, "Following a colleague survey we made some changes to our assessment and reward process to introduce greater clarity and transparency. The early feedback we've had so far has been very positive." Pay now depends on four elements: internal relativity (a colleague's salary relative to others carrying out the same or similar work); external relativity (the going rate earned by people doing comparable jobs outside Ofcom); performance; and potential.

The starting salary for graduates is currently £26,000 – assuming good performance a colleague can be earning up to £36,000 three years later. Bonus pay is set at anywhere between 8% and 20% of base salary, according to level of experience, and using a number of forms of measurement. Examples include effectiveness in budget management and in people management, level of responsiveness to the public, and success in delivering projects and regulatory outcomes.

Ofcom operates a flexible benefits system called 'Choices'. Among benefits that can be exchanged are holiday time (up to 10 days above or 5 days below the 25 days standard), life assurance for a partner, private medical insurance, childcare vouchers and bicycles. Other benefits include a defined contribution pension, life assurance and private medical insurance.   »

"The interests of citizens and consumers are at the heart of everything we do at Ofcom" (Ed Richards, chief executive)

"People who work for us need to have a real interest in the communications industry. It's a fast-moving, ever-changing environment and that's reflected in the way we work"
(Janet Campbell, head of HR)

Managers can award discretionary bonuses to high-performing colleagues. These are usually awarded on-the-spot and are non-cash awards, such as tickets for events or meal vouchers.

Career Development

It is usual for 10 graduates to be recruited each year by Ofcom and each is given a comprehensive introduction to the organisation, starting with an initial week-long Induction programme. Participants on this two-year programme experience life in different parts of the organisation; though by necessity generalists move around more frequently than colleagues in specialist roles.

"We've also just revamped our induction process for all colleagues from beginning to end to improve the experience colleagues get when they first join us," explains Campbell. "People now participate in a longer, modular-based Induction programme, the purpose of which is to explain what Ofcom is and what our duties and regulatory principles are."

In addition to the formal Induction, all colleagues can opt to attend a series of introductory guides to aspects of the regulatory environment. These are allocated on the basis of the individual's job description, so, for example, an economist might receive training in telecom market analysis. These tailored training modules are available to all colleagues but form an integral part of the graduate training programme. These are in addition to the structured graduate training programme.

Campbell says, "The size of our organisation means we don't have structured career paths. We don't say to people that if they start in a particular job, after two years they'll be at such and such a level. However we strongly encourage each person to have a personal development plan and to work with their line manager to look at their training needs over the coming six to twelve months."

Ofcom provides support for colleagues studying for professional qualifications, for example in finance. It has also designed an accredited professional development programme (in conjunction with Warwick University) for those in field operations.

The role of the EU in shaping European-wide telecoms regulations means there are opportunities for international travel for some Ofcom colleagues. This also applies to members of Ofcom's international spectrum team who work with various agencies on behalf of the UK.

Corporate Social Responsibility

In the last few years, Ofcom has been particularly active in promoting diversity, both internally and to external stakeholders. A working group has been established to co-ordinate efforts and one important outcome is a diversity toolkit for telecom businesses – which aren't subject to the same level of scrutiny as the broadcast sector. The toolkit was successfully launched at a conference attended by many leading industry operators. Upcoming plans include sharing best practice ideas with other organisations and incorporating commitment to diversity as a criterion of overall procurement strategy.

Another key area of focus has been the environment. In 2007 Ofcom launched a 'footprint' initiative designed to reduce its carbon emissions, part of which included replacing many fleet vehicles with new, more energy-efficient models. Another transport-based initiative saw car parking space converted to house bicycle racks, to encourage people to cycle into work. In addition, on-site environmental champions have been appointed with responsibility for encouraging sustainable work practices. Examples include switching off computer monitors when not in use, using double-sided printing, drinking from reusable paper coffee cups and the separate disposal of different types of waste for recycling. Its efforts to become a carbon-neutral organisation also included planting a tree for each completed questionnaire in the last colleague survey – in all over 650 trees were planted.

Ofcom colleagues participate in a limited number of volunteering activities. These centre on literacy and foreign language assistance at local schools and sixth form colleges. Last year, for the first time, the organisation provided six-week long internships to half a dozen students from local colleges.

Colleagues choose, by a vote, the selection of the charity Ofcom supports. For 2008-9, the winner was Childline.

Responsibility for regulating Ofcom's own activities and operations lies with the main Board and various committees. The Content Board sets and enforces quality standards in the broadcast industry and reports to the main Board. Like other committees its membership represents all parts of the United Kingdom in order to reflect the different national concerns. An advisory committee operates on behalf of older and disabled customers; while technical input comes via the Spectrum Advisory Board. A Consumer Panel operates independently of Ofcom to provide advice to customers in the markets it regulates.

Facts and figures

Total number of staff: 850 (600 in London, the remainder at other offices)
Office location: London (HQ), Glasgow, Cardiff, Belfast, Manchester, Birmingham, Caterham and Baldock
Industry sector: Media and Communications
Operating expenditure: £130m

Be Humankind

Oxfam

Oxfam House
John Smith Drive
Cowley
Oxford OX4 2JY

Telephone: 0300 200 1300
www.oxfam.org.uk

Pay and Benefits	★ ★ ★ ★ ☆
Training and Development	★ ★ ★ ☆ ☆
Career Development	★ ★ ★ ★ ☆
Working Conditions	★ ★ ★ ⯨ ☆
Company Culture	★ ★ ★ ⯨ ☆

Biggest plus
Absolute clarity about why they're here.

Greatest challenge
Ensuring we have the right people with the right skills in the right places at the right time to support our mission to bring about an end to poverty and suffering.

Summary

Oxfam was founded in Oxford in 1942, in response to the famine in Greece caused by the Nazi occupation. Since then it has developed to become a leading international non-governmental organisation (NGO) spending about £300m a year delivering aid and development work in 65 countries around the world, from Albania to Zimbabwe. Of its 6,500 staff, about 5,000 operate overseas, but it also has a programme tackling poverty in Britain. Still based in Oxford, it fights poverty by campaigning for change, by supporting development work designed to help poor people help themselves and by responding to emergencies.

About the organisation

Oxfam is probably best known within the UK for the chain of charity shops it operates. There are 630 of these spread around the country, with 500 of them having paid managers. The rest are run by some of the organisation's 22,000 volunteers.

Oxfam remains true to its roots, with the original Oxfam shop still in Oxford city centre, but it has developed significantly and become much more structured and professional in the half century since its establishment by a group of concerned individuals. David Benson, resourcing manager, says: "Donor reporting is becoming tighter and tighter. We're totally accountable for every penny that we spend and we are expected to have much greater rigour and control."

Another factor making Oxfam more like a business than the traditional idea of a charity is the growing complexity of its operations. It is affiliated to Oxfam International, a confederation of NGOs doing the same sort of work that it is, and works with many other aid and development organisations in various different ways in a wide range of countries. Moreover, its own activities are run from regional centres with some support from the Oxford headquarters.

In addition to having increasingly to account for how money is spent, Oxfam must compete with other similar bodies for funds from individual and corporate donors as well as funding from the Government and this requires an increasingly professional approach. As a result, Oxfam is putting a lot of effort into promoting its brand within the UK. "We're recognising that a good brand presence is incredibly important to the successful recruitment of excellent staff," says Benson.

»

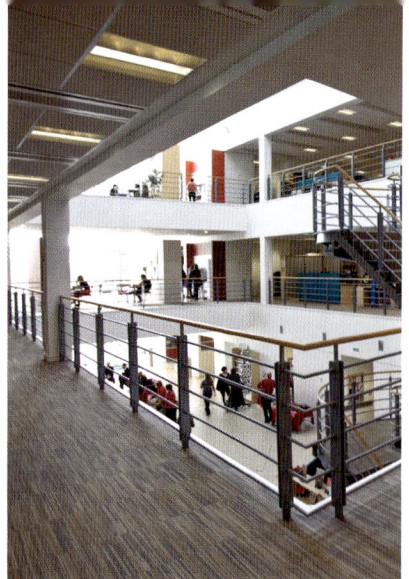

"We're recognising that a good brand presence is incredibly important to the successful recruitment of excellent staff" (David Benson, resourcing manager)

Consequently, marketing is one of the functions represented on the top team led by recently ennobled chief executive Dame Barbara Stocking. The others are finance, human resources, international operations, communications and campaigns and policy development.

Company Culture

Under Stocking, a former regional director of the NHS, Oxfam is a businesslike place, with clear strategies and policies. But – thanks in part to its modern headquarters building on a business park outside Oxford – it is also an open organisation with plenty of communication between Stocking and her fellow executives and between them and the rest of the workforce. She shares "not just our achievements and challenges but also visits locations around the world and emails staff regularly with her observations," says Benson.

Oxfam has three core values guiding its work – empowerment, accountability and inclusivity. Making sure that these values run throughout the operations is key, whatever the role of the individual and wherever they are operating.

In the staff handbook, Stocking says: "Each type of work is vital, and every member of Oxfam GB has an important role to play. That means that in everything we do, we have to be committed to the highest standards ourselves. We have to be good at what we do, and aim constantly to be the best. We owe it to our donors to be as efficient and as effective as possible. We believe we are accountable to the people living in poverty and seek ways to achieve that. We should demonstrate by the way we behave to others that we are committed to building the bridges, networks, and alliances that will enable us to go forward together."

The top team is small, but its members are easily accessible by everybody within the organisation. "There's a very clear line of sight to the people who make the decisions," adds Benson.

The human resources role is similar to that in a private sector organisation, with a human resources director and centres of expertise. Because of the huge diversity created by Oxfam operating in so many different parts of the world, it tends to have HR managers in each country, with some degree of support coming from the regional centres.

There is a strong emphasis on learning, from induction for new recruits to training for new managers and for specific responsibilities. Work-life balance is encouraged through initiatives on flexible working and home working and the general approach is that most of the employees have sacrificed financial rewards to work at Oxfam and are passionate about the job so will get the work done. This strength of commitment is demonstrated by surveys showing that 97% of the staff enjoyed working at Oxfam.

Innovation and Creativity

Oxfam prides itself on its ground-breaking work – not just in the field, where it has become expert in improving sanitation in disaster zones – but also in how it goes about raising the funds that enables that relief effort.

It was, for example, the first charity to have high street shops and led the way in encouraging donors to make regular monthly donations. Many of its shops are now specialist, so that, as well as the regular charity shops, there are some that just sell bridal wear and others that concentrate on 'retro' clothing. Book selling has been a particular success, to the extent that Oxfam now claims to be Europe's largest second-hand bookseller. In an effort to make the most of donations, it has established a 'Wastesaver' centre in Huddersfield, where skilled operators sort donations for recycling.

Most recently, Oxfam has teamed up with retailer Marks & Spencer to run a scheme whereby donors receive a voucher for every M&S item donated to an Oxfam shop. There is, says Benson, "a lot of thinking going on," with the aim of making sure that Oxfam receives as big a share of the public's charitable donations as possible.

Pay and Benefits

Oxfam's policy is to be reasonably competitive on pay rather than rock-bottom, aiming to be on about the 80th percentile, although its status as a charity means that it cannot match the top private-sector salaries. "You don't come here if you're chasing the pound," says Benson.

Junior staff start out on about £14,500, with shop managers typically receiving between £18,500 and £25,000. Senior managers are paid between £40,000 and £54,000. Unsurprisingly, the organisation does not pay bonuses, but employees can see their salaries progress in accordance with their ability. Each pay scale has a minimum and maximum.

Salaries also rise in accordance with the inflation rate. But the bigger problem is paying appropriate salaries in different parts of the world, particularly those where – like Zimbabwe – inflation is rampant. »

"There's a very clear line of sight to the people who make the decisions" (David Benson, resourcing manager)

"Each type of work is vital, and every member of Oxfam GB has an important role to play" (Dame Barbara Stocking, chief executive)

Staff are also eligible for defined contribution pensions, where their contributions are matched by the organisation up to 4% of salary, and receive 25 days' holiday a year. At the Oxford headquarters there is also a crèche to help with childcare. However, many of the other benefits typical in large organisations are not available. Medical insurance, for example, is only offered to those posted overseas.

Despite this, Oxfam has no problem recruiting in the UK. It has 40,000 names on a database waiting for the right job, while staff turnover is about 15%.

Career Development

Oxfam's avowed approach is to grow its own executives. Sixty-seven per cent of senior roles are filled internally, while for middle-tier personnel the figure is 52%. To this end, the organisation supports and encourages staff to acquire professional qualifications, such as those from CIMA for finance specialists and from the CIPD for HR specialists.

There are also great opportunities to go overseas on secondments, a factor that helps offset the comparatively low pay in the organisation's attractiveness to recruits.

In keeping with one of its aims being to help communities develop, Oxfam tries to recruit locally wherever possible. But local staff are often supplemented for varying periods of time by experts flown in from Britain or the regional centres.

Flexibility is the key, since staff can often find themselves deployed to a disaster zone at very short notice. The pressure is perhaps most intense at the large warehouse Oxfam runs at Bicester. This is filled with all sorts of emergency equipment with the aim of enabling the organisation's teams to be "on the ground within 48 hours with all the right kit."

Employees are expected to stretch themselves and there are regular performance reviews during the year as well as more informal opportunities to discuss progress and opportunities with managers. In addition to backing professional learning, Oxfam offers various training programmes, including one on how to be an Oxfam manager for those newly promoted or aspiring to be managers. There are also courses run in conjunction with such well-known centres as INSEAD and Henley Management College. However, much of the training is on-the-job, with some online learning introduced recently, while great emphasis is also placed on learning from past experiences.

Corporate Social Responsibility

Since Oxfam is a charity, all of its work falls into the CSR category. However, it endeavours to do this work as effectively and as transparently as possible. Since it relies on donations, it is vital that it accounts for every penny raised. In addition, its work around the world is monitored by compliance teams in order to ensure that it is spending the money it receives appropriately.

In the staff handbook Stocking reminds employees that: "Our mission, as an organisation and as a charity, is to overcome poverty and suffering, wherever it occurs. But our vision goes far beyond that. Our goal is a world where everyone is able to live a life of dignity and fulfilment, free from misery, want, and exploitation… To achieve this goal our philosophy is to work with others – with groups of poor people seeking their rights and with groups of like-minded people everywhere. The work we do takes many forms: from relief in emergencies, to grass roots development work, to advocacy, lobbying popular campaigning, influencing and persuading. To do it we continually have to persuade people of the justice of our cause and convince them that we are deserving of their support, financial and non-financial."

As far as environmental responsibility goes, the organisation has equipped its Oxford offices with extensive recycling facilities, while staff are helped with cycling to work through the provision of extensive cycle racks. The Wastesaver initiative enables recycling.

Facts and figures

Total number of staff: 6,500 (1,500 in Britain, the rest overseas)
Office location: Oxford
Industry sector: Non-governmental organisation/charity
Turnover: £300m

Peter Brett Associates LLP

Caversham Bridge House
Waterman Place
Reading
RG1 8DN

Telephone: 0118 950 0761
Email: reading@peterbrett.com
www.peterbrett.com

Pay and Benefits	★ ★ ★ ☆ ☆
Training and Development	★ ★ ★ ★ ☆
Career Development	★ ★ ★ ½ ☆
Working Conditions	★ ★ ★ ½ ☆
Company Culture	★ ★ ★ ☆ ☆

Biggest plus
Carrying out interesting and variable projects that make a real difference to society and the environment.

Greatest challenge
The current economic climate and the effect that has on clients being able to fulfil their aspirations.

Summary

Peter Brett Associates LLP (PBA) is a multi-disciplinary consultancy, bringing engineering, planning, and scientific skills and experience together to deliver sustainable development and infrastructure projects worldwide. PBA was established as a private partnership in 1965 in Reading, originally providing structural advice. In 2008 the consultancy converted to LLP status and it is now one of the UK's leading independent multi-specialist consultancy companies. The mission statement sums up PBA's ethos neatly: "To be personal, trusted advisors, creating value for our clients, opportunity for our staff, and deliverable, sustainable solutions worldwide." There are 24 partners.

About the organisation

PBA has grown organically over the past 40 years and now employs around 600 staff in 11 UK offices: Reading (HQ), Ashford, Birmingham, Bristol, Cardiff, Exeter, London, Northampton, Taunton, Warrington and West Malling. There are international offices in the Czech Republic, Germany, India, Mauritius, Romania, Slovakia and South Africa. PBA is now one of the largest independent consulting practices in the UK. The consultancy has developed a reputation for providing quality and innovation, working in close collaboration with its clients and associated professionals.

Turnover has increased by nearly 50% over the past three financial years, for both the UK and international operations. Turnover for the whole operation in 2008 was £49m, up from £38m in 2007 and £28m in 2006. The business has managed to maintain profit levels of around 10% throughout this period.

PBA currently offers over 40 services covering water, environment, infrastructure, land development, transport and buildings. "We adopt a client-focused approach to business, valuing long-term relationships," says Richard Puttock, partner. The organisation has won many awards, with a typical example being the 2008 British Cartographic Society's award in the e-mapping category for PBA's production of the Thames Estuary Coastal Habitat Atlas. Work done for other clients has led to further awards such as the Institution of Highways and Transport Manual for Streets Award. "We feel that the way in which we value all our stakeholders and the way in which we approach our business helps to define the nature and success of our practice," says Puttock.

Company Culture

"Our employees are the key to the success of our business, because our clients buy their enthusiasm and service as well as their technical expertise," says Puttock. "A happier and more satisfied workforce is good for the community where their skills are employed."

〉〉

"Our employees are the key
to the success of our
business, because our
clients buy their enthusiasm
and service as well as their
technical expertise"
(Richard Puttock, partner)

"We are passionate about our work. We apply new ideas and encourage all within the practice to be creative, develop their skills and challenge traditional thinking," says Felicity Griggs, head of HR Operations. "We provide knowledge and expertise in our respective fields and leadership to our teams of engineers, environmental and transport planners, modellers and scientists. We adopt a personal approach that consistently results in satisfied clients, repeat business, recommendations and referrals."

At PBA individuality is important – it's an organisation where people are encouraged to express ideas and display critical thinking to help solve clients' problems. "Adding value is key," says Puttock. Staff are not pigeonholed or constrained. Indeed there is a family feel, which staff often say in opinion surveys. "People are valued and it is essential we strive to maintain that."

Communication is vital. The business has 360-degree feedback sessions for senior managers to help them manage better. Coaching and mentoring are available to help them develop their management and communication skills.

"We like people who can think freely, be innovative, challenge ideas, but most importantly be prepared to work as part of a team," says Griggs. A team spirit is vital in an organisation that has nine business groups (or divisions) and an international division. "We are constantly working so people can work with teams in other business groups, and working for other teams for a client. Staff also work with client teams both here and abroad," says Puttock. The underlying ethos is very much 'work hard but have fun.'

Innovation and Creativity

There is an active R&D programme in which the company asks staff in groups to monitor areas of the business that would benefit from R&D. The business then funds relevant projects. "The (new) Equilibrium tool kit was developed for delivering sustainable developments for clients," says Puttock. "It takes clients through their development project, to ensure they understand all the sustainability issues and obtain the maximum benefit for what they are trying to do. This will be done for each stage of the development cycle. We have shown it to clients and had a great reaction. Clients like the tool kit." PBA is constantly looking to maximise new technologies for the benefit of its clients.

Although many of PBA's ideas result in a construction project, it's equally true that to achieve the vision of a sustainable future, it's essential to create an environment that leads to changes in behaviour.

PBA is constantly looking to maximise new technologies for the benefit of its clients. "We are advising on ways of obtaining energy from waste using all available processes including anaerobic digestion," says Puttock. "Waste after minimisation should be seen as a resource and managed appropriately." This is not just something for large-scale projects, but is also relevant at the local level. "It means approaching the issue of sustainability in the best way you can."

Pay and Benefits

PBA always pays a fair salary in the upper quartile and benchmarks against similar-sized businesses. There is a profit-related bonus for all, with 10% of attributable profits allocated to the bonus scheme and paid in two tranches, in December and June. More senior staff (for example associates, senior associates and divisional directors) also receive a further profit share, paid quarterly and at year end.

There is a defined contribution pension scheme, where PBA matches contributions up to 7% of gross salary, with a further 4% depending on years of service. "If anyone leaves us and returns within 10 years we will add the previous years' service to whatever the staff member has accrued," says Griggs.

Company cars or travel allowances are given to associates and above – below this level (principal and senior grades of technical and administrator staff) a travel allowance is paid. Interest-free loans are available to all for bicycles, motorbikes and season tickets, with access to Toyota Prius cars from the car pool for special assignments. There is a preferred car sharing parking arrangement with a guaranteed lift home policy should the car driver have to go elsewhere at short notice.

Holiday entitlement is in the range of 23-30 days, with the flexible benefits scheme enabling staff to buy benefits and sell holiday. There is death-in-service of five times salary (can be flexed up to eight times), permanent health insurance (the first 13 weeks on full pay, weeks 13-26 on 75%, and after that 75% less state benefits, until retirement at 65), private medical insurance, dental plan, annual health screening and childcare vouchers. There is free parking at most offices for staff first (before management, who typically will have to park in a public car park nearby and walk to the office), critical illness cover for staff and partners, gym membership and an employee assistance support programme. There are long-service gifts for staff notching up 10, 15, 20 and 25 years' service. »

"We like people who can think freely, be innovative, challenge ideas, but most importantly be prepared to work as part of a team" (Felicity Griggs, head of HR Operations)

"We are passionate about training staff"
(Richard Puttock, partner)

Career Development

"We recognise that the continual growth and development of our staff is key for PBA to evolve, indeed some of the Partners started as graduates which demonstrates our commitment to the development of our staff and promotion from within," says Puttock.

All staff, from administration support to Partners, are encouraged to maximise their full potential through an extensive training and development package tailored to them as an individual and developed in conjunction with experienced training professionals. This includes day release to college for technicians, graduate training schemes, sponsorship for existing staff to study for post-graduate qualifications part-time and a range of technical and managerial training initiatives. Other training and development programmes are managed via the PBA Training Academy.

"We are passionate about training staff," says Puttock. "We budget for four days training per year per employee with the associated cost and allowance for training courses, MSc and technical college fees accumulating to over £1m per year." There are formal training schemes available for staff to obtain professional recognition through the four main technical disciplines. There are close relationships with universities and the sponsoring of undergraduates at Portsmouth, Surrey, Imperial College and Southampton in addition to involvement with the ICE Quest Scholarship. Of PBA's total staff, 31 are studying either part-time or full-time for MSc degrees, 10 BSc degrees, 28 HNC and seven ONC qualifications; one is doing an MBA at Henley Management College and two are doing PhD studies – into transportation and underground non-coal mining cavities.

Some staff join as technicians or school leavers and progress through stages to become chartered engineers. A number of administrative staff have transferred to professional roles after training. A postman joined and received help in completing modules of an Open University degree – he is now working as a technician. "We give opportunities to staff and get the best out of them," says Puttock. "The key is people believing they can do it."

Corporate Social Responsibility

"Corporate Social Responsibility is a key part of our ethos," says Puttock. "Our commitment to our clients, suppliers, employees and the communities in which we work is of paramount importance to us. Whilst delivering our services we seek to support the needs of our stakeholders in an ethical and empathetic manner."

Through encouraging innovative thinking and pioneering new concepts, PBA has embraced its economic, social and environmental responsibilities on a local, regional and international scale. The consultancy seeks to deliver sustainable benefits through the work that it does, and the way in which it operates.

PBA makes annual charitable donations and supports regular fundraising events for international, national and local charities. In an independent survey, staff rated PBA very highly for giving something back to society. The firm also has a Give As You Earn (GAYE) system operating through the Charities Aid Foundation, allowing staff to donate to charity in a tax-efficient manner.

When competing in the WaterAid Six Peaks Challenge in 2008, PBA's team finished first and raised nearly £5,000 for the charity. The winning team completed the challenge well within the 72-hour target, ahead of 21 teams and more than 160 competitors. A second PBA team stayed hot on their heels to ensure it was also one of three teams to make the demanding time limit.

PBA is a founding member of Reading Initiative for Tsunami Action (RITA), which is an association committed to the longer-term rebuilding of the areas affected by the Asian tsunami. "RITA is committed to long-term targeted support in Sri Lanka, where we are acting as technical consultant and treasurer with representation on the steering group," says Puttock.

On environmental issues, PBA has implemented an Environmental Management System which includes commitments to energy efficiency, various recycling schemes, and the review of the potential to build-in environmental benefits to projects that the consultancy works on.

Facts and figures

Total number of staff: 550 in the UK, 600 in total
Office location: Reading (HQ); 10 other locations in the UK and 8 overseas
Industry sector: Engineering and environmental consultancy
Turnover: £49m

Pret a Manger (Europe) Ltd

1 Hudson's Place
Victoria
London SW1V 1PZ

Telephone: 020 7827 8000
Fax: 020 7827 8787
Email: recruitment@pret.com
www.pret.com

Pay and Benefits	★ ★ ★ ☆ ☆
Training and Development	★ ★ ★ ⯨ ☆
Career Development	★ ★ ★ ★ ⯨
Working Conditions	★ ★ ★ ⯨ ☆
Company Culture	★ ★ ★ ★ ☆

Biggest plus
A great team-based culture, a real passion for food.

Greatest challenge
Managing to avoid changing it as it grows.

Summary

Since it opened in London 1986, Pret a Manger has become firmly established as one of the leading sandwich shop chains and a byword for high quality, freshly prepared food. A private company, Pret owns 200 shops in the UK, 20 in New York and 10 in Hong Kong. Pret employs nearly 4,000 people, 3,887 in the UK. Pret continues to expand. It opened 32 new shops in 2008, 23 in the UK, and recruits new Team Members every week. Turnover for 2008 is projected to be £222m with an operating profit before interest and tax of £17.7m.

About the organisation

Pret opened in London in 1986 when college friends Sinclair Beecham and Julian Metcalfe insisted on making 'proper' sandwiches using natural, preservative-free ingredients. The two had little business experience but were rather good at creating the sort of food they craved but couldn't find anywhere else.

Good, natural food is sacred to Pret. So too is friendly service, and a pleasant environment. Its sandwiches and other offerings are freshly made throughout the day in each and every Pret kitchen – one of the things that make Pret special.

Pret has 110 shops in London and 90 in the regions and airports. The traditional format of the 'City takeaway' is changing and many new shops have a more café or coffee lounge feel, appealing to tourists and shoppers. The airport shops, including Heathrow Terminals 3 and 5 and Gatwick South, are massive operations. Pret is now 'motoring' in the US, with a slightly different and focused offering aimed at healthy women and hungry men, which roughly translated means more salads and more meat.

What you do see in all Pret restaurants are the words 'Just Made.' Pret slavishly sticks to a few key principles: simple, freshly prepared food on the premises, using stylish ingredients you would recognise from your own kitchen. The Pret larder has been extended, with no fewer than 117 new products launched this year, and now includes offerings such as vitamin drinks, fresh carrot juice and Viennese-style luxury coffees. Pret is sensitive to price points too, introducing products below £2.50 such as slim baguettes. "Whatever your pocket is, Pret will be able to look after you," says chief executive Clive Schlee.

»

Pret now has private equity firm Bridgepoint as its principal shareholder. "They have been extremely respectful of the Pret culture and the Pret brand. We've not been pushed into anything that doesn't fit with the Pret story and our measured rate of expansion," says Schlee.

Company Culture

Pret has built a strong culture that its people are really proud of. The company is determined to maintain, not change it. As the business grows, it is like splitting a cell, with the same shop-opening ceremony, the same recruitment policies, and the same values. At the core is a deep respect for the motivation of Team Members, getting up early, community and respect.

"There are three behaviours that we expect to see in all Pret people," says Andrea Wareham, director of People. "These are passion, clear talking and teamworking. We have an almost religious duty to develop all Team Members on the way up. Each day you can climb another rung on the ladder."

'The Team' means a close integration of the shops and head office. Twice a year every Head Office employee spends two days ('Buddy days') in a shop, wearing the uniform, working in teams and attending social events.

To work at Pret you must have not only a respect for but also a real passion for food. "When people join we want to see a massive love of people and of food," says Danilo Martinelli, general manager of the Victoria shop. "And you won't get them caring about sandwiches if they don't care about people." Pret people really 'own' their sandwiches.

'The Pret Recipe' is in fact an articulation of how it wants its people to run the shops, and how to get the wheels turning. "We want to get a focus on getting the people-products-service right, then sales will follow," says Schlee.

Pret is quite transparent in all that it does, from food ingredients to promotion opportunities to reporting financial performance. Pret is also renowned for its enormously diverse culture. It employs many different nationalities, and highly values the cosmopolitan flavour this gives the company.

Innovation and Creativity

Pret was aware that CHIP and PIN credit cards would be difficult to introduce without lengthening queues and increasing 'fumble time.' So Pret developed in conjunction with HSBC a solution that waives the requirement of a PIN, with the company taking the risk on orders below £15. Over time it anticipates that transactions will migrate to touch cards like Oyster.

Pret has strived hard to develop hot products that don't require the customer to wait while they are cooked. Pret A Manger means 'ready to eat,' after all. Pret has become very good at developing heat retention packaging and new products like its Italian Prosciutto Artisan Baguette have become roaring successes.

"Whatever your pocket is, Pret will be able to look after you"
(Clive Schlee, chief executive)

"The behaviours we expect of Pret people are passion, clear talking and teamworking" (Andrea Wareham, director of People)

Pret has its own in-house 'ideas department'. Online idea submissions are reviewed each month from the thousands of bright ideas put forward, aimed at helping Pret become a better, kinder, easier place to work and shop. Prizes this year include an expenses-paid trip to New York for an entire shop. There are two categories. The best service idea to Wow! customers, which has seen dance classes for the queues; raffles; and free coffee and sandwich for any customer wearing the day's designated accessory, for example a red tie or scarf! There's also a category for best new food product idea, with Pret staff voting on which go into the range. These have led to the introduction of luxury hot drinks, or 'Velvet Jolts'; fresh carrot juice; and smaller baguettes at a £1.50 price point.

Pay and Benefits

"We pay our hardworking staff as much as we can afford rather than as little as we can get away with," says Wareham. Pay is based more on you as an individual – the bonus on how your shop is performing.

Team Members up to manager level are paid hourly, each week, at levels 114-131% ahead of other company averages. Performance-related pay has been introduced within the shops, based on mystery shopper visits, with resulting scores above 90% providing an extra £1 an hour. Pret's compensation stands out at Team Member level.

General and assistant managers receive a bonus based on sales, gross profit, personal targets and quality standards that can add up to 30% of salary. Every quarter, Pret identifies the highest achieving shops. The top three managers have their bonus tripled while the next seven managers see their bonus doubled. Pret also offers doubled bonuses for the two best mystery shopper ratings, two best quality surveys and two best manager-controlled profit figures. "It's a huge incentive. We know from recruiters that these bonuses really set Pret apart," says Wareham.

Head office staff are rewarded for meeting environmental as well as financial targets. If the company does well, everybody receives a share of the profit and bonuses across the board can be substantial. Shareholding is possible through the Partners in Pret scheme. An employee has to be nominated by members to be invited to join; each member has three votes and two of these must go to shop-based people rather than head office management.

»

"When people join we want to see a massive love of people and of food"
(Danilo Martinelli, general manager)

Holidays are 28 days including Bank Holidays, rising by one day per year worked after five years' service to a maximum of 38 days. There are also flexible and part-time hours working contracts that can be tailored to suit individuals.

Twice a year, the company throws a massive party. Some have passed into Pret legend. Everyone at Pret is invited.

Career Development

Pret has a strong tradition of developing its people. Currently, 75% of managers began their Pret careers as Team Members. "Someone can join as a Team Member and if they are proficient and excel could be a general manager in two-and-a-half to three years," says Wareham.

Pret runs many courses at its hectic Training Academy in Victoria (most of which have nothing to do with sandwich making). There has always been a clear training programme for Team Members up to line management but a big step this year has been the creation of the Pret Academy to act as an umbrella for all training and offering a clear pathway for all managers.

Another recent development is improved clarity of the roles of general manager and assistant manager. The latter role has been split into front of house and kitchen, which supports Pret's move to its more café-style proposition. "The effect on general managers has been amazing," says Wareham. "Previously they were trying to do everything." With well trained people below them, they can now rise above many of the day-to-day, hour-to-hour issues and become more of a leader.

That means focusing on getting six things right: having the right people, offering amazing service, delicious food and drink, a well-loved shop, shop profitability and growing sales. "It has to be done in that order too," says Wareham. Progression for general managers used to mean moving from a smaller to a larger shop. Smaller shops often need better managers and with pay now based on individual ability, this issue has been solved.

There is a rigorous recruitment process. Team Members vote on new recruits and only one in 20 is successful. "It makes people feel valued and engenders a genuine teamworking atmosphere," says Wareham. This year Pret has added a graduate recruitment programme.

Corporate Social Responsibility

Pret doesn't believe in long-winded 'eco policies' that rarely ring true. With a dedicated Sustainability Manager, Pret examines each part of its business that affects the environment and establishes a list of priorities under the banner 'Making Sustainability Stick.'

The Pret Foundation Trust supports many different charities but primarily the Pret Charity Run – literally a drive to feed the homeless. Previously shops dropped off food to hostels directly or outsourced delivery to a charity. Pret has now assumed this responsibility with real gusto, taking the whole operation in-house including three full time employees and a dedicated fleet of six electric vans to distribute food at a cost of £250,000 each year.

Pret Foundation raises funds by donating profits from certain products (for example the Tuna Baguette and Christmas Sandwich), loose change boxes in the shops, and its own efforts including a big auction event – Julian Metcalfe donated two days' use of his Aston Martin while Clive Schlee threw in a week's skiing!

Pret has really grasped the food recycling problem by the scruff of the sandwich box – the only fast food company in the UK to really do so. Pret's recycling project in the shops has food disposal stations that segregate liquids, food and tea bags, and empty packaging, with a target of 96% recycled. "We've spent £0.5m in developing this project," says Schlee. "We're probably ahead of our customers on this but employees, many of whom come from Europe which is ahead of the UK in food recycling, are really pleased."

Thermo mugs instead of paper cups; managing a waste budget; and asking customers whether or not they want a paper bag all add to the effort. In Hudson's Place there are similar recycling stations; china mugs instead of paper cups; notes to switch off PCs and monitors; and instructions to switch off lights and air conditioning and to print paper and emails only if strictly necessary.

Pret believes that air freighting food and veg is completely unnecessary and (with the exception of basil leaves) it doesn't do it. Wherever possible Pret buys British and seasonal produce and insists on very high standards of animal welfare. That's why you will find Wiltshire cured ham, Alaskan wild salmon, Fairtrade mango, free-range chicken and Rainforest Alliance coffee in Pret products.

Facts and figures

Total number of staff: 3,887 in the UK; 4,000 worldwide
Office location: London head office. 200 shops in UK, 20 in New York, 10 in Hong Kong
Industry sector: Food retail
Turnover: £222m

Quest Diagnostics

Unit B1 Parkway West
Cranford Lane
Heston
Middlesex TW5 9QA

Telephone: 020 8377 3300
Fax: 020 8377 3350
www.questdiagnostics.com/uk

Pay and Benefits	★ ★ ★ ⯨ ☆
Training and Development	★ ★ ★ ☆ ☆
Career Development	★ ★ ★ ★ ☆
Working Conditions	★ ★ ★ ★ ☆
Company Culture	★ ★ ★ ★ ☆

Biggest plus
A friendly and inclusive culture based on innovation through working together as a team.

Greatest challenge
Making its name in the UK, where the US-based company is less well known.

Summary

Quest Diagnostics is a large US organisation employing some 43,000 people globally, of which around 350 are based in the UK in Middlesex and Central London. The company has two business units – one providing laboratory testing to the NHS, where Quest has recently secured a contract with West Middlesex Hospital to conduct all the testing of patient samples on the hospital's behalf, and the other providing testing services for pharmaceutical companies who are running clinical trials to develop new drugs. In the UK, the company employs biomedical scientists to work in its laboratories, as well as data management staff to process information and deliver results to clients in an efficient and timely manner.

About the organisation

Quest Diagnostics was the laboratory testing business of Corning Incorporated until it was spun out as an independent company in 1996 and listed on the New York Stock Exchange. In 1999, the business acquired SmithKline Beecham Clinical Laboratories and became America's largest provider of diagnostic testing, information and services.

Quest launched its UK operation in 1996, investing more than £3.5m in state-of-the-art laboratory facilities. The business has tripled in size over the past eight years. In Europe there is also a site in Belgium and sales people based in Germany, France and Spain, with further laboratories in India, Singapore, Australia, Mexico and Brazil. Nevertheless, around 40,000 of the company's 43,000 staff remain based in the US.

Quest's global turnover in 2007/08 was US$7bn, of which the UK last year contributed £50m, a figure that continues to increase.

Surya Mohapatra, chairman, president and CEO of Quest, says: "We have a successful strategy based on three simple but profound words: Patients, Growth and People. We have a mission to be the undisputed world leader in diagnostic testing, information and services."

Quest in the UK is seeking to hire first-class biomedical scientists, the vast majority of whom are currently working in the National Health Service (NHS). The company believes it can offer employees something different. Linda Smith, the UK director of human resources, says: "This is a slightly different organisation doing the same sort of work. We are much smaller than the NHS, so we are more flexible. We are working in an industry that is quite altruistic in that it is concerned with human health, and yet we are also participating in some of the most advanced clinical trials going on in the country and worldwide. Working here is all about cutting-edge technology and innovation; those are principles that are part of the company's values." »

Company Culture

The business's values of quality, integrity, innovation, accountability, collaboration and leadership are in evidence day-to-day, and there is an intrinsic focus on high-quality service.

Smith says "Because Quest is in the private sector, there may be a perception among people who have worked in the NHS that the business is about cutting costs. In fact, quality is of the utmost importance, and providing a high-quality service is key."

That commitment to delivery for the client is at the heart of the culture in the UK. Smith says that all staff appreciate the importance of delivering diagnostic results as quickly as possible. "If somebody has had a biopsy done, a lot of people working here know that this could be their own mother or brother who is waiting for the results," she says. "It is somebody's relative, and so we are dealing with information that is critically important to individuals."

A common phrase used around the business refers to the importance of getting things 'right first time,' but whilst it's unacceptable to make mistakes, the aim is to avoid that by having a collaborative team mentality rather than a blame culture. The managing director meets with a representative group of employees once a month for lunch, to exchange ideas and discuss issues, and whilst there is an element of pressure to the company's culture, staff feel they are doing a job with real value, according to Smith.

"There is an element of urgency," she says. "But we know what we are doing is something of value. We are not just producing another widget; we are doing something that's going to make a difference to someone's life."

The HR team's objective is to nurture that culture within the organisation, and help each individual feel part of the end product, whatever their role. With most employees aged between 20 and 35 years old, there is a very sociable and informal feel to the place.

Innovation and Creativity

Innovation is one of the core values at Quest, and the business is focused on process improvement and enhancing the way that people work. If staff have suggestions of ways in which things might be handled more efficiently, they are encouraged to make them known and, wherever possible, ideas are acted upon.

One area in which Quest is cutting new ground is through a product called Results View, which allows private sector customers to go online and see the results of the tests that they are running, instead of having to wait for a paper results report to be delivered.

"We have a successful strategy based on three simple but profound words: Patients, Growth and People"
(Surya Mohapatra, chairman, president and CEO)

"We know what we are
doing is something of
value…we are doing
something that's going
to make a difference to
someone's life"
(Linda Smith,
UK director of
human resources)

Similarly, the company is trying to revolutionise the way it deals with requests from doctors. Presently, doctors complete forms stating what they would like the samples to be tested for, but this paper-intensive process can be hindered by illegible or badly completed forms, so Quest is moving to an electronic format.

Each team at Quest has an individual responsible for process improvements, and that person communicates with the managing director on a regular basis. On a practical level, it was an employee that recently suggested introducing a flexible working policy allowing staff to start late the following day if they have had to stay late the night before, as is often the case when dealing with colleagues in the US.

Pay and Benefits

Quest's compensation policy is based on providing a competitive package, including both a competitive base salary and a bonus scheme for all employees. The bonus scheme is tied to the performance of the business as a whole, rather than that of the individual, such that if the company hits its objectives there is a bonus for everybody of 10% of salary, from the secretaries to the managing director.

If the business exceeds objectives, bonuses can be as high as 15%, but if they are missed, there is no bonus. "The scheme helps people feel that their job really makes a difference, because management are not the only people who affect our success," says Smith.

The benefits packages are based on the same principle and are not restricted to senior employees. All staff can participate in a private medical plan, receive life insurance and permanent health insurance cover.

There is a pension scheme that is open to everyone, with a generous company contribution based on the age of the individual, with the company sometimes contributing as much as 15% of base salary.

Smith says: "Because we work in the health industry, quite a lot of our focus is on the health of our employees. All employees get an annual health check that includes blood tests and cholesterol testing, and those are very popular. We also offer all employees flu vaccinations each year if they want them." »

"Because we work in the
health industry, our focus
is on the health of
our employees"
(Linda Smith,
UK director of
human resources)

There is a flexible working policy that allows staff to adapt their work hours to suit them, so that if they are required to work late some evenings they can either take longer lunch hours or start later as a result, for example. Smith says, "In the laboratories we have got people working all sorts of days and hours to fit with their own personal commitments, and we welcome that."

Career Development

Quest is very training-focused as an organisation, with every single employee receiving a personal Training and Development Plan, which outlines the minimum training that they should be doing in their role. If they want to do additional career development programmes they are encouraged to do so.

There are performance reviews for all employees twice a year, not just looking at performance but also updating their development plans to suit their individual needs and ambitions.

Quest has a history of supporting staff through academic endeavours, and has supported UK employees studying bachelor degrees and master's degrees, while the company is currently sponsoring an employee studying for a PhD.

The business runs an array of internal training courses once a month, ranging from project management skills to things like time management, dealing with customers and handling difficult people. These are open to anyone, as are the online training sessions that are run out of the US and to which people are able to log on and participate as and when it suits their schedules.

Occasionally staff opt to shift between departments within the business, and that is encouraged so as to foster the team-based culture. There are individuals in the HR and IT teams who used to work in the laboratories, and who the company has supported through retraining. "If individuals in the laboratories want to work in other functions, it's great," says Smith." They understand the business and can liaise with other departments to help everyone understand what the company does as a whole."

There are opportunities for staff to travel to other offices of the company, with a new Quest laboratory in India recently opened to which several UK employees were seconded to help with its start-up and make sure there was global consistency of approach.

Corporate Social Responsibility

Quest has a full-time Environment, Health and Safety Officer within the UK business, working to make sure the company is recycling waste wherever possible and minimising its environmental impact. Because of the nature of Quest's business, much of its waste is chemical and cannot be recycled, but the company nevertheless goes to considerable efforts to make sure waste is separated effectively so that everything that can be recycled or re-used is treated appropriately.

The officer holds monthly meetings to which people from across Quest are invited and suggestions and contributions are encouraged. The efforts being made as a result include small-scale initiatives such as the replacement of all water cooler machines with facilities that are plugged into the main water supply, thereby removing the need for large plastic containers to be transported to and from the building.

There is a programme called Green Quest that measures the company's impact on the environment and sets annual targets for improvements in areas such as energy use, water use, and recycling.

Quest in the UK supports people who want to do charity work, and provides backing to staff taking time out to work on large-scale projects. One UK employee is currently working in India on a charity project and has been given a sabbatical and financial assistance. Another went to work in an orphanage in Sri Lanka with the company's backing.

A team from Quest completed the Walk for Life and was sponsored by the company and there is an annual summer social event that includes a raffle and other fundraising activities on behalf of local charities.

Diversity as an issue is taken extremely seriously at Quest, and the company has a Diversity Action Plan and a Diversity Committee that meets regularly and includes people from across the business. The committee discusses ways in which Quest can better recruit and retain people from diverse backgrounds.

As part of this initiative, Quest holds a Diversity Day when people throughout the company are encouraged to dress in the clothing that is traditional in their own culture. Whilst many arrive to work in saris and the like, Smith says one English employee arrived wearing braces and a string vest. She adds, "We are quite a diverse population already so for us it's about trying to maintain that and make sure that's valued by everyone in the company."

Facts and figures

Total number of staff: 43,000 worldwide, 350 in the UK
Office location: Central London; Hounslow and Heston, Middlesex
Industry sector: Healthcare
Annual turnover: US$7bn worldwide; £50m in the UK

Reliance Security Group Ltd

Boundary House
Cricketfield Road
Uxbridge
Middlesex
UB8 1QG

Telephone: 01895 205000
Fax: 01895 205085
Email: info@reliancesecurity.co.uk
www.reliancesecurity.co.uk

Pay and Benefits	★ ★ ★ ★ ☆
Training and Development	★ ★ ★ ⯪ ☆
Career Development	★ ★ ★ ★ ⯪
Working Conditions	★ ★ ★ ⯪ ☆
Company Culture	★ ★ ★ ★ ⯪

Biggest plus
The friendly, helpful workforce.

Greatest challenge
Providing the highest levels of customer service in the face of financial restraints.

Summary

Reliance is a privately owned company that has grown from its beginnings in supplying staff for the security industry to become a leader in facilities management and business process outsourcing as well as a range of security activities. Chairman and founder Brian Kingham is still actively involved in all aspects after 35 years. In the financial year to April 2008, turnover grew 10.7% to £382.6m, with profits before tax and exceptional items up 5.5% at £14.3m. It employs more than 13,000 people from a network of offices throughout the UK and has won many awards for its operations.

About the organisation

Reliance Security Group began in 1973, when Brian Kingham, then running a recruitment business, saw an opportunity to supply quality security services staff. This activity remains the core of the business to this day, with 9,500 people employed in various activities, ranging from patrols and key holding, through to specialist services including policing demonstrations and protests.

The company has grown organically and in 1987 was floated on the London Stock Exchange. Two decades later, Brian Kingham bought back the shares and the company is once again privately owned.

There are four main operating companies: Reliance Security Services, Reliance Secure Task Management, Reliance Facilities Management, and Reliance High Tech. Security Services is based around supplying security patrols, but has developed to include managed entry and exit of premises, alarm response and key holding and – through Project Security and Goldrange – security for major projects, events and the entertainment industry. Secure Task Management employs 2,900 people on contracts, chiefly within the criminal justice sector. Its activities include secure transport of prisoners, custody management, forensic medical services, secure logistics and administration. Facilities Management has about 700 people involved in all facets of running offices and other buildings, from M&E, landscaping and catering, to security. Clients are mostly in the private sector. High-Tech has 140 people engaged in developing ever more sophisticated security and associated remote monitoring technology for use in both the private and public sectors. As such, it works closely with the other operating companies to support them in their work.

In an increasingly competitive environment, Brian Kingham and his executives believe that through the combination of exceptional people, innovative solutions, a commitment to service excellence, plus a culture of continuous improvement, the business can develop long-term relationships with customers and so thrive. »

"If we can enable and support the Reliance team to work better each day than they did the day before, and to be more valuable than they were in previous employments, we will have competitive advantage" (Julian Nicholls, managing director)

Company Culture

Reliance sets great store by the quality of its people. In its annual report and accounts for 2007-08, Brian Kingham writes "It has been their [employees] professionalism and commitment, their willingness and enthusiasm to 'go the extra mile', which makes the Reliance Difference." Managing director Julian Nicholls adds "Our people approach is influenced by the belief that, if we can enable and support the Reliance team to work better each day than they did the day before, and to be more valuable than they were in previous employments, we will have competitive advantage."

Consequently, Reliance staff receive much more extensive training than is normally expected in the security industry. As well as running comprehensive on-the-job training initiatives, the company has set up an Academy programme, which involves the chairman and senior executives spending six days a year with managers and supervisors as well as outside specialists developing the organisation's people leadership skills. Feedback from these sessions suggests that participants find them useful, with well over 80% regarding them as good use of their time and beneficial to their jobs.

With so many employees spread around the country – in more than 30 centres – and many working inside other organisations, communication is seen as very important. Each company has its own newsletter, which also includes articles about the group as a whole.

Line managers have responsibility for managing their teams, but each unit has a human resources specialist, while more strategic initiatives are handled by the central HR teams.

Reliance works around the clock, but it stresses that employees are not expected to work long hours. In fact the company goes to great lengths to accommodate requests for flexible working from staff at all levels. Charmyn Hall, HR director at Reliance Secure Task Management, says she has senior employees working part-time, while some staff work only weekends or nights.

Innovation and Creativity

In its mission statement Reliance aims 'to add maximum value for our customers through innovative work practices.' One way in which the company puts this into practice is through the 'Red Book Scheme,' described by Iain Kennedy, director of people innovation, as "a supercharged suggestion scheme." Every site and every centre has a copy of the Red Book with the aim of encouraging employees to write down any ideas they get about how Reliance's services to its customers can be improved.

"Mostly it's security officers making very significant suggestions about how customers can improve their business," says Iain Kennedy. It is a measure of the commitment of the staff to the company that last year 15,000 suggestions were received. Many of them generated substantial savings.

In the same vein is the company's Continuous Improvement Programme, aimed at bringing about the goal of being 'one per cent better at 1,000 things we do' that is at the heart of what it calls 'The Reliance Difference.' Iain Kennedy says, "We are constantly talking to people about how we can do things better."

The company is also highly innovative in harnessing technology to improve its services. At the heart of this is the company Reliance High-Tech, which supports each of the business units through developing ever more sophisticated techniques in areas such as electronic surveillance and security. One particular example is a piece of equipment that helps protect guards working on their own by linking them to a monitoring station via a device worn around their necks.

Pay and Benefits

The company makes much of its attempts to be an exceptional employer in the security industry. It is proud of its Investors in People status and says that its employees are 'the cornerstone' of its business. "Working in partnership with our customers, we employ innovative management practices to promote employee involvement, skills enhancement, and exceptional work performance and recognition," says Brian Kingham. "With a policy of above-average remuneration and training, we are proud that we are able to recruit and retain personnel of the highest calibre."

Reward varies considerably between the companies within the group because in many cases Reliance is taking on government employees and needs to keep their terms and conditions on the same basis as those of their former colleagues in the public sector. Charmyn Hall stresses that because the company has to provide good value for its public sector customers, it needs to be innovative in how it rewards staff, for example with bonus schemes based on service delivery.

However, Reliance still claims to offer most workers packages that are well above the industry average. In particular, the company provides sick pay and pensions for employees, both of which are extremely rare in ≫

"We are constantly talking to people about how we can do things better"
(Iain Kennedy, director of people innovation)

"It has been employees' professionalism and commitment, their willingness and enthusiasm to 'go the extra mile', which makes the Reliance Difference" (Brian Kingham, founder and chairman)

the security industry. This treatment pays off in the form of considerable loyalty on the part of employees, with many receiving long-service awards.

The standard salary package for a senior manager includes a potential bonus, a car or car allowance, as well as use of mobile telephones and laptop computers. "Whatever they need to do the job," says Gwyn Jones, head of HR for Reliance Security Services.

Pensions are provided for all staff, with the company contribution starting at 1% of salary and rising to 10%. There is also life assurance and private medical cover.

Reward and recognition are a demonstration of the importance the company places on its people and it actively promotes an extensive awards scheme for all employees. In recognition of the outstanding service provided by people at locations across the UK, it receives hundreds of letters of commendation from customers each year. These commendations are acknowledged through Continuous Improvement Awards.

Career Development

Proud of the loyalty it attracts from its workforce, Reliance goes to great lengths to develop its employees. The Reliance Academy is the clearest manifestation of this. In his latest chairman's report, Brian Kingham says the academy's commitment to lifelong learning "has given renewed vigour and impetus to the work to support and inspire our people."

Each quarter, managers work with outside specialists from organisations such as Brunel University and Newcastle University's leadership centre, as well as customers, to develop people leadership skills within the business. All those responsible for one or more colleagues meet regularly to learn from one another and to hear about the latest techniques in leadership.

Charmyn Hall points out that the company makes a substantial investment in education. For instance, it sponsored her MBA and at any time there are many people gaining external qualifications in such areas as finance, marketing, human resources and security management. Staff taking such courses are given time off to study as well the funding to pay for them. Iain Kennedy says that one of the big benefits of external education is the exposure to outside ideas it brings.

But, conscious that the company does not have a huge budget for training and development, managers have become quite innovative in how they go about developing their teams. Throughout the business, for example, there are people on secondments and special projects. Another initiative involves HR departments recording the roles that employees have performed in the past, even prior to joining Reliance, so that managers can call upon that experience when the company enters new markets.

In addition, the company has begun running development centres for security officers. As part of this scheme, they are given personal development plans with the idea that the training forms part of the company's succession planning for the future.

Corporate Social Responsibility

Reliance is very active in the community, working nationally and through its sites around the country on crime-fighting initiatives, learning and development schemes for young people, support for the victims of crime, assistance in rehabilitating offenders, and support for football teams and other recreational and cultural activities.

One recent initiative was Reliance Secure Task Management's support for Kids Taskforce, a charity set up in 2007 to educate children aged between six and 16 about the dangers of modern life. In addition to giving the organisation money, the company is working in partnership with it, seconding staff to help schools learn how to use the Kids Taskforce resources.

On sustainability, the company is working hard to reduce its carbon footprint. It has introduced electric utility vehicles and operates a vehicle leasing scheme that provides vouchers to offset the carbon emissions of its mobile response vehicles. It has also attained accreditation for ISO 14001 and 18001. Last year, it sponsored 'Greening Your Office,' an A-Z guide to reducing the carbon footprint on the administrative side of a business. In addition, it is about to introduce video conferencing to reduce the need for travel. "There's a real commitment from the top that CSR will remain extremely high on the agenda," says Charmyn Hall.

The company is also committed to diversity in its employment policies. Managers point out that there is a lot more variety to the workforce than might be imagined. Steps have been made to hire more women in such roles as prisoner custody by stressing that the job is about 'having the people skills.' In one recent quarter, 70% of management appointments were female.

Facts and figures

Total number of staff: Over 13,000, mostly (9,500) in the core Security Services operations; 2,900 in Secure Task Management; 700 in Facilities Management; and 140 in High-Tech
Office location: HQ in Uxbridge, and over 68 sites around Britain
Industry sector: Security
Turnover: £382.6m (year to April 2008)

RLB | Rider Levett Bucknall

Rider Levett Bucknall UK

Millennium Point
Curzon Street
Birmingham B4 7XG

Telephone: 0121 503 1500
Fax: 0121 503 1501
Email: info@rlb.com
www.rlb.com

Pay and Benefits	★ ★ ★ ★ ★
Training and Development	★ ★ ★ ★ ★
Career Development	★ ★ ★ ★ ⯨
Working Conditions	★ ★ ★ ★ ★
Company Culture	★ ★ ★ ★ ★

Biggest plus
Freedom to develop and encouragement to go as far as you can.

Greatest challenge
Maintaining momentum and motivating staff in a difficult economic climate.

Summary

Rider Levett Bucknall UK (RLB) is a professional firm specialising in project management, quantity surveying and building surveying. Its client list ranges from BAE Systems, Tesco and Waitrose to the Ministry of Defence, the Prison Service, housing associations and other public sector bodies. The firm has around 390 employees, mostly based in Birmingham, Bristol, London, Manchester, Sheffield, the Thames Valley and Welwyn Garden City. Wholly owned by its staff, RLB is part of a successful international alliance with partners in Australasia and the Pacific Rim. Turnover and pre-tax profit for 2007-8 were £31m and £2.6m respectively, up from £25m and £2.2m in 2006-7.

About the organisation

Rider Levett Bucknall claims to be the world's third largest quantity surveying and project management practice. It was formed in June 2007 as a tripartite alliance between Bucknall Austin, a British project management and surveying firm, Rider Hunt, Australia's largest quantity surveyor with interests throughout Australasia and in the USA, and Levett & Bailey, the largest quantity surveyor in Hong Kong which also operates in China, Malaysia, Singapore and Macau. The three companies remain independent but work as a team, sharing expertise and clients across six continents, with expansion plans in booming economies such as India and the Gulf States.

"The alliance is all about an exchange of global clients and establishing an international brand," says RLB's operations director, Ann Bentley. "We were already well known in our own industry but we weren't big enough to be really competitive. The alliance has given us critical mass, enabling us to develop business from our alliance partners, explore new markets, and bid for the kind of global contracts that we couldn't have hoped to win on our own."

For the UK company the alliance marks a high point in a 60-year roller coaster ride that has embraced a stock market listing and delisting, rapid growth, diversification, near-collapse, receivership, and rebirth through a management buyout early in 2003.

The firm foresaw the slump in the commercial property sector, and since early 2007 has deliberately switched its main focus from commercial to public sector work, which now accounts for around 60% of its business, including defence, education and social housing. RLB also has a strong presence in the booming nuclear sector.

We're pretty conservative in how we spend our money and we're totally self-financed with no bank borrowings, so we're not a hostage to interest rates," says Bentley. "We're as confident as we can be given the current state of the economy."

Company Culture

"We're not yes-men," says Bentley. "Clients come to us because they genuinely believe we'll give them trustworthy and impartial advice – even if it means saying, 'That's a daft idea, why not do this instead?'"

This attitude permeates the whole company, which has retained a very flat structure despite a significant growth in headcount in recent years. Managers are very approachable, a style set by the UK firm's founder and chairman, David Bucknall, who is only slowly letting go of the reins at the age of 70. "David is so involving, he sees the firm as a kind of extended family," says Bentley.

"We give almost unlimited headroom to those who want it," says Hilary Richardson, RLB's HR manager. "People who are prepared to push boundaries may find these don't actually exist, and our managers are the sort of people who just pick things up and do them. If you want a hierarchical environment where you're checked up on and told what to do all the time, this isn't the place for you."

"Being wholly owned by our staff is very motivating," adds Bentley. "People are prepared to go the extra mile because ultimately they're doing it for themselves."

This is just as well, because RLB's professional staff may find themselves covering a lot of extra miles to make site visits and attend client meetings. "As a service business we are at people's beck and call," admits Bentley. But high pressure and long days are sporadic rather than continuous, and when you are not busy nobody will mind you fitting in a round of golf or picking the kids up from school. Flexible, home-based and part-time working are all feasible, thanks to new technology and the project-based nature of RLB's work. Sickness rates and staff turnover are low, and each of the firm's seven offices has an active social life.

Innovation and Creativity

"We have a reputation in the industry for assertive cost management, based on our unique 'four-dimensional' cost model that takes account of running costs over time as well as construction costs," says Bentley. "It enables clients

to model a number of fully costed options before the first stone is laid, depending on whether they want, say, cheaper capital outlay, lower maintenance costs or better resale prospects."

The model can show how installing fewer doors would reduce security costs or more expensive construction could improve insulation. Now it is being extended to take more account of sustainability issues.

Some of RLB's internal processes are equally forward-looking, such as its early adoption of smart pensions, and its enthusiasm for recruiting trainees from non-construction disciplines puts it ahead of competitors. A new performance management training course for line managers that focuses on encouraging outstanding performance rather than rectifying failures, is so innovative that RLB's training provider is marketing it to other clients.

The firm runs innovation forums in each of its core focus areas – people, service, customers and profit – and welcomes thoroughly researched business proposals from its staff. For example, someone spotted that some of RLB's UK customers were starting operations in the Caribbean and suggested that RLB followed them, so the firm opened a Caribbean office.

Pay and Benefits

RLB aims to pay top quartile salaries and commissions an annual peer review to benchmark this. "We conduct exit interviews and it's really rare for us to lose someone on pay," says Richardson. Staff are divided into half-a-dozen broad salary bands. Junior people are paid a small bonus that reflects the firm's performance, but for senior staff up to 30% of their remuneration is dependent on their personal performance and that of their business unit and the firm as a whole.

Unusually for its sector RLB is entirely owned by its employees and just over a third are shareholders. Although it is keen that more senior executives should own a significant stake in the firm, a proportion of shares are reserved for junior employees. The firm is also unusual in offering a 'smart' pension scheme that allows employer's National Insurance to be added to the employee's pension pot, with staff contributing 4% of salary and the company 5%. The scheme is very popular, with more 90% of staff participating.

The firm has an extensive flexible benefits programme. Staff can add or subtract five days from the standard 25-day holiday allowance, vary their working hours, and take various tax-efficient, salary-sacrifice ››

Managers are very approachable, a style set by the UK firm's founder and chairman, David Bucknall

options such as private health and dental cover, and cycle purchase, and nursery and child care vouchers (particularly popular with male staff, apparently). Other benefits include discounted air travel, spectacles and AA membership, interest-free season ticket loans,and the option of a company car for professionally qualified staff. The firm gives maternity and paternity benefits above the legal minimum, an employee assistance programme for staff and their immediate families, private health insurance guaranteeing 75% of salary for two years plus lump sum payment during long-term sickness, and life insurance of eight years' salary if in the pension scheme, one year's salary if not.

Career Development

RLB recruits between five and eight school leavers a year and provides work experience placements for secretarial trainees, school pupils and undergraduates. It also recruits about eight graduates annually. Half are from non-construction related disciplines. "Their ability and enthusiasm are phenomenal, and a different skill base such as languages can be very valuable to us, because we can train people in technical skills," says Bentley. Widening the scope of its recruitment has enabled RLB to raise the bar substantially in terms of the quality of applicants it accepts. "It costs us a few more grand to train them, but who cares if it means we get the cream?" says Bentley.

RLB's work covers three broad disciplines: quantity surveying (focusing on building techniques and cost analysis), building surveying, and project management. Once they have mastered the basics, recruits are assigned to live projects very quickly. "One of our graduates said he was surprised to be doing work of value within a couple of months," says Richardson. "Our work is also hugely varied, and we try to make sure trainees don't get bogged down on a single project."

RLB aims to fill at least half of posts through internal promotion and able people can move up quickly. "We're training people all the time and there's a significant drive to lift the lid and allow people to move up," says Richardson. The firm has around 70 partners, most of whom achieved this status before the age of 40. The chief executive is 40 and the head of the Welwyn office is 37.

As well as surveying and project management, staff can take professional qualifications in accountancy, marketing, HR, IT, and law, and MBAs and MScs. All managers are taught coaching and motivation skills. Annual staff turnover is 8.7% but it is common for leavers to return later in their careers.

Corporate Social Responsibility

"We're making a really big effort on the environment this year, both in our own operations and in ensuring that we provide sustainable advice to our clients," says Bentley. Sustainability is becoming a major part of RLB's unique 4D cost modelling, helping its clients to reduce a building's carbon footprint or limit energy usage and waste creation during construction.

RLB aims to cut its own CO_2 emissions by 20% this year. It has installed video conferencing in all offices to reduce travelling to meetings, is looking at how site visits can be reduced, and is doing some lateral thinking on promoting greener commuting. It has banned desk-side rubbish bins in favour of recycling points, uses smart light switches, low-energy bulbs and recycled paper, and has a personal carbon footprint calculator for staff. Season ticket loans and tax-efficient bicycle purchase encourage staff to leave their cars at home, and the company car scheme encourages them to choose low-emission vehicles.

Construction remains predominantly a white, male industry but RLB is working to increase its diversity. With women accounting for more than a quarter of staff and one of four directors, the firm is above the industry average, especially since the female director (Bentley) is a professional engineer. Ethnic minority representation has almost doubled in the last two years to 7% and RLB takes advice from the charity Scope on recruiting disabled people.

The firm donates a small amount of cash to charity and encourages payroll giving by staff, but it prefers to make gifts in kind, giving the equivalent of nearly £100,000 in professional time via pro bono (unpaid) work. It works extensively in schools through organisations like the Salford Business Education Partnership and Sandwell Council in the West Midlands, and has two 'construction ambassadors' who visit schools to support teachers and give kids a hands-on impression of how rewarding a career in construction can be.

The firm allows staff up to a week's paid leave for voluntary work, gives free professional advice to charitable organisations through Business in the Community, and is involved with the Birmingham Foundation that gives direct support to community entrepreneurs. A dozen senior staff are qualified external assessors for the Royal Institution of Chartered Surveyors.

RLB has Investor in People certification.

Facts and figures

Total number of staff: 390
Office location: Birmingham, plus Bristol, London, Manchester, Sheffield, the Thames Valley and Welwyn Garden City
Industry sector: Professional services
Annual turnover: £31m

RPS Group Plc

Centurion Court
85 Milton Park
Abingdon
Oxon OX14 4RY

Telephone: 01235 438151
Email: rpsmp@rpsgroup.com
www.rpsgroup.com

Pay and Benefits	★ ★ ★ ★ ★
Training and Development	★ ★ ★ ★ ★
Career Development	★ ★ ★ ★ ⯨
Working Conditions	★ ★ ★ ★ ⯨
Company Culture	★ ★ ★ ★ ★

Biggest plus
An intellectually stimulating but commercially successful workplace.

Greatest challenge
Maintaining communications across a global enterprise.

Summary

RPS is an international consultancy. It advises on the development of natural resources, land and property, environmental management, and the health and safety of people. Its 4,600 employees operate out of offices in 70 major towns and cities worldwide. In the financial year ended 30 April 2007, Group pre-tax profit was £45m, up 30% on the previous year. Fee income was £305m, a rise of 24% on 2006.

About the organisation

RPS is a British success story. Over the last 10 years, its growth rate has averaged 27.4% per annum. This expansion, the combination of acquisitions and organic growth, has resulted in the Group majoring on ambitious staff development and recruitment strategies. It focuses on the premium end of consultancy in the international private sector, and also advises governments. This focus allows RPS to maintain high margins (18% plus), far above many of its ostensible competitors.

The Group offers integrated services through three divisions. RPS Energy provides technical, commercial and project management support to the energy sector in the fields of offshore wind, exploration geosciences, reservoir engineering, carbon capture and storage, environmental management, decision risk management and H&S support services. RPS Planning & Development offers town planning, urban design, transport planning, architecture, civil and structural engineering, onshore wind, solar and tidal energy consultancy and the full range of environmental assessment services. And RPS Environmental Management provides advice and services in a range of areas including water management, safety and environmental liability consultancy, occupational health, occupational hygiene, environmental laboratories, and risk management systems to the property sector.

RPS trades in the UK, Ireland, the Netherlands, Poland, the Russian Federation, the United States, Canada, Australia, Malaysia and Singapore, and undertakes projects in many other parts of the world. To give an idea of its scale of operations, its energy division alone has an annual portfolio of over 500 projects, in over 100 countries, for over 100 clients. The Group is also known and respected for its very high-calibre people, who continue to power its growth by satisfying and exceeding its clients' expectations.

Among its many current projects, RPS is working on preparations for the 2012 London Olympics, advising on planning, transport, environment, and building design and urban design; and assisting Centrica Renewables on the development, engineering and construction of the largest wind farm under construction in UK waters. It also recently aided Scottish Power in developing Scotland's largest dedicated biomass-fired energy plant, through rigorous air quality, health risk and ecological studies.

»

"Over our 38-year history RPS people have shown remarkable ability to seek out and develop opportunities, whatever the difficulties"
(Alan Hearne, chief executive)

Company Culture

RPS is a company at ease with itself. People are expected to work really hard – but that work is satisfying and stimulating. It makes a difference in society and aims to add value to its client's activities – as the amount of repeat business from existing clients testifies. As Chairman Brook Land says, "Our mix of skills and the depth of experience of our staff enable us to advise our clients on some of the major issues of the twenty-first century."

The generally relaxed working environment and flat management structure encourage everyone to socialise with their colleagues. This may be the one of very few companies where "having fun" appears to be written into the five-year plan! Graham McMorran, technical director: "Working with RPS is about total commitment – but at reasonable levels. We won't expect people to work at weekends, for example. Some industries, architecture for instance, are notorious for asking ridiculous hours of employees. That sort of thing means that deadlines are not being managed properly."

Individual offices have their own character, partly reflecting regional differences and the varied professions, although increasingly, a Group culture is emerging. Projects often involve liaising with different offices and even different divisions, and many employees will find themselves working in multi-disciplinary teams with people in other RPS locations.

The Group culture overlays a very strong departmental ethos reinforced by regular team meetings, with directors definitely a part of the team rather than closeted in inaccessible locations. As Douglas Lamont, the Group's business information manager, puts it, "Everyone is totally committed to achieving a positive result and works closely with colleagues to make it happen."

If you are a team player who is articulate, and displays practicality and creativity in equal measure, you probably have what's needed to succeed at RPS. Good communication skills are vital, since you will have to deal professionally with other in-house experts, clients and often many other stakeholders. A poor communicator, however brilliant, is unlikely to shine here.

Innovation and Creativity

Instances of the Group's innovative and creative solutions are too numerous. RPS assisted OpenHydro with the design of the first grid-connected tidal device in the UK, a 250kW tidal turbine demonstrator unit at the European Marine Energy Centre test site in Orkney. This novel multi-bladed turbine is operated by the ebb and flow of tides rather than by wave movement, and its open centre minimises the effect on marine life.

Drilling for oil and gas in offshore waters less than 120m deep uses a technology known as jack-up drilling – and RPS is at the forefront of such consultancy. Its Joint Industry Project analyses data from previous installations around the world, verifies new geotechnical predictive analytical methods, and produces international guidelines for the safe emplacement and removal of jack-up rigs.

RPS in Newcastle, New South Wales, won the 2007 Infrastructure Category Award at the NSW Awards for Excellence in Surveying and Spatial Information. It won the award for works undertaken on behalf of Hunter Energy for the Seahampton to Rutherford 34.4m gas pipeline. The challenges set by the client's needs, and the often-rugged terrain in ecologically sensitive areas, demanded an integrated approach involving input from all specialist aspects of the business, including ecologists, planners, surveyors and GIS (Geographic Information System) mapping.

Pay and Benefits

RPS is acknowledged as one of the better payers in its sector, and is in the upper quartile. This is no accident. Lamont: "We have to recruit and retain the best people if we are to maintain our rate of growth. We promote from within, but we also need very talented individuals from elsewhere." That includes some high-flying women looking for challenging and rewarding work to return to after career breaks, and RPS has recruited a number of these in recent years.

A bonus is paid, but more as an added extra. When the team's targets are met, the bonus is good; if they're not met, there may still be a divisional bonus element as appropriate. However, the approach at RPS is more about boosting wages rather than making people rely on bonuses to sustain their standard of living.

There is a range of flexible working possibilities, supported by the i-zone project management system in place at many larger offices across the UK and Ireland. There are also outstanding Intranet and Extranet systems that allow people to identify colleagues by skill set, project experience and so on.

Non-cash rewards are included in an excellent flexible benefits scheme. This comprises everything one would expect of a top Plc, including life assurance, childcare vouchers, a private healthcare plan and discounts at nurseries and gyms. There is also a portable, independently administered, contributory pension scheme »

If you are a team player who is articulate, and displays practicality and creativity in equal measure, you probably have what's needed to succeed at RPS

"We have to recruit and retain the best people…we promote from within, but we also need very talented individuals from elsewhere"
(Douglas Lamont, group business information manager)

that allows users to put in as much of their salary as they wish; the employer also contributes up to 10% depending on the job level.

RPS also has various tax-free share purchase plans open to most employees, including one that doubles the number of shares purchased after three years. "We have one of the best share purchase plans in the industry," says Lamont. Senior staff have a share plan linked to their performance which gives them some free shares.

Career Development

As McMorran puts it, "graduates are the lifeblood of RPS." The Group operates more than one graduate recruitment scheme, and upwards of 100 new graduates will be taken on worldwide each year. One graduate entrant to the Group became a senior director less than 10 years after joining. RPS also operates a scheme whereby undergraduates can join the company for a year's industrial work placement, then go back to university to finish their course. The Group has strong relationships with many universities from Oxford and Cambridge to those more local to its many regional centres, such as Imperial College, UCL, Brunel, University College Cardiff, Dundee, Loughborough, Southampton, Nottingham, Lincoln, Sheffield, Huddersfield, UAE, UWA, Manchester and Leeds Metropolitan Universities or Queens University Belfast.

RPS has plenty of young minds – but there is certainly no ageism in the organisation. There are also large numbers of people in their thirties, forties and fifties and even those aged 65 and over!

The Group invests heavily in training, well above the industry average. It runs its own training schemes, many accredited with professional bodies. There is also considerable day-release degree study, combining salary-earning work with a professional qualification.

Succession management and staff mobility are particularly well handled at RPS. It encourages staff to register their areas of interest on a central online jobs database so that they automatically receive immediate notification by email of all relevant job opportunities a week before adverts appear in the press. During 2008, RPS introduced new online staff appraisals as part of its developing centralised HR system. These allow all employees to check and update their own personal records, qualifications and working requirements; employees can apply for annual leave (which includes a degree of buy-back flexibility). Staff can also apply for further training using this system. Managers can then approve applications in real time online.

There is plenty of opportunity to move around within the Group, and to undertake projects overseas. As Lamont says, "People can add to their knowledge and get a lot of additional experience without leaving the company."

Corporate Social Responsibility

The Group's success is in large part a result of its reputation as a trustworthy business partner that promotes sustainability within its own operations and in client projects. It is proud to have been included in the FTSE4Good index of leading companies since its inception in 2001.

RPS is heavily involved in many of its local communities. During the financial year to 30 April 2007, the company and its staff gave or raised over £214,000 in charitable contributions. Adding in the £153,000 spent on academic bursaries and educational initiatives not connected to staff training, the Group's total contribution to the communities in which it operates was over £367,000.

The Group supports Tree Aid and its educational, tree planting and woodland conservation programmes in sub-Saharan Africa with charitable donations towards its work in Mali.

During 2008 and 2009, RPS will commit £45,000 annually to provide three Urban Design Scholarships, working in partnership with the publishers of the Architects' Journal and in association with Design for London (now part of the London Development Agency).

The Group contributes to environmental management in many of the projects that it undertakes for clients. It advises international bodies, governments, local authorities and private companies on improving their environmental performance. Internally, 52% of the electricity purchased by RPS in the UK in the last financial year was from a 'Green' tariff, and this figure will continue to rise in the coming years. It is also switching to lower-emission vans and company cars, reducing the energy consumption of its offices and introducing minimum environmental standards for all new offices and office refurbishment.

RPS maintains and implements documented Quality Management Systems in certain parts of its business to ensure compliance with ISO 9001. The Group also has a detailed financial reporting management system that includes checks and reviews, financial modelling, accountability and transparency at every level.

Facts and figures

Total number of staff: 4,600 worldwide, 2,550 in the UK
Office location: Abingdon, Oxon and 70 major towns and cities globally
Industry sector: Consultancy
Turnover: £45m

Saffery Champness

CHARTERED ACCOUNTANTS

Saffery Champness

Lion House
Red Lion Street
London
WC1R 4GB

Telephone: 020 7841 4000
Fax: 020 7841 4100
Email: info@saffery.com
www.saffery.com

Pay and Benefits	★ ★ ★ ★ ⯪
Training and Development	★ ★ ★ ★ ☆
Career Development	★ ★ ★ ★ ⯪
Working Conditions	★ ★ ★ ★ ⯪
Company Culture	★ ★ ★ ★ ☆

Biggest plus
One of the best-kept secrets in the sector.

Greatest challenge
Recruiting and retaining excellent people.

Summary

Saffery Champness is an independent top 20 firm of chartered accountants. It focuses on advising owner-managed businesses in a variety of commercial sectors, wealthy individuals, families and trusts, charities, other not-for-profit organisations, and landed estates. The firm has nine offices across the UK, one in Guernsey, and one in Geneva. It also has worldwide associations in over 100 countries through member firms of Nexia International, the ninth-largest international accounting network.

About the organisation

Founded in 1855 by Joseph Saffery, the modern firm can be dated to the 1980s. In that decade, it set up its Guernsey office, which today is one of the largest independent firms of its type on the island. In addition, Saffery merged with Champness Cowper to create Saffery Champness.

October 2008 saw a further significant development with the opening of the Saffery Champness Geneva office. This allows the firm to serve international private wealth owners more directly and doubled its offshore locations.

Also in 2008, the firm opened a new office in the heart of Manchester. This expansion, although impressive, is controlled. Rather than arbitrarily growing its network, Saffery Champness tend to be where large concentrations of its clients are. Its partners are also conscious that its smaller size and nimbleness compared to some top 20 firms are what make it special, and it is keen to preserve those qualities.

Having dabbled in non-core activities such as portfolio management and financial services in the 1990s, the firm today is definitely focused on its strengths: mainstream audit, tax and private wealth. Within that ambit is a series of national practice groups. These are landed estates; private wealth; media and entertainment; not-for-profit; owner-managed businesses; professional and consultancy services; and property. The firm has a leading role in a number of these areas.

The approach of Saffery Champness is distinctively proactive, very different from the traditionally reactive accountancy model. Its concept of service is to solve problems, exploit opportunities and turn advice into action.

In the financial year 2007/8, the firm grew its mainland billings by 11% on the previous year to £35.6, and its total billings (including its international earnings) by 9.5% to £48.9m. Fee income has increased every year since 2001/2.

Company Culture

Saffery Champness has a distinctive culture, the result of three factors: size, relationships and integrity. On the issue of size, the firm is large enough to handle all client needs but small enough to tailor its services. Relationships are key. As managing partner Rob Elliott says, "The personal and professional relationships with our clients and our staff have been the foundation upon which the firm has been built." And integrity came out strongly in a recent customer survey commissioned by the firm through an independent consultancy. One client quote, typical of the majority, was, "I find them very competent and very trustworthy."

Refreshingly in a top 20 firm, there is a distinct lack of ego. As Nigel Boniface, head of HR, puts it, "Nobody seems to tell you how you should work. You're free to work the way that suits you, and nobody criticises it." There is also considerable scope to develop, but no one is overlooked; good work gets noticed.

Although Saffery Champness people work hard, this is definitely not a sweatshop. The board and managing partner take a genuine interest in staff, and it has been known for them to tell fee-earners to ease up. The firm does look for hard work and effort, and inevitably there are some long hours. But Saffery Champness is not about stress and burnout.

The firm has a strikingly wide range of flexible working options: at the last count, there were no fewer than 12 different arrangements, from full time to four days a week, short hours on one day and longer on others, etc. Females make up 50% of the firm, with 20% of them doing some form of part-time work.

Another difference is that Saffery Champness has no grapevine, no rumour mill. If people have heard something, they've done so officially, aided by the excellent internal communications programme.

Innovation and Creativity

Unlike some accountancy firms, Saffery Champness never stands still. A good example of this was the opening of

The firm has a strikingly wide range of flexible working options: at the last count, there were no fewer than 12 different arrangements

"We rarely lose people because of money: pay is not a key issue" (Nigel Boniface, head of HR)

its Geneva office, a decision it researched extensively before proceeding. Jonathan Fox, executive partner: "Our offering in Geneva is unique: we're providing bespoke fiduciary, banking and private wealth services all mixed into one – almost like a consultancy. No other accountancy practice has ever done this."

The firm has also made a name for itself with its sector publications. Its *Creative Industry Survey of 2008*, for example, received considerable press coverage. Researched by the firm, this survey looked at a UK sector comparable in size to financial services. Despite worries about the credit crunch, it found that 55% of respondents were positive about the coming 12 months.

Again unusually perhaps for a firm in its sector, Saffery Champness warmly embraces the latest communications technology. Its website boasts a series of podcasts, while its employees can view and select their own total reward statements through its intranet or online. The new 'mybenefits' system allows them to monitor the value of their pay, pension, bonus, healthcare and other parts of their package.

Pay and Benefits

The firm aims to recruit bright and ambitious people from a variety of backgrounds looking for challenging professional careers. In return it provides exciting development opportunities and excellent promotional prospects, together with the chance to work in a friendly, progressive environment.

Boniface: "We rarely lose people because of money; pay is not a key issue." This was confirmed in 2008 by the global human capital consultancy Watson Wyatt, which found Saffery Champness well positioned in terms of salary.

As a partnership, the firm has no stock options. However, every member of staff participates in profit sharing, geared to the gross profitability of the business. The firm pays overtime for all grades up to the senior level, with those above this level receiving a performance-related bonus. There are also cash payments for introducing new clients, which can be significant: 10% of the first year's fee, or 5% if a one-off fee.

Saffery Champness was one of the first providers of flexible benefits in the chartered accountancy sector. This has proved to be a big incentive in recruiting and retaining top people, and the firm continues to add »

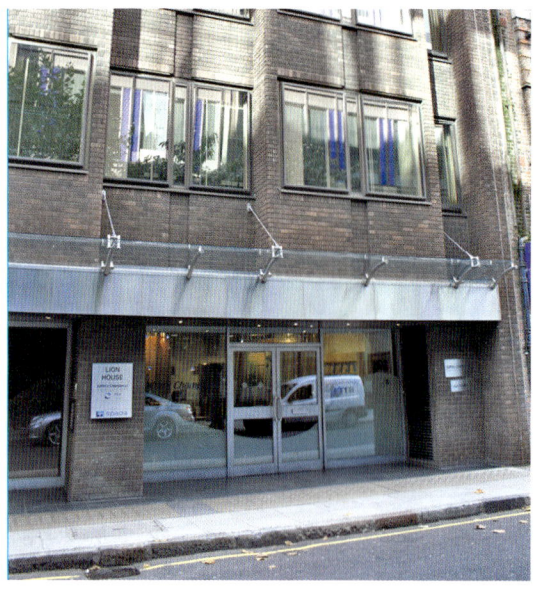

"Having previously worked for a Big Four firm, I'm definitely glad I made the move to Saffery Champness" (A Corporate Tax Senior at Saffery Champness)

to its range. Its benefits now include a pension scheme, health assessment and GP support, group life cover, childcare vouchers, critical illness insurance, home and contents insurance, worldwide travel insurance and more. Staff can take up to five extra days' holiday by salary sacrifice; similarly, they can take up to five fewer days and take that entitlement as cash. Its cycle-to-work scheme allows staff to lease a bike from the firm up to a value of £1,000.

The firm has a fun day for every office, and also a social event that brings all staff together once a year. Each of the offices has its own year-end celebrations, and there is an active sports and social committee.

Career Development

The firm has an impressive and well-designed training and development package. Technical training is first class, supplemented throughout by people management abilities to help graduates and other trainees build a balanced set of skills. By the time they qualify, they are ideally placed to develop their careers as they would want.

Saffery Champness people certainly seem to be more content than those in some other top 20 firms. This quote, from a Corporate Tax Senior, is typical: "Having previously worked for a Big Four firm, I'm definitely glad I made the move to Saffery Champness. I've found it to be a much more relaxed environment. My work has been varied and interesting from the start, with plenty of direct client contact and opportunities for taking ownership of the work."

This appreciation extends to non-technical staff. An IT support analyst said: "Saffery Champness has a reputation of looking after its staff and I've certainly found this to be the case. The work is challenging and varied, so being part of such a supportive and knowledgeable team makes for a great working environment." It's not necessary to be a graduate to join the firm's trainee programme – something which definitely sets it apart within the top 20. It takes both non-graduates and mature students.

Exceptional performance is recognised, in some cases by job titles such as supervisor, manager and senior manager, all below partner level. There is an in-depth discussion about everyone at the time of their salary review,

and appropriate development opportunities are identified through individual performance and development reviews.

There are openings for overseas secondment through the Nexia connection, and also through the firm's own international offices in Guernsey and Geneva.

Partners in each office act as mentors to junior staff, and to colleagues if appropriate. The firm also pays for specific and high-level external coaching, which it sees as an investment in its future.

Corporate Social Responsibility

The firm has a spread of most ethnic minorities, particularly of Asian backgrounds. And females are well represented: with 50% for the firm as a whole and 19% at partner level which is a higher percentage than many other top 20 firms.

Saffery Champness helped found the Holborn Business Improvement Partnership, an initiative created by businesses in the area to improve the local environment. It initially gave free accountancy advice to the partnership and now has a number of staff sitting on various committees to assist it.

It also does pro bono work, offering its services where they can make a difference. One recent case in point was a small charity, which was eligible for funding if it could produce audited accounts – but couldn't afford accountancy fees. A member of the firm stepped in and offered his services to them for free.

The firm has a vigorous environmental policy that continues to develop. In the year to March 2008, for example, it reduced its paper consumption by 200,000 sheets – the equivalent of 24 trees. Its various recycling schemes in the current year saved 25 tonnes of waste from going to landfill, nearly double the previous year's saving. It monitors its water consumption in its London head office, and used 560,000 litres less water in 2007/8 than in 2006/7.

Saffery has strict environmental guidelines. These include buying paper from sustainably managed forests, using double-sided printing for internal documents, returning junk mail to senders and recycling wherever possible. Its bottled water comes from a company whereby all profits go to help the third world.

Facts and figures

Total number of staff: 455 (UK and overseas)
Office locations: Head office in London, plus eight other UK offices and offices in Guernsey and Geneva
Industry sector: Accountancy
Total billings: £48.9m

Shaw Trust

Fox Talbot House
Bellinger Close
Greenways Business Park
Chippenham
Wiltshire SN15 1BN

Telephone: 01225 716364/716300
www.shaw-trust.org.uk

Pay and Benefits	★ ★ ★ ★ ☆
Training and Development	★ ★ ★ ★ ☆
Career Development	★ ★ ★ ★ ☆
Working Conditions	★ ★ ★ ⯪ ☆
Company Culture	★ ★ ★ ★ ⯪

Biggest plus
Impeccable social goals combined with impressive business drive.

Greatest challenge
Maintaining culture as Government policies and contracts change and new players enter the market.

Summary

Shaw Trust is a national charity that provides training and work opportunities for people who are disadvantaged in the labour market due to disability, ill health or other social circumstances. It is the UK's largest voluntary sector provider of employment for disabled people, but sees lots of opportunity to grow: nearly one in five people of working age in the UK is disabled but only about half of them are in work. The Shaw Trust assisted 67,355 clients in 2007/08, getting 13,030 of them into employment. It has 1,353 employees across 160 sites nationwide, an income of £72.9m, and runs 200 projects.

About the organisation

Shaw Trust was formed in 1982, in the Wiltshire village of Shaw, during the International Year for Disabled People. A group of local business people had the plan to help a small group of severely disabled people get jobs by focusing on what they could do, rather than what they could not. They set up a horticultural project to achieve this. Director general of the Trust, Tim Papé OBE DL, was one of this original group.

The Trust has grown quickly. In 2000 Shaw Trust had 488 staff, helping 10,000 clients with income of £30.6m. By 2008 it had worked with more than 294,000 people since its start, empowering more than 64,000 of them to find and stay in employment.

Shaw Trust helps its clients achieve their aims by providing guidance on finding jobs; training and benefits; supporting increased independence for disabled people; creating jobs through social enterprise; and working in partnership with employers, local authorities and health trusts. "Our drive and determination to do the best for every single client is what drives our success, and raises our aspirations every year," says Papé. Many of its services are tailored to the specific requirements of people with issues such as mental ill health, substance misuse problems or learning disability.

It is the largest provider of the Government's new Pathways to Work and New Deal for Disabled People programmes, and is the only not-for-profit organisation viewed as a major bidder for these contracts. The Government's Workstep programme is a big source of income for the Trust.

Shaw Trust also offers a range of services for organisations, from support in employing disabled people to advice on how to make their websites more accessible. Its 36 shops are used to raise money, and promote awareness of the Trust's work. In addition to donated goods, the shops sell new goods, including items made by people with disabilities.

"Our drive and determination to do the best for every single client is what drives our success, and raises our aspirations every year"
(Tim Papé OBE DL, director general)

Company Culture

Shaw Trust delivers social purpose in a thoroughly businesslike way. Papé is driving the business the way any corporate would attack its goals. "Growth is crucial for us because it means we can support more people to achieve their work ambitions and greater independence," he says.

But there's no losing focus on the Trust's mission 'to provide the resources and opportunities for disabled and disadvantaged people to engage more fully within society and realise their potential, principally through access to employment.' Shaw Trust's approach to delivering on this mission is effective. "Our results and reputation for efficiency, matched with our passion for the clients we serve, has seen us rewarded with unparalleled success in securing New Deal for Disabled People contract renewals and brand new European Social fund money," says Papé.

Staff are keen to make a difference to society, and they're skilled and professionally equipped to do this. About 75% work directly with clients and tend to have well-developed life skills. "They've got to have enthusiasm to work in quite often challenging environments," says business performance manager Nick Lee. "It's about the rewards not only being financial, but more around the work and the outcomes of the work." Similar roles can be found in mainstream recruitment businesses but there the focus is on how much money you get.

Realising potential is at the forefront of the Trust's mind, and a highlight of its year are its STAR Awards that recognise the achievements of clients, employers, partner organisations and staff. The finals are major events and in 2007 Duncan Bannatyne from TV's Dragon's Den presented the awards.

Employee Nik Brooks, who won a staff award last year, said, "It's typical of Shaw Trust to publicly congratulate their clients, staff and supporters. I feel revitalised and even more determined and motivated."

Innovation and Creativity

Always ambitious, and with a grand vision, Shaw Trust has extended the reach of its services by launching its first venture with an organisation outside the UK – a working partnership with Integracja in Poland. And exploiting its experience and in-house skills to the full, the Trust has developed a web accreditation service that offers a comprehensive audit of web accessibility combining a full technical audit with rigorous disability use testing. It's a revenue stream for the charity and is considered the best of its kind in the UK. It has also created a free online web resource detailing how organisations can support their staff who are suffering from mental health problems.

Openness and communication are seen as vital to the Shaw Trust culture. The organisation produces the weekly 'Shaw Thing' internal bulletin to ensure that employees are kept up to date with changes and developments within the business. But going beyond this, director general Tim Papé has made himself available to answer any question put to him by staff. The service is called 'Ask Tim' and though he might seek advice and assistance, he does answer all queries himself.

Pay and Benefits

"We need to attract people who have the skills," says Carol Alexander, chief officer, People & Performance. "Our salaries are competitive against other charities, and on the higher side including our benefits. But we pitch it that there is real job satisfaction. What we do changes peoples' lives."

You can't expect a private sector pay cheque. Salaries are benchmarked with an external survey each year, and the Trust checks out what its competitors are paying. The basic salary average for a front-line adviser is about £20,000-£22,000. Around 10% of staff earn more than £30,000. There is also a significant contribution payment scheme, which runs annually, so people delivering sustained performance can earn additional amounts, picked up in appraisals.

Beyond salary the Trust offers a flexible benefits scheme (considered unusual in the sector), contributory pension scheme, health insurance, income protection insurance and medical insurance. It also offers childcare vouchers, five weeks' holiday per year and disability, maternity and paternity leave, and flexible working.

"We value people," says Alexander. "We give paid time off when someone's having a crisis; it eases people when there's pressure on, and we get it back in bucket loads."

Managers have a budget for recognising and rewarding exceptional performance on an ad hoc basis. This typically involves small 'thank you' presents or additional time off.

"...there is real job satisfaction. What we do changes peoples' lives" (Carol Alexander, chief officer, People and Performance)

...a highlight of its year are its STAR awards that recognise the achievements of clients, employers, partner organisations and staff

Career Development

One thing that new starters at Shaw Trust can be sure of is that they get thorough training in disability equality, mental health awareness, and employment law. It's fundamental to the business. Much of this is delivered through e-learning modules in conjunction with management supervision and assistance.

The organisation has a £1m training budget, which is spread across a thorough induction programme of two to three months, right through to its leadership development programme. The induction process is intended to give new employees a feel for the business from day one then build on it over subsequent weeks. "It's also welcoming," adds Alexander.

The leadership development programme involves around 40 days in total, and is a mix of conventional classes, coaching, job shadowing and action learning. Those involved will take responsibility for a particular business project for the Trust. Any employee can apply for it, and those who aren't able to go on it get access to other staff development modules.

Most of the organisation's staff work directly with clients, but the Trust also funds professional qualifications where appropriate in finance, IT, and HR and marketing.

Alexander estimates nearly 40% of Shaw Trust people are involved in some kind of continuous professional development. Managers are also encouraged to shadow frontline staff to stay connected with how the Trust operates at the sharp end.

Another opportunity for development comes with the Employee Forum, which meets at least four times a year. As well as taking an active role in staff issues and reviewing policies, the 14 forum members contribute to the development of the following year's business plan.

There are opportunities to work abroad following the Trust's expansion overseas. It has links with organisations in Romania and Australia as well as Poland.

Corporate Social Responsibility

The very nature of Shaw Trust's work is putting something back into communities. Just one example is its local partnership with Disc and Mental Health matters in Middlesborough. Through this initiative, 360 participants with disabilities, mental health illnesses, or a history of substance or alcohol misuse, found work or achieved qualifications.

And as you'd expect, Shaw Trust is determined to support equality and diversity in its own workplace as well as encourage and assist it in other organisations.

Managers check at least once a year with employees that its practices are not disabling them from developing and using their abilities. The proportion of its employees declaring a disability is 18.55%, close to the 19.0% of the population as a whole. To keep pushing this it will also interview all disabled candidates who meet the essential/minimum criteria.

Shaw Trust has also taken positive action in recruitment to help increase the number of staff from black and ethnic minority groups by offering work trials and tasters. On top of this the Trust has been recognised as one of the UK's top employers by Stonewall, the organisation working for equality and justice for lesbians, gay men and bisexuals.

The Trust has a Code of Conduct for staff, clients, employer partners and sub-contractors to adhere to. The Code asks them all to challenge discriminatory behaviour. A confidential helpline is available for people suffering from harassment, bullying or illegal discrimination, and runs regular employee surveys to check for harassment and discrimination, and it acts upon the findings.

The Trust is expanding its diversity policy by having a supplier diversity manager to make sure the businesses it deals with represent an ethnically diverse and rich group of companies. "We're not just using the big boys," says Alexander. "We think we're ahead of the game with this, and it'll help us move forward."

Shaw Trust has just agreed a new environmental strategy recognising there's more it can do in this area. Its sites recycle the usual suspects: paper, print cartridges and computers. It is embracing teleconferencing and video conferencing to reduce the impact of staff car journeys.

Amongst the Trust's social enterprises are garden centres and a plant nursery.

Facts and figures

Total number of staff: 1,353
Office location: Chippenham, Wiltshire, with 160 sites and 36 shops nationwide
Industry sector: Charity
Turnover: £72.9m

SYBASE®

Sybase (UK) Ltd

Sybase Court
Crown Lane
Maidenhead
SL8 8QZ

Telephone: 01628 597100
Email: emea-recruiting@sybase.com
www.sybase.com

Pay and Benefits	★ ★ ★ ⯨ ☆
Training and Development	★ ★ ★ ★ ☆
Career Development	★ ★ ★ ★ ☆
Working Conditions	★ ★ ★ ☆ ☆
Company Culture	★ ★ ★ ☆ ☆

Biggest plus
Steady growth over the past five years, which shows no sign of slowing.

Greatest challenge
Uncertainty as to where the market is going next.

Summary

Sybase is an enterprise application software company whose focus is managing information from the data centre through to the point of action – everything from database systems to mobile messaging. The aim is to have a virtual platform across the complete product suite. Based in California, Sybase employs 4,000 people in 94 global locations. Sybase (UK) is the largest subsidiary with 250 staff, based mostly in Maidenhead, the others being in two London offices and Bristol. Rapid growth through acquiring one/two companies per year for five years has resulted in Sybase being the world leader in delivering "the unwired enterprise". Subsidiary Sybase365 is world leader in mobile messaging.

About the organisation

Initially Sybase found fame as a client/server database developer. For the past five years, a fresh strategy and a series of well-planned acquisitions of small, specialist software companies – although the most recent was of a part of Cable and Wireless – have seen the company conquer the leading position in the field of mobile data. Sybase's software products link central databases or portals and then through data analysis, mobilise information to get it to the point of use, such as laptop computer screens and/or hand-held devices. Currently there is no other company making whole applications available across mobile platforms.

Under the leadership of chief executive John Chen, Sybase is witnessing good growth and changes while simultaneously returning excellent profits. In the 2007 financial year, Sybase lived up to its forecast and became a billion dollar turnover company – indeed group turnover was US$1.026bn in 2007 (US$876m in 2006, US$819m in 2005) while operating income increased to US$169m in 2007 (US$134m in 2006, US$122m in 2005). "The company's strong business pipeline, combined with our proven ability to execute, enables us to raise our 2008 financial targets," says Chen. While UK-specific figures are not published, the financial performance is testimony to Sybase's competency in its core enterprise software and services business. Over 60% of firms in the City, 75% on Wall Street, and 81% of Fortune 100 companies run on Sybase applications, which are widely recognised for their robustness and scalability.

In October 2008, Sybase repeated its success in Mobile Village's annual awards by securing four Mobile Star awards, cementing its global market leadership positions in mobile and embedded databases, mobile management and security, mobile middleware and synchronisation. "Our challenge in mobile applications is to know where the market is looking to grow, moving forwards," says HR director Brendan Coyne. "This is very much unknown territory, knowing what the next big thing or development is going to be." »

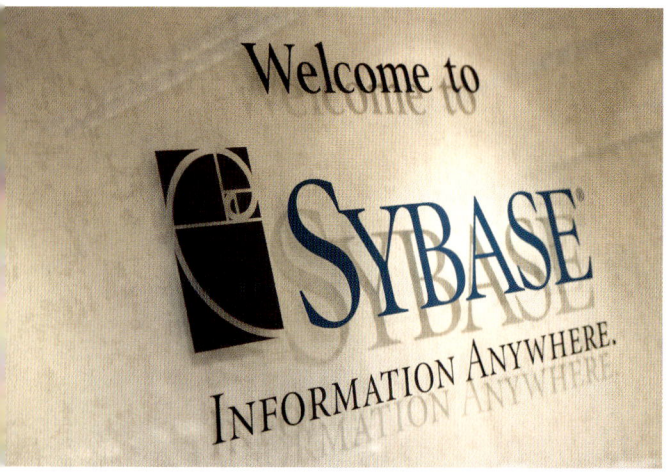

"The company's strong business pipeline, combined with our proven ability to execute, enables us to raise our 2008 financial targets" (John Chen, chief executive)

Company Culture

Sybase is pragmatic in its approach. To be a part of Sybase is to be part of the Sybase family. People who do well here are those who enjoy autonomy, without always being told what to do. Meeting deadlines is the goal. No-one is micro-managed and there is a lot of freedom in the way people do their jobs. The term work-life balance actually starts to mean something. This is a friendly company where employee opinion surveys show 89% of staff saying the key reason they work at Sybase is the people they work with (up from 85% the previous year).

Senior management is open and approachable. Indeed, Coyne says that anyone who needs to ask a question can pick up the phone or email a senior manager, even if that person is the global head of a division. "You can always expect a straight and honest answer," says Coyne. Global heads give quarterly webcasts to all staff at which questions are encouraged and ensure they host face-to-face staff meetings whenever visiting offices.

Many teams are international and one-third of UK employees have a line manager outside the UK. With a US West Coast HQ and thriving subsidiaries in South East Asia, there could be pressure on hours. "It's a question of establishing a balance and not doing long hours just because Sybase is global," says Coyne. Smart working around time zones is a byword, with much calculated use of 'telepresence' suites and videoconferencing. Everyone has a mobile phone and laptop.

Working hours are flexible and if someone puts in extra time they can take time in lieu. Some staff work part-time or from home, and much effort is expended to try to arrange people's hours to suit family commitments. On overseas trips staff are encouraged to take a day off to look around the city.

Innovation and Creativity

There are updates of Sybase product suites regularly. For the past five years, Sybase has been particularly busy acquiring one or two small companies in the UK every year. In the past 12 months however only one acquisition was made, that of a small part of Cable and Wireless, to develop mobile messaging services.

"There are many new releases planned for the first quarter of 2009," says Coyne. R&D is split globally with 10% of the workforce in the UK working on R&D. "A lot of mobile applications are developed in the UK at Bristol," says Coyne. When a new product is launched the whole company is invited to suggest product names with prizes for winners. It gets people involved and embeds understanding of the products, including self-awareness.

"There are our Star Performer awards where anyone can nominate any other employee, and it can be at departmental level, divisional or country level, or global level," says Coyne. "The nomination can be for anything – a business process, modifying a product – anything. "We have them quarterly with prizes of up to US$1,000 (about £500) for the successful nomination."

Pay and Benefits

"All of our benefits apply from day one of employment," says Coyne. Sybase aims to pay salaries near to the 60th percentile – which means 'better than average' – and benchmarks itself against similar companies. There is a grading structure but that doesn't restrict people's salaries, Coyne indicates.

Salaries for support engineers can start at around £35,000, while experienced salespeople can earn above market base salaries with the opportunity to add a further 100%+ through commission. Non-sales staff can earn up to 25% bonus based on overall group performance and seniority. Sybase's strong performance over the last four years has meant near-target bonuses. All staff can purchase Sybase shares at a 5% discount and new hires and promotions receive stock options. Further stock options are awarded to high-performing 'key contributors' – about 10-15% of staff a year.

The stakeholder pension scheme is considered to be generous, with the company contributing 6.75% of gross remuneration – including bonus – for all staff from day one. The minimum individual contribution is 3%. In the event of death in service, disability or serious accident, payouts of up to four times salary are made. Private health insurance cover ensures any long-term sick receive full pay for six months and up to 75% of salary thereafter until retirement age. Compassionate leave is offered.

Other benefits include 25 days' holiday, (plus public holidays) a year, which everyone is encouraged to take. There is travel and medical insurance for all staff and their families, discounted gym membership, 'vitality days' (health assessments, nutrition advice and so on), car allowance and a fuel card for most staff (not just those who travel on business), childcare vouchers, cycle-to-work scheme, employee assistance programme, and a money club promising to procure anything from washing machines to holidays at the cheapest available price.

"People who do well here are those who enjoy autonomy without always being told what to do" (Brendan Coyne, HR director)

At 6.25 years, the average length of service is long for the IT industry. People stay because of the opportunity to grow a career

Career Development

"Historically, this is not usually the first job for staff," says Coyne. "Most have a technical background." At 6.25 years, the average length of service is long for the IT industry. People stay because of the opportunity to grow a career.

Sybase expends much effort in succession planning and prefers to promote internally, which accounted for 75% of senior posts filled over the past 12 months. Promotion is merit-based. The average age in the company is 41 – up from 34 just a year previously – with some senior managers in their mid-20s, others in their mid-40s. "We are focusing this year on a management development programme called AIM – Advance Into Management – about recognising our next generation of managers, and also for people thinking about line management responsibility," says Coyne.

At annual performance reviews – although monitoring is pretty much constant, certainly happening quarterly – clear individual goals are set, as is an individual training plan. Most staff can expect 10-15 days' training a year, delivered through internal and external courses, and online. "With online learning, objectives are discussed quarterly to see if this is what the person is seeking to do," says Coyne. There is a good uptake of Sybase's own technical qualifications and foreign languages also feature strongly with staff.

There is a structured two-year management development programme for all managers – in the UK 42 managers are currently working through this module, and are 18 months into the work. "The next six months are very important, being concerned with putting everything into perspective," says Coyne. "This is an ongoing programme." All new recruits are mentored for their first six months and executive coaching is available for senior managers. Sybase also encourages studying for MBAs and other masters degrees, providing study leave and assistance with fees of up to €6,000 a year.

Corporate Social Responsibility

Sybase has a declared statement of business ethics and values that every employee signs up to. This covers how the company conducts business ethically, treating people fairly, and who it does business with to avoid any conflicts of interest. As a US listed company, Sybase is governed by Sarbanes-Oxley and the rigorous internal fiscal reporting controls that the Act demands. There are rigorous checklists, often requiring five different

approvals for sign-off. These approvals are needed at local and global levels up to the chief executive. Each manager has training on what needs approval and by whom. All the approval checklists can be referenced online, and managers are trained on how to use this tool – it cannot be bypassed.

Sybase is a meritocracy and an equal opportunity employer – diversity is not an issue here. "Everyone is employed for the role," says Coyne. "Race, gender, age, disability simply do not come into it. There is a job description and skill sets are matched against it." In the UK 34% of employees are female. Anyone working overseas is paid the going rate in that country, wherever the employee has come from. Sybase is a culturally sensitive organisation – being global, the company has to understand different people and different cultures in order to do business.

The company supports charities favoured by employees with which they have links or can relate to – for example individuals running marathons to raise money for charities, perhaps connected to family members suffering from a serious illness.

Within the company, recycling of paper, plastic, cans, and printer supplies is carried out as much as possible. Computer equipment that becomes outmoded (for example, staff laptops are replaced every three years) is donated to the charity Computer Aid for re-use in developing countries. In the Maidenhead building there are checks to see that all computer screens are switched off when unattended. The building itself is being refurbished in 2009 and staff are being asked to make suggestions as to where redundant office equipment can be sent or recycled – and how the company can become more environmentally friendly going forward. Of course there is the argument that Sybase, by the nature of its business, is improving efficiency in business and thus contributing to environmental efforts. But Sybase intends to do more than that.

Facts and figures

Total number of staff: 4,000 worldwide, 250 in the UK
Office location: Maidenhead, London, Bristol, and 94 other global locations
Industry sector: Software and services
Turnover: US$1.026bn for global operations

TATE & LYLE

CONSISTENTLY FIRST IN RENEWABLE INGREDIENTS

Tate & Lyle Sugars

Thames Refinery
Factory Road
Silvertown
London E16 2EW

Telephone: 020 7540 1223
Email: recruitment@tateandlyle.com
www.tateandlyle.com

Pay and Benefits	★ ★ ★ ★ ☆
Training and Development	★ ★ ★ ★ ☆
Career Development	★ ★ ★ ★ ☆
Working Conditions	★ ★ ★ ★ ☆
Company Culture	★ ★ ★ ★ ⯪

Biggest plus
Open employee communications and a real appetite for change.

Greatest challenge
Overcoming external factors that provide barriers to growth.

Summary

Tate & Lyle Sugars is a main operating division of Tate & Lyle PLC. It is renowned for its refined cane sugar products. Tate & Lyle produces 1.4 million tonnes of cane sugar each year from its two refineries in Europe, 1.1 million tonnes from its main refinery at Silvertown on the River Thames. Tate & Lyle Sugars employs around 1,300 people, 550 at the UK refinery. The Guinness Book of Records lists Lyle's Golden Syrup, produced at its Plaistow factory in East London, as the world's oldest branding (packaging).

About the organisation

Britain might not manufacture a lot these days, but don't tell Tate & Lyle that. The company has been refining sugar continuously at its Thames refinery since 1878 and hosted a visit by Her Majesty the Queen for its 130th year celebrations.

Tate & Lyle's sugars business can trace its roots back to the 19th century to the sugar-cane refining businesses of Henry Tate – who introduced the sugar cube to Britain and went on to found the Tate Gallery – and Abram Lyle.The products might not have changed much but the business and its processes certainly have.

Tate & Lyle sources sugar cane from African, Caribbean and Pacific countries and least developed countries under the EU sugar regime. Tate & Lyle is converting all of its UK retail cane sugar to Fairtrade by the end of 2009, the largest ever switch to the ethical labelling scheme by any major UK food or drink brand.

"It's unique in the UK to have lasted this long at the same site," says Michael Grier, Corporate Social Responsibility manager. "The size and location of the refinery, close to London City Airport, is not what people expect." Tate & Lyle is the biggest user of the River Thames and its refinery is clearly visible on the map of the TV soap Eastenders.

Tate & Lyle is an enduring tale of defiance and optimism. It has survived the Blitz in World War 2, environmental changes, and the considerable obstacles created by the European Union's Common Agricultural Policy (designed to protect the European sugar beet industry by raising tariffs on imported raw ingredients).

Tate & Lyle has strived in recent times to be ever-efficient and survive. But in so doing, it has achieved more than this. With open communication with its loyal and responsive workforce, EU reforms underway, and fresh investment including new cranes and an environmentally friendly biomass boiler, Tate & Lyle has positioned itself for a bright future.

"What you hear most is how friendly the place is"
(Rachel Tofts, HR director)

Company Culture

"What you hear most is how friendly the place is," says Rachel Tofts, Human Resources director. "People here talk, smile, and that's the impression visitors always take away."

That Tate & Lyle has remained on the same site for 130 years and undergone continual change in the face of constant challenges is testimony to their resolve. "We've come through better and stronger, because employees have actually welcomed change," says Grier. "We've had to, to survive." Changes have included introducing technology, different ways of working, and process improvements. At all times 'safety first' is the highest priority. They really mean it.

"The business has always recognised the importance of employee input," says Sarah Freeman, HR manager. Strong employee communications, including roadshows, Q&A sessions, listening and feedback, is a hallmark of Tate & Lyle. The company involves its employees in all issues, whether on Health & Safety teams, change exercises, transparency over profits, reporting why investment is or isn't being made, or lobbying the EU on its sugar regime. The way the company communicates openly with employees has made life for the business and employees considerably better. "If we're not thinking about the next change, then our employees certainly are," says Tofts.

Tate & Lyle supports work-life balance through flexible working policies including homeworking, sabbaticals and shift-swaps. Shifts are 12 hours long but people work four days on, four days off; then four nights, but then eight days off. "No one asks to get off this shift system," says Grier. Working fewer total days and chunks of free time to spend with family, do DIY or take extra holidays, it's little wonder.

Many employees have been here so long that there are generations of families on the same site. Tate & Lyle certainly appears to be one big happy family.

Innovation and Creativity

There's a benefit of the pressure Tate & Lyle has been under in recent years: "There's been a massive effort to become as efficient as possible," says Grier.

Investment in modern 'super cranes' sent a message that the company was here to stay. The 60-metre high cranes can offload a ship's cargo in a single day, leading to massive savings.

Project Husky saw Tate & Lyle invest in a renewable biomass boiler to supply 70% of the refinery's energy. Named from the wheat husks being burned, the technology was not bought in, but designed by Tate & Lyle's own engineers.

Tate & Lyle Process Technology is a specialist unit which provides consistently high quality and profitable technical, engineering and project management solutions to the cane sugar and associated industries, within and external to the Tate & Lyle Group.

If you think sugar is sugar, think again. The famous Lyle's Golden Syrup is now available in pouring and squeezing bottles as well as the iconic tin. Project teams are always working closely with customers to develop new products, such as flavoured syrups including maple and banoffi.

Outside the sugars business, Tate & Lyle's US ingredients division has developed innovative new uses for ingredients, including the conversion of corn into clothes and even aircraft de-icing fluid.

Pay and Benefits

Tate & Lyle benchmarks pay and benefits at least annually. It aims to be a median payer, but for certain roles with market shortages, it will compete as necessary. The annual pay review is in April and pay increases are merit based.

Everyone participates in a bonus scheme, relating to their division or area of business. "The refinery is a team, all pulling together," says Tofts. "It's right that the bonus is team-based." On-target bonus for represented group is 5% of salary and is seen as a bonus – not pay at risk. For managers, the variable component is higher, with on-target bonuses starting at 10%.

A high percentage of employees participate in the Employee Sharesave Scheme, which is open to all with no minimum period of service.

Holidays are generous at 26 days, plus public holidays. Maternity benefits are above statutory and other benefits include childcare vouchers, season ticket loans and the cycle-to-work scheme. There's a large on-site, free »

"The business has always recognised the importance of employee input" (Sarah Freeman, HR manager)

"If we're not thinking
about the next change,
then our employees
certainly are"
(Rachel Tofts, HR director)

car park and the company encourages the use of public transport by running a free minibus between the refinery and the nearest Tube station. The on-site canteen is subsidised, with a centrepiece of a full scale model cow, called Chrissy, made entirely from sugar cubes.

Tate & Lyle is proud of its best practice occupational health programme. It's for everyone, and includes vaccinations, health check-ups, free physiotherapy sessions, counselling and support, and education on health and fitness. There are discounts on local (and national) sports facilities.

Long service is celebrated after 25 and 40 years (with plenty of takers), the latter by a solid silver sugar sifter, £500 vouchers and a beautifully catered lunch at Tate & Lyle's corporate head office at Sugar Quay, overlooking HMS Belfast.

Career Development

Tate & Lyle Sugars is primarily a refining business and recruits graduates into a number of roles, particularly chemical and process engineers, and logistics backgrounds. "We give graduates a broad view of the refinery, so they work in different areas including distribution, sales, customer service and packing, so that when they move on they have a good understanding of the business," says Tofts. Graduates are encouraged to take on leadership roles early on. The same is true of support services like finance, IT, HR and sales professionals, who are also given a depth of experience early on.

Tate & Lyle is also keen to recruit locally. "We work with local schools and the University of East London to encourage local people to view Tate & Lyle as the employer of choice," says Tofts.

There are sometimes overseas assignments to places like Israel and Portugal. One role in Italy was created specifically to be filled by different people every six months. One graduate career route started with working on shifts, to shift manager, to process engineer, then an assignment to Mexico, promotion to area manager and another assignment to Israel. All in just three-and-a-half years.

Employees at all levels can apply for Tate & Lyle's 'Grow Your Own' programme of training and development to gain experience as either a shift manager or area manager.

Whoever you are, you receive excellent training and development. The annual performance review is an opportunity to request training – in safety, IT skills, foundation management skills and teambuilding, for example. "We also sponsor further development and education, including masters' degrees, HNCs and chartered status for professionals, if it's

mutually beneficial," says Tofts. There's an on-site Resource and Learning Centre that offers self-help tutorials in just about anything.

Vacancies are advertised internally and the company promotes from within wherever possible. "It sometimes means we need to give a bit more support and guidance, but the benefit is that our own people already know the company and its culture." Over 20% of Tate & Lyle Sugars directors joined the company early on in their careers.

Corporate Social Responsibility

Tate & Lyle says that "corporate and social responsibility equates to applying our four core values – safety, integrity, knowledge and innovation – to the way we run our business."

Tate & Lyle is the first sugar company in the UK to make all its retail sugars Fairtrade. Tate & Lyle absorbed the premium given to farmers rather than passing it on as a price increase. "It's not fair that the customer should pay," says Simon Houghton-Dodd, head of Quality & Sustainability.

The industry typically sends raw sugar suppliers 'self audits' to cover issues such as child labour and excessive hours. "We were uncomfortable with this approach," says Houghton-Dodd. "It's only a bit of paper." So Tate & Lyle did its own ethical audits on suppliers, going into the fields and visiting the mills to check all aspects of certifiability and producing a 50-page audit on each one.

Sugar cane milling is practically carbon neutral, as cane fibre powers the mills and the company ships rather than flies all its cane to its refineries. It's more efficient than transporting sugar beet. Tate & Lyle has also switched its sugar deliveries from road to rail, saving 2 million road miles. Meanwhile its new biomass boiler has cut fossil fuel usage by 70%.

As a UK company, community work has a UK bias and an emphasis on education. Tate & Lyle runs the Gifted and Talented programme, where students visit the refinery and Tate & Lyle employees reach into the community. In all, Tate & Lyle supports no fewer than 300 organisations, to which it gives money, goods and employee volunteering. It also hosts the Junior Citizens scheme by the Metropolitan Police, teaching safety skills to thousands of children. Tate & Lyle won a silver 'Big Tick' at the UK's Business in the Community 2007 Jubilee Awards in recognition of its long-term partnerships with local organisations.

When WWF approached Tate & Lyle and representatives of the sugar cane growing industry to discuss environmental issues at the growing stage, Tate & Lyle grasped the mettle and established the Better Sugar Cane initiative, which puts together new standards for the industry.

Facts and figures

Total number of staff: 1,300
Office location: UK – London (refinery); Merseyside, Hull, Bristol, Dagenham; and 15 countries worldwide
Industry sector: Food manufacturing
Turnover: £1.4bn (Sugars)

sure *we can*

TNT Express Services UK & Ireland

TNT Express House
Holly Lane
Atherstone
CV9 2RY

Telephone: 01827 303030
www.tnt.co.uk

Pay and Benefits	★ ★ ★ ★ ☆
Training and Development	★ ★ ★ ★ ☆
Career Development	★ ★ ★ ★ ✦
Working Conditions	★ ★ ★ ★ ☆
Company Culture	★ ★ ★ ★ ☆

Biggest plus
A market-leading secure employer with a track record of respecting and empowering its employees.

Greatest challenge
Continuing to drive its environmental targets in tough trading conditions.

Summary

TNT Express Services UK & Ireland is a business-to-business express delivery carrier, employing more than 11,500 people and operating 3,000 vehicles out of 70 locations. The company is market leader in the UK, and TNT's Express division became intra-European market leader in 2007. It is ranked third in the global market and is continually expanding its network in Europe, Asia, Australia, South America and the Middle East. Parent company TNT N.V. is based in The Netherlands and serves more than 200 countries and employs approximately 161,500 people. The group reported total revenues of €11bn (£9bn) in 2007.

About the organisation

TNT has introduced a global strap line - 'sure we can' - which will be appearing on all vehicles, aircraft and in communication materials and campaigns. CEO Peter Bakker says: "It's a mentality that applies to all TNT businesses. 'Can do' is simply the way we do things."

TNT's roots illustrate this. They can be traced back to 1946 and a single truck operation in Australia started by Ken Thomas. This became Thomas Nationwide Transport in 1958. TNT Express Services UK & Ireland was established in Britain in 1978. This operation is led from the front by managing director, and former driver, Tom Bell.

Bell has pictures of Thomas on his office wall and recalls meeting him many times. "He believed if you treat your people right they'll look after the business for you," says Bell, who subscribes to the same view.

After growth of 12.1% in 2006, the revenues of TNT's express division (of which UK and Ireland is a part) increased by 13.8% in 2007 to €6.5bn (£5.33bn). Operating income rose 7% to €599m (£491m). He expects 2009 trading conditions to be tough, but knows how to handle it. "We'll maintain levels of profitability," he says, "and come out stronger."

TNT has also fought off a lot of competition and is now much more than a parcels carrier, as its divisional structure shows. This comprises Express (its core parcels division); Fashion (delivery of clothing for leading retailers); and Value Added Services (including mail room and office services, financial services such as cheque clearing and consumables for banks, archiving, and document services).

Company Culture

TNT's mission is 'to exceed customers' expectations' through going the extra mile with its service. Bell sets the tone at TNT to ensure its culture helps achieve this. He or his management team visit all TNT's depots, »

"If you treat your people right they'll look after the business for you"
(Tom Bell, managing director, TNT Express Services UK & Ireland)

he tries to speak to as many staff as he can, at all levels, and insists on being called Tom. He believes it's respectful to make time for your team. Bell, happily gave up his office to host a jumble sale to raise money during the breast cancer campaign week. "We're a big business, but we're a family business," he says.

Standards are important, and trucks are washed twice a week, for example. "We've always run the cleanest, most modern fleet. Drivers have always been very proud of their vehicles," Bell says. "If you work in dirty shoddy conditions your service will be shoddy."

Employees certainly believe it's a good place to work and don't want to leave. The company has over 450 employees who've worked there for more than 25 years. In 2008, 90 people reached this milestone and were honoured at a formal presentation ceremony including an overnight stay at a hotel with their partner.

The company likes to promote from within. More than 80% of supervisory and management positions are filled internally. "If you want to progress within this organisation you can do," says Sue Barnes, director of HR. "We'll give you every development opportunity we can if you have the right attitude and aptitude." Staff encourage their friends to join too. Almost a quarter of appointments come through TNT's 'recommend a friend' scheme.

Innovation and Creativity

TNT has an impressive record of innovation. It's an essential approach in a fiercely competitive market. It has been trialling 50, 7.5-tonne zero emission electric vehicles in major UK cities and is considering ordering 50 more for delivery by June 2009. The company helped develop the vehicles, intending to be first to market exploiting the new green technology. "They're brilliant," says Bell. "Driver acceptability is excellent and the performance is very good".

Bell believes that in five years he'll be running approximately 300 of them. The move is environmental and business minded. Though they cost twice the price of a normal truck he thinks TNT will break even on the trucks in five years because of the reduced maintenance and fuel costs, plus the fact they'll last longer than standard diesel vehicles.

TNT runs an employee suggestion scheme entitled Grand Ideas to encourage the innovation and creativity of its people. Employees receive a scratch card with cash payouts of up to £100 for every idea they suggest to improve the company's business. So far TNT has received 5,000 suggestions and paid out £13,000. Three ideas have been so good they'd earned their originators £1,000 each. "We get our people on board and they generate some fantastic ideas," says Barnes.

Pay and Benefits

TNT describes its salaries as in line with the market, and in some cases above it. "We want to keep our best people," says Bell. "If you're asking people to outperform the market conditions it is only fair you reward them."

It continually reviews its remuneration packages with reference to surveys such as Watson Wyatt and Hay Paynet.

Target-beating performance is rewarded by a variety of incentive and bonus schemes at all levels. For depot general managers, the bonus element is up to 50% of salary, representing a significant amount of money. Senior managers also benefit from a share scheme.

The company also offers a group pension scheme open to all after six months – it makes a 7% contribution of pensionable earnings, and employees add 3%. There's also non-contributory life insurance scheme; private health insurance and company car scheme for managers; enhanced company maternity pay and a childcare vouchers scheme.

TNT introduced a voluntary benefits scheme in 2008, where employees receive preferential rates on a variety of products and services including health care, gym membership and holidays.

TNT also runs a reward and recognition scheme called Delivering More. This is designed to empower management to reward everyday examples of excellence and first class service using a selection of high street retail and leisure outlet vouchers. "A manager can say 'job well done, thanks, here's £20'," says Bell. "There's no formal process."

TNT will always try to look favourably on requests for flexible working, from part-time working to job sharing, if this meets the requirements of the business.

Career Development

TNT has won six National Training Awards and is one of only 36 UK companies to be awarded the title of Investor in People Champion. In the course of a year it delivers more than 20,000 delegate training days through 1,700 courses and it employs 50 people in its People Development team. »

"If you're asking people to outperform the market conditions it is only fair you reward them"
(Tom Bell, managing director, TNT Express Services UK & Ireland)

"People are actively encouraged to move between functions to boost their knowledge of the business" (Tom Bell, managing director, TNT Express Services UK & Ireland)

As well as driving, TNT has opportunities in sales, operations, customer service and all the support functions needed by any major corporation.

Managers of the future are constantly being created. An 18-month Corporate Development Programme has been established with Nottingham Trent University to award accredited qualifications to successful TNT employees who graduate. The company puts 15 to 20 people through each time, and of those that participated to date, 88% are still with the company and 70% have enjoyed positive career moves. TNT has also introduced a three-day leadership training programme for its top 200 managers.

People are actively encouraged to move between functions to boost their knowledge of the business. As part of a global group, there are opportunities for secondment abroad. There is an open-job website, with all internal vacancies advertised, including global opportunities. "The opportunities when I was coming through were fantastic," says Bell. "But nothing like they are today – you can work in the States, Australia and China to name but a few."

The company took on five graduate trainees in 2008, out of 700 applicants. TNT promises graduates a challenging job, with genuine responsibilities, while taking part in its Introduction to Management programme, externally accredited by the ILM (Institute of Leadership & Management). Graduates will spend their time managing key projects across Head Office and within the operation with potential budgets of up to £100,000, and can expect to be in a management position within five years.

Corporate Social Responsibility

TNT takes its social responsibility very seriously. CSR is a key differentiator between the Company and other players in the express market. Since 1997 it has donated more than £2.3m to Wooden Spoon: a charity which funds projects for physically, mentally or socially disadvantaged children. The company's website carries fundraising stories, almost weekly, from across its network of depots and head office.

TNT also supports the United Nations World Food Programme (WFP) and the UK operation generates funds and awareness of global hunger. The UK business is aligned to the WFP programme in Tanzania, helping feed and educate thousands of malnourished children, as well as providing sustainable resources for the future. High performing sales and customer services representatives are rewarded with a trip to Tanzania to help with the programme and also witness the work first hand. "Ask any one of our people who has been down there, and they say it's life-changing," says Bell.

The company helps fund an initiative to feed and educate youngsters, but also delivers hands-on assistance by enabling employees to go on three-month paid secondments to developing nations to contribute to community projects such

as designing and building water-recycling units, wood-burning ovens and even school kitchens. Globally TNT has contributed €29.4m (£24.1m) to WFP operations in recent years, and, in addition, TNT employees' have generated further contributions of €9m (£7.4m) via various fundraising activities.

In 2007 and 2008 TNT topped the prestigious Dow Jones Sustainability Index, which tracks the financial performance of the leading sustainability-driven companies worldwide. The achievement was all the more worthy given that the company operates in the transportation sector.

TNT has an explicit equal opportunities policy, enforced by management and formal grievance procedures. It also runs group-wide networks, connecting and supporting gay and lesbian employees, the professional development of women, and inter-cultural diversity.

In 2006 the company launched its Integrity Programme to formalise its approach, guided by its business principles. It also offers clear guidance, and policies and procedures, for handling whistle blowing, fraud prevention, conflicts of interest, gifts and entertaining, and pre-employment screening.

In 2007 TNT launched Planet Me, a global initiative with the bold quest to become the first zero emission mail and express delivery company. TNT will record the carbon emissions of its full chain of operations and report annually on those emissions, just like it reports its financial figures. Mandatory targets are also set across all of TNT's divisions for the reduction of carbon emissions in the following areas: aviation, buildings, business travel, green investment, company cars, operational vehicles, partnering with customers, and procurement. The UK's zero emission vehicles are a primary focus of Planet Me, and TNT is seeking to expand the fleet and deploy the 'green' vehicles in other parts of the world.

The company is exploiting video conferencing technology, with Bell being one of its leading exponents. Bell cut the number of return flights he made from 18 in 2007 to just one in 2008, attributing the drop to video conferencing. Currently, TNT's five-year fleet replacement programme ensures that all commercial vehicles benefit from the most current fuel-efficient and emission-reducing engine technology. Its fleet of 3,000 vehicles runs on ultra-low sulphur diesel (50 parts per million), which produces significantly lower sulphur emissions. Drivers are also trained in safe and environmentally friendly driving.

Facts and figures

Total number of staff: 11,500 in UK and Ireland, 161,500 worldwide
Office location: Head office in Atherstone, Warwickshire. 70 locations nationwide
Industry sector: Transport
Turnover: £849m (2007) UK and Ireland. Worldwide €11bn (£9bn) in 2007

The UNITE Group plc

The Core
40 St Thomas Street
Bristol
BS1 6JX

Telephone: 0117 302 7000
Fax: 0117 302 7403
www.unite-group.co.uk / www.Unite-students.com

Pay and Benefits	★ ★ ★ ★ ★
Training and Development	★ ★ ★ ★ ⯪
Career Development	★ ★ ★ ★ ⯪
Working Conditions	★ ★ ★ ★ ⯪
Company Culture	★ ★ ★ ★ ⯪

Biggest plus
Stimulating, enjoyable work based on an interesting business proposition that is doing good for the communities it serves.

Greatest challenge
Keeping the entrepreneurial spirit going while it grows in size and matures as a business.

Summary

The UNITE Group is an integrated property investment, development and management company. It is the UK's leading specialist provider of branded student accommodation offering both academic institutions and NHS Trusts integrated solutions to their accommodation requirements. UNITE provides modern, safe homes to around 37,000 customers in 23 UK cities, with 50% concentrated in London, Sheffield, Liverpool, Bristol, Manchester and Leeds. UNITE properties are purpose-built and professionally managed. Based in Bristol, and with regional offices throughout the UK, UNITE is a publicly listed company that ranks in the FTSE 250.

About the organisation

UNITE is a fast growing, entrepreneurial success story in a niche property area. UNITE's accommodation is pitched at the top end of the student accommodation market – high quality apartments designed for modern living. Smart exteriors, warm friendly interiors and ensuite bathrooms are standard, while services like all-inclusive rents, broadband, insurance and gymnasiums in the building are typical. UNITE even offers a top-floor penthouse/VIP floor at a property in Leeds.

The company builds its own properties, making extensive use of groundbreaking modular construction methods at its facility in Gloucestershire.

UNITE began as a developer, and became skilled at intuitively finding the best urban locations. It evolved into property management and its approach was originally paternal, providing students with security. "Then the students told us 'you're our landlord – not our parents,'" says Shane Spiers, Group HR director, and the emphasis switched to providing superb levels of customer service.

Typically, UNITE's property assets are invested in a property fund, or other joint venture vehicles. The UK Student Accommodation Fund ('USAF'), in which UNITE holds a 20% stake and manages on behalf of other investing institutions, is the largest such vehicle that UNITE manages.

Although UNITE is by some considerable distance the largest property company of its kind in the country, it is still a small fish in a large pond. There are 1.43 million students in the UK, an increase of 8.4% over 2007 levels, with 18% from overseas. Although it faces a tight housing and land environment, little direct competition for this type of product means it adds up to ongoing opportunity.

"Against a challenging UK property market, and contracting credit and finance markets, we continue to deliver a resilient performance," says Spiers. That 'resilient' performance means UNITE entered 2008/09 »

"Our philosophy is that all stakeholders – customers, employees and shareholders – are equal" (Shane Spiers, Group HR director)

with 99% of its beds let, and a 9% growth in like-for-like sales, which reached £72m in 2007. Healthy property valuations have been maintained as a result of strong occupier demand and USAF is the highest performing fund in the IPD Pooled Property Fund Index.

Company Culture

Established in 1991, UNITE saw its entrepreneurial CEO step out of the business two years before. UNITE today is in transition from a niche enterprise to a long-term sustainable business. But it's determined to take the enterprising spirit with it. "It's why we focus on customers and deliver a consistent customer experience," says Spiers.

UNITE is some 12 months into a two-year change programme called 'Blueprint.' "We said at our annual conference, 'we have to truly change this year,'" says Spiers. This is intended to increase levels of professionalism throughout the organisation and get better value from how money is spent. In other words, a performance-based culture has been introduced. Some jobs and processes have had to change. "Periods of change are always testing times for employees," says Mark Allan, chief executive. "It is a testament to the commitment and professionalism of our people that the business has been able to perform strongly through this period," adds Spiers.

Values play an important part in shaping a performance culture and at UNITE these include caring, working together, and taking the lead. The employee surveys endorse this, citing the effectiveness of line management, teamwork, and providing stimulating work.

HR philosophy is changing too. "The spirit of HR here is to provide central support but to take roles into the business units, which means within individual cities. That gets us as close to the customer as possible," says Spiers.

Who flourishes in UNITE's performance culture? "Someone who truly wants to be a high performer, is committed, energetic and pioneering," suggests Spiers. This drive towards higher levels of professionalism is attracting high calibre people from leading blue chip companies. "We also want to take the warmth of the organisation with us," says Spiers. "The challenge is to get the balance right."

Innovation and Creativity

UNITE was the first to pioneer constructing 11-storey-high prefabricated housing. From the rolling of lightweight steel, using modern technologies of a car production line, UNITE produces fully furbished bedrooms with ensuite bathrooms and fitted kitchens. The units are loaded onto trucks and turned into homes "like a big Meccano set being put together," suggests Spiers.

UNITE uses pioneering research methods to understand the science and the sub-conscious that influence what customers really want. UNITE probably has one of the most Internet-savvy demographic customer groups, including many overseas students who cannot view onsite and need to trust the brand and buy online. Consequently UNITE's website is crammed with innovative functionality and features, including virtual tours and an online booking system.

As part of the 'Blueprint' initiative to improve core processes, UNITE has been pushing the boundaries on the cycle of selling and allocating rooms, check-in, check-out and room service. Using process mapping, online tenancies (which previously required a physical signature), and hand-held technologies, UNITE aims to reduce check-in times to just 10 minutes by the next academic year. UNITE pioneered the sector, creating a new asset class on the Stock Exchange and a new financial vehicle by developing an investment fund into which its properties are placed.

Pay and Benefits

UNITE's overall remuneration strategy is to benchmark pay through the 'usual' surveys, and then aims for the median point, but on the overall package it aims for the upper quartile. UNITE ensures its reward structure is both fair and transparent.

Everyone is eligible for a bonus, which is linked to individual performance and the results of the business unit and company. Potentially this can boost salaries by 10% and up to 30% in the case of senior managers. The bonus is based on a pot and multiplier system linked to a performance rating, where 75% is 'on target,' 100% is over-performance, and can go as high as 144%.

The Sharesave scheme is open to all employees. Senior managers participate in a long-term incentive plan (not share options) where they are granted shares and the company vests them on their behalf. "We've taken this down to business unit manager level," says Spiers. "It has a considerable motivational effect. They know we're here for the long term and they can profit from a nice windfall."

There is a contributory pension plan with matched contributions, 25 days' annual holiday, and a one-month sabbatical after seven years' service. Other rewards include £250 for recommending an employable friend; matching contributions up to £250 for charity events; 10% discount on student accommodation for family members; life insurance; and maternity leave that exceeds statutory requirements. »

Values play an important part in shaping a performance culture and at UNITE these include caring, working together, and taking the lead

"Periods of change are always testing times for employees. It is a testament to the commitment and professionalism of our people that the business has been able to perform strongly through this period"
(Mark Allan, chief executive)

Recognition plays its part. Simple 'thank you' cards are given by managers for little things that have a big effect in showing esteem. Meanwhile annual long-service awards for five, seven and even 15 years' service are celebrated at the annual garden party. On a lighter side, the 'UNITE Academy' delivers its rendition of 'Britain's Got Talent' at an annual charity fundraising event.

Career Development

There is such a variety of roles within UNITE. Land acquirers, research professionals, planners, architects, construction engineers, manufacturers, supply chain specialists, production engineers, property managers, customer service, fund managers, sales, marketing, HR, and IT to name but a few.

There are 1,200 people working in the business today compared to 800 three years ago, which gives an indication of the level of recruitment activity. UNITE has recently introduced a training academy and all new recruits spend two weeks there (staying in student accommodation of course) by way of an induction to the fundamentals of UNITE's business.

UNITE has focused a lot on management and leadership development. It operates a number of core management programmes to teach basic line management skills, coaching, values-based recruitment, performance feedback and executing strategy. The same applies to the leadership development programme at lower levels. "It's vital to the success of the business that these core skills are instilled," says Spiers.

This is supplemented by personal development training, 360 degree feedback, coaching and mentoring. UNITE sponsors professional qualifications including MSc's in Business Entrepreneurship and Real Estate Management.

A career development plan provides the framework for developing current roles and broader career aims and the skills required to realise these ambitions. All this is linked to the performance culture of the business and those who deliver and perform tend to get the more challenging promotions.

Responsibility can come quickly. Regional directors, looking after accommodation in 3-4 cities, are often running a £20m turnover business. Construction managers and land purchasers deal with huge sums. Even an individual property manger is responsible for £1m annual sales.

The Board of UNITE is home grown – nearly everyone started in the business. "We're now getting a balance, attracting people from outside, particularly from the larger branded organisations," says Spiers. With UNITE's business expanding rapidly, there's ample room for both.

Corporate Social Responsibility

UNITE is committed to ethical business behaviour with its own code of ethics. "We're responsible to all of our stakeholders – customers, people and shareholders – and our philosophy is that all are equal," says Spiers. UNITE follows the principle that if you provide people with good careers, they will give good customer service and that will in turn deliver rewards to shareholders. An element of performance pay is based on a customer satisfaction index.

A 'higher purpose' of the organisation is to provide quality accommodation and service, "to give students and their parents one less things to worry about, as they begin one of the most enjoyable but also one of the most vulnerable periods of their lives," says Spiers.

UNITE regenerates brownfield sites, bringing derelict urban land to life. With students being nocturnal creatures, UNITE nurtures local communities carefully through consultation, good planning, providing CCTV and staff on site, overnight, to deal with any issues.

UNITE's wider approach to the community is about putting something back. UNITE founded the charity, Unity Aid, which provides bursaries to provide accommodation to people who could not otherwise afford university accommodation. Other projects include helping to build a medical centre in the Cameroon, big charity balls, and local community work.

UNITE employs local people in the cities it operates in and its workforce reflects those communities. The age demographic of the workforce tends to be relatively young, reflecting the type of people attracted to these roles, but people of all ages are found across the organisation.

"There are a number of sustainable environmental initiatives baked into everything that we do," says Spiers. UNITE runs a Carbon Management programme in association with the Carbon Trust. Perhaps the biggest impact it can make is in what it does and how it produces it. UNITE conserves energy through improved insulation and the use of efficient heating and lighting systems. It also incorporates renewable energy into its new buildings and actively encourages customers to use less energy and recycle more – such as providing real incentives for switching off lighting and heating when they are not needed.

UNITE favours the use of building materials and furnishings from sustainable sources. It makes extensive use of modular construction. Off-site manufacturing significantly reduces material waste compared to traditional construction methods. What's more, it uses around 30% less material by weight than traditional methods.

Facts and figures

Total number of staff: 1,200
Office location: Head office in Bristol and offices/operations in 23 UK cities
Industry sector: Housing
Turnover: £72m in the 2007 financial year

View

The Penthouse
Long Island House
1-4 Warple Way
London W3 0RG

Telephone: 020 8740 9751
Fax: 020 8740 9857
Email: careers@view.uk.com
www.view.uk.com

Pay and Benefits	★ ★ ★ ★ ☆
Training and Development	★ ★ ★ ⯪ ☆
Career Development	★ ★ ★ ★ ⯪
Working Conditions	★ ★ ★ ☆ ☆
Company Culture	★ ★ ★ ★ ⯪

Biggest plus
An innovative agency with real opportunity for individuals to grow.

Greatest challenge
As it grows, putting in place the right infrastructure at the right time.

Summary

View is a leading corporate brand communications agency that provides a comprehensive range of online and offline communications services. View's blue-chip client list speaks for itself, including The Army, GSK, Rolls-Royce, BlackBerry, Astra Zeneca, Rio Tinto, Tate & Lyle, Smith & Nephew and Thames Water. View helps them speak to audiences more effectively by delivering, among other services, best in class Internet and Intranet solutions. View is an independently owned agency of 35 people and growing quickly.

About the organisation

View has a vision. And that is to be the brand communications agency of choice among FTSE-100 companies. "View symbolises blue sky thinking, innovation and perspective," says Bernard Guly, executive director, from the agency's penthouse office in West London. Its vision is quickly being realised as the agency expands by delivering groundbreaking work for clients.

In just 16 years View has evolved from a print design agency into one of the more innovative service providers in online brand communications. View considers corporate brand communications to encompass messaging, ethos, positioning, and how a corporation touches internal and external audiences. "It's about communicating consistently and effectively, engaging audiences, and reinforcing clients' real points of difference," suggests Guly.

These days online represents the most important communication channel, and designing and building Internet/Intranets for corporate clients now accounts for 70% of View's revenues. Overall, fee income increased from £1.65m in 2005 to £2.0m in 2006 and £2.1m in 2007.

View remains confident both about its position in the marketplace and future growth. "We are poised for the next jump forward, and how changing technology will affect the way people and businesses communicate," says Guly. This includes media convergence, rapid broadband take-up and increasing customer expectations of the online experience.

Company Culture

"View aims to be the best agency in its sector to work for – and to work with," says Jason Ross, chief executive. There is a real focus on client service, and in particular on developing long-term relationships. "A number of agencies are perceived to have good creative output, but it's how you service your clients and apply that creativity that really matters," adds Ross.

"View aims to be the best agency in its sector to work for – and to work with," (Jason Ross, chief executive)

On the surface, there's an informal atmosphere at View, without too much 'suiting and booting.' But don't be fooled. Lurking underneath is a totally professional work ethic and a commitment to best practice and service.

Creative businesses tend to see people move around a lot, but View tends to hang onto its people. Helen Thain, project director, has been at View for six years. "I enjoy working here because I enjoy the people here," she says. "They are fun, everyone looks after one another, and the chemistry is really good between teams."

The operational board of three is working on a 'View Manifesto' for 2009, covering all dynamics from new business and studio resources to infusing innovation and rewarding success. "We're a small, growing agency, and you need to put in place the right infrastructure and processes when you're growing," notes Ross. "And within that, we have a responsibility to recognise and reward the commitment made by our people."

Like any agency with immoveable client deadlines, everyone pulls their finger out when needed. "But there's no culture of working late for the sake of it," says Ross. "We also allow staff to work from home occasionally, to address work-family balance issues, and there's sometimes time off in lieu of hard work."

Friday afternoon 'show and tell' sessions are very much part of the View culture, where the whole agency gets together to share with one another what is happening. There's an active social committee, whose brief is to deliver a mix of social and teambuilding events to improve agency cohesion and break down any barriers. The penthouse rooftop terrace has hosted memorable parties and barbeques away from prying eyes, fuelled by silly games and free drinks, while karaoke and tenpin bowling are popular activities outside the office.

Innovation and Creativity

"We're creative, but in the corporate arena," says Mark Smith, creative director. "We're always looking to push back the boundaries in the corporate environment. What makes View stand out is its ability to ensure that large brands communicate consistently, but with subtle differences adapted to different audiences."

View has produced visually inspiring and engaging websites to represent international companies in a more holistic way, for example with RioTinto.com and GSK.com. On the latter, View provided the company with a better online platform from which to manage its reputation, communicate good work, and respond to any media criticism

by elevating information on GSK's CSR activities such as World Aids Day and medicine distribution in Sri Lanka. It created a constantly refreshing series of corporate storytelling features on the home page that reflected the current environment or responded to media coverage – the first site of its kind to do this.

View is striving constantly to raise the bar and anticipate the next wave of Internet and Intranet sites, and the underlying technologies that will become the norm. "Blogs, Wikis, video and podcasts are rapidly becoming more mainstream, especially in areas such as careers and the mobile environment," says Guly. "Corporate websites are increasingly affected by audience expectations as consumers, and the two are definitely converging. View aims to stay ahead of this curve."

To maintain its innovative edge, View's creative team is constantly monitoring other companies and what they are doing, online and visually. "We also get out of the office and look beyond the usual environments," says Smith. "Good creatives also understand what the strengths of other team members are, and any technical limitations there might be to a project."

Pay and Benefits

View benchmarks salaries against league tables and through frequent conversations with recruitment specialists. "We always pay top quartile," says Guly, "and market rate if not better if we have to, in order to get the best people." Pay is reviewed annually.

The agency has recently initiated a monthly bonus scheme to reward extraordinary teamwork and recognise outstanding work during that month. It's a discretionary cash bonus, and could be given to anyone in any role. There is a Christmas bonus, which is a lump sum and designed to make everyone feel part of the same team. There's a 'bounty' payment of £750 for introducing candidates that View subsequently employs. Senior members participate in an equity scheme.

Creative and new media employees can earn overtime – at 25% of their hourly rate for daily hours above $7^{1/2}$, and time-and-a-half for anything in excess of 10 hours. The standard holiday entitlement is 20 days, rising to 22 days after two years and 25 days after six years. Work-life balance is supported through part-time and home working.

>>

"Any member of staff has the opportunity to work their way up and become a member of View's senior management team"
(Bernard Guly, executive director)

Like many agencies, View eschews elaborate benefits packages in favour of good salaries, good bonuses and being a great place to work.

Career Development

This is a View with room… room to grow and to realise ambition. There are broadly three types of role within the agency: client account and project management; creative, planning and research; and a technical team of web programmers and developers.

"The next step on the ladder is always available," says Thain. "You get better opportunities at a smaller agency. There's no room to hide – that takes you out of your comfort zone and encourages you to be the best you can be."

Directors heading up teams put in place a number two. "We prefer to promote internally and so we look at ways people can expand their career – within the same and across different roles, cross transferring skills," says Guly. "Any member of staff has the opportunity to work their way up and become a member of View's senior management team."

The annual, formal appraisal and a six-monthly informal performance review are opportunities to discuss career ambitions and training requirements. A target 10% of time is spent on training, creative thinking and brainstorming, which has the dual benefit of enabling employees to develop their talents and also enhance the level of service to clients.

"As the agency grows, it's about people growing as well," says Ross. "It's important that each year people feel they are worth more than last year."

A mentoring system is supplemented by training courses, attending industry events and knowledge sharing. The 'View Skool' is one that has few rules and is more about innovative brainstorming sessions and informal presentations. One internal course 'Inside the Client's Mind' helps employees understand what clients look for in pitches and how

the agency can respond effectively. Developers are sent on relevant technical courses such as .Net or Plum Tree.

According to Guly the type of person who does well at View is someone who is a smart thinker, flexible with a 'can do' attitude, and constantly wants to improve work quality. "It's those that add 10% to 100% who tend to get noticed, stay long term, and be promoted," says Guly.

Corporate Social Responsibility

Many of View's clients aspire to be leaders in ethical business behaviour and where practicable View also takes this position. View helps to set benchmark standards for clients and through them is influencing the whole CSR debate.

View is an ethical employer and always aims to do business in a manner that is honest, proper and safe. All new joiners are given 'The Way We Work' manual to read, outlining the agency's behaviours and HR policies.

If anyone is concerned about any facet of working practices, there is a whistle-blowing policy to encourage them to contact senior management. And if a situation arises where individuals may have ethical objections to working on particular projects, the agency does everything it can to take account of strongly held views when putting together project teams.

View employs a wide range of nationalities from all continents, including people from Spain, Ireland, Argentina, Netherlands and China. View values the strength that it derives from having a diverse workforce, although being a service agency, recruitment and promotion are, of course, on merit. "It must always be like that," says Guly. "Race, gender, age and sexual orientation just don't enter into it."

"We support good causes where and when we can," says Guly. View entered a team in the Three Peaks Challenge, raising over £10,000 for the Anthony Nolan Trust (child leukaemia), generously supported by its clients. Entering a team for the BUPA London 10,000 charity run is currently under discussion and regular charity raffles and other events ensure that fundraising is a year-round effort.

View has recycling processes in place for all excess paper, print and cartridges; documents are printed on both sides; and the agency ensures it's 'lights out' unless they are absolutely needed. Of course, as an agency specialising in online communication, View is actively helping others to embrace a paperless environment.

Facts and figures

Total number of staff: 35
Office location: London
Industry sector: Corporate Brand Communications
Turnover: £2.1m

Writing team

Paul Donkersley (Editor)

Paul is a professional writer and communications consultant, specialising in marketing, media, transport, employment and sports. This is the third time he has edited *Britain's Top Employers*. He has had freelance journalist work published in UK and European newspapers and magazines, and has won British Association of Industrial Editors awards for producing the best company newspapers. He also wrote the UK's first book on fantasy football. Paul has his own consultancy, Terrier, producing original web, internal and external communications for business clients small and large.

Alana Juman Blincoe

Alana Juman Blincoe has been a journalist for 17 years, working freelance for the past 10. She writes for business/technology news sites and publications, including *Estates Gazette*, *Channel4 Homes website, The British Journal of Midwifery* and various consumer gardening titles. When she had a regular job she was editor of IT business and IT consumer magazines. She is currently working on a project concerning eco-friendly design.

Robert Blincoe

Robert Blincoe started his journalism career as a crime reporter in Manchester's Moss Side in 1991. He has been news editor of Europe's largest technology news website, promoted the UK's biotech and green fuel industries for The British Council, and was a senior member of Getty Images' award-winning customer magazine *Edit*. Robert writes about business, science, crime and gambling and has contributed to many magazines as well as the *Financial Times*, the *Guardian*, *The Independent* and *The Sun*. He has an MSc in Business and IT and is married to Alana Juman Blincoe.

Frank Booty

Frank Booty has been a freelance editor and writer for over two decades, contributing to many market-leading titles, books and websites in the fields of business, facilities management, IT and networking, and manufacturing. Frank is also the editor of *Top IT Employers United Kingdom*, and has contributed to other books in CRF's portfolio. An award-winning journalist, he has also devised and chaired many conferences in the facilities management market, and is the editor of the highly-acclaimed *Facilities Management Handbook* (now in its 4th edition), published by Butterworth-Heinemann, an imprint of Elsevier.

Jim Dow

Jim Dow has been a newspaper journalist for more than 50 years. He spent 23 years at *The Scotsman* (latterly as business editor for nine years), is chairman of a public relations company, runs a freelance journalist business in Edinburgh and has found the time to write a couple of books.

Paul Bray

Paul Bray read Modern History at Oxford, and spent five years in the computer industry before entering journalism in 1988. He was deputy editor of *Which Computer?* for two years and went freelance in 1991. Since then he has written for the *Daily Telegraph* and *Sunday Telegraph*, the *Guardian*, *The Times* and *The Sunday Times*, many magazines including *Computing*, *Director* and *Nasdaq International*, as well as more exotic publications such as the *Hutchinson Encyclopaedia* and *Almanac*.

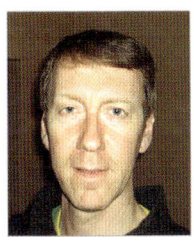

Jon Lamb

Jon Lamb is a writer on business and organizational issues. He has contributed to national newspapers including *The Times* and the *Guardian* and worked on online projects for the DTI and HMRC. Jon has an MSc in Business Psychology.

Claire Smith

Claire Smith is a freelance journalist with more than 10 years' experience writing about the legal and financial services industries in the UK and globally. She was editor of *Top Legal Employers UK 2009*, and is currently contributing editor to *Legal Business*, and a regular writer for *The Times*, the *Financial Times*, *Financial News*, *Private Equity News* and *CityAM*. She is also a tutor with the College of Law in London, and runs her own research consultancy focusing on the legal profession.

››

Rachelle Thackray

Rachelle Thackray is a freelance writer and editor, and author of *20/20 Hindsight*, published by Virgin Business Guides. She works for a range of clients from different sectors.

Roger Trapp

Roger Trapp is an experienced business journalist and corporate writer with in-depth knowledge of management issues, enterprise and a variety of related topics. He was on the business staff of the *Independent* and *Independent on Sunday* for more than a decade and as part of his focus on enterprise took responsibility for the *Independent on Sunday's* pioneering annual survey of fast-growing companies. He has also been a regular writer for a variety of magazines covering a range of subjects, but particularly management, finance and enterprise.

David Vickery

David Vickery is a corporate writer, web editor and communications consultant who runs his own writing business, Davang Ltd. An honours graduate in economics, he held senior writing positions at Henderson Investors, Abbey and the London Stock Exchange, and worked for the advertising agencies Valin Pollen and DMB&B. David now writes brochures, websites, magazine articles, internal communications material and annual reports for clients throughout the UK and internationally.

About CRF

For more than 18 years CRF has been conducting international research into Top Employers. Top employers and their unique propositions are presented in the publications *Britain's Top Employers, Top IT Employers United Kingdom* and *Top Legal Employers United Kingdom*, as well as dedicated websites. Our research projects have proven their effectiveness when recruiting new staff and holding on to the existing workforce. More than 2,000 organisations – many of which are blue-chip companies – around the world have participated in our projects. CRF operates in 12 countries and three continents globally.

Book Order Form

I would like to purchase _____ additional copies of BRITAIN'S TOP EMPLOYERS 2009 at £14.99 each.

Please return this form by fax to **+44 (0)20 8387 1410** or by post to:

CRF, Kinetic Centre, Theobald Street, Elstree, Herts WD6 4PJ

Your details

Company name:

Address:

Postcode:

Contact person:

Title:

Email:

Telephone:

Signature:

IDENTIFYING**TOP**PERFORMERS